# CROWN HILL

## HISTORY | SPIRIT | SANCTUARY

Text by DOUGLAS A. WISSING, MARIANNE TOBIAS, REBECCA W. DOLAN, and ANNE RYDER
Photographs by MARTY N. DAVIS and RICHARD FIELDS

INDIANA HISTORICAL SOCIETY PRESS | INDIANAPOLIS 2013

© 2013 Indiana Historical Society Press

Printed in China

This book is a publication of the
Indiana Historical Society Press
Eugene and Marilyn Glick Indiana History Center
450 West Ohio Street
Indianapolis, Indiana 46202-3269 USA
http://www.indianahistory.org
Telephone orders 1-800-447-1830
Fax orders 1-317-234-0562
Online orders @ http://shop.indianahistory.org

The paper in this publication meets the minimum requirements of American National
Standard for Information Sciences—Permanence of Paper for Printed Library Materials,
ANSI Z39. 48–1984

Library of Congress Cataloging-in-Publication Data

Crown Hill : history, spirit, and sanctuary / text by Douglas A. Wissing ... [et al.] ;
photographs by Marty N. Davis and Richard Fields.
        p. cm.
Includes index.
ISBN 978-0-87195-301-8 (cloth : alk. paper)
1. Crown Hill Cemetery (Marion County, Ind.)—History. 2. Crown Hill Cemetery
(Marion County, Ind.)—Pictorial works. 3. Indianapolis (Ind.)—History.
4. Marion County (Ind.)—History, Local. 5. Indianapolis (Ind.)—Biography.
6. Marion County (Ind.)—Biography. 7. Indianapolis (Ind.)—Social life and customs.
8. Marion County (Ind.)—Social life and customs. I. Wissing, Douglas A. II.
Davis, Marty N. III. Fields, Richard.
F532.M4C76 2013
977.2'52—dc23
                        2012016569

"The history of a cemetery can never be complete
any more than the history of a city of the living.
After all has been done, after we have made this place as
beautiful as human hands may, bending nature and art
to our purpose, the place where we lay our dead is
consecrated not only by the use to which it is put, but by
the tears, the broken hearts, the bitter anguish of the
living as they murmur the last farewells."

ANNA NICHOLAS, *THE STORY OF CROWN HILL* (1928)

# Benefactors

## Leader
The Ruth Lilly Philanthropic Foundation

## Patron
Nancy Ayres | Mr. and Mrs. John H. Holliday | The MacAllister Family
The Mothershead Foundation | Charles and Peggy Sutphin | Marianne Williams Tobias
The Van Riper Woodard Family Foundation | Mrs. William A. Wick

## Friend
Frank and Katrina Basile | Marguerite Ayres Ferguson | William L. Fortune Jr. and Joseph D. Blakley
The Griffith Family Foundation | James H. and Nancy S. Johnson | Stanley Malless
Mr. and Mrs. H. Roll McLaughlin | Doctor and Mrs. George F. Rapp | Evaline Rhodehamel
Mr. and Mrs. Ronald G. Salatich

# In Memoriam

Ulysses S. Adair and Steven Adair
BY ADA A. ADAIR

Mary Jo Bradley
C. Harvey Bradley and Carolyn C. Bradley
BY C. HARVEY BRADLEY

Fred H. Day and Susannah M. Day
BY THE DAY FAMILY FOUNDATION

Mary Jewell F. and Berkley W. Duck Jr.
Frances M. and Warren T. Ruddell
BY NANCY R. AND BERKLEY W. DUCK III

John M. Howie
BY MARGARET M. HOWIE

Mardenna Johnson Hunter
(Mrs. Curtis Winston Hunter)
BY SCOTT J. AND VIRGINIA H. BROWNING

Evan Lilly Noyes
Marguerite Lilly Noyes and Nicholas Hartman Noyes
BY LINDA NOYES AND FAMILY

Sylvia Griffith Peacock
BY JOHN E. D. PEACOCK JR. AND SALLY BRADLEY PEACOCK

Slavo Randjelovic
BY MARIA RANDJELOVIC AND FAMILY

Howard Waldemar Sams
BY BARBARA H. SAMS

# CONTENTS

# PREFACE

The term cemetery comes from the Greek language, meaning "sleeping place." Concepts of eternal rest, eternal repose, and eternal peace are common attributes of final burial. As opposed to graveyards, cemeteries are usually landscaped, spacious places that are legally protected, sometimes consecrated by a church or other religious entity, sometimes private, or owned by a municipality. Whatever the description or physical outcome, there is in every cemetery an ineffable sweetness. Such is the case with Crown Hill Cemetery.

Crown Hill sits majestically in the midst of a large city, Indianapolis, Indiana. The cemetery's quietness speaks not only of finality but also of hopes, beliefs, beauty, and acceptance of destiny.

Crown Hill speaks of life. It reflects perennial rebirth in the rhythms of the seasons and offers sanctuary not only to those placed in its grounds and those grieving their loss, but also to deer herds, innumerable songbirds, flowers, and hundreds of species of thriving trees. Its grounds are sites of picnics, concerts, tours, botanical education, human history, and life celebrations. Crown Hill tells many stories.

This book marks not only 150 years of a remarkable history, but also reflects the beauty of life itself. With this in mind, *Crown Hill: History, Spirit, and Sanctuary* is dedicated to the citizens of Indianapolis.

MARIANNE TOBIAS

*Opposite: Waiting Station and triple-arched limestone gate designed by Adolph Scherrer in 1885 located at Thirty-Fourth Street and Boulevard Place. The archway was completed in time for the funeral procession of Vice President Thomas A. Hendricks. The Sentry House to the left of the archway, designed by the Vonnegut and Bohn architectural firm, was constructed in 1904.*

# INTRODUCTION

In recognition of Crown Hill Cemetery's 150th anniversary, the Crown Hill Heritage Foundation and the Indiana Historical Society are very pleased to present *Crown Hill: History, Spirit, and Sanctuary*. With more than 200,000 burials, Crown Hill serves as a chronicle of the history of our city, as seen through the thousands of stories of those who are buried within these sacred grounds. These are the stories of politicians and statesmen who shaped our government; authors, poets, and artists who reflected the emotions and feelings of their time through their work; and soldiers and military leaders who fought in the nation's wars and conflicts, many of whom gave their final sacrifice to protect the freedoms that we enjoy today. Equally as important are the mothers, the fathers, the children, and the individuals who have represented the basic tenets of life—faith, goodness, sacrifice, and happiness, who have made up the fabric of our society.

Families and visitors find Crown Hill to be a place of great beauty, a place for solace, reflection, and reverence for those who are interred within. And we are also fortunate to have a great legacy in the historic structures of Crown Hill. These structures include the Gothic Chapel (1875), the Waiting Station and Gothic Gate (1885), the Sentry House (1904), the Service Yard, Barns and Workshops (1920s), the Subway (1925), and the Community Mausoleum (1948). It is because of the ongoing preservation and restoration of these structures undertaken by the Crown Hill Heritage Foundation that these valuable historic structures serve the community and the families of Crown Hill today.

Since 1985 the Foundation has raised more than ten million dollars to fulfill its mission to restore Crown Hill's historic structures and provide educational and public awareness programs through special events and historical tours. The success of the foundation is a result of the generosity of our donors—the families of Crown Hill, who recognize and value that Crown Hill is "exquisitely planned, laboriously tended, and watered by the tears of generations, becoming one with Indianapolis."

KEITH O. NORWALK

*President, Crown Hill Cemetery and
the Crown Hill Heritage Foundation*

# 1

## THE BEGINNING

First there were the glaciers, carrying rocks and sand from a thousand miles north. Beginning 2.6 million years ago in the Pleistocene Ice Age, the immense ice sheets alternately built and scoured the land that came to be Indianapolis. About 18,000 years ago, a mere blink in geologic time, the last glaciers receded from the region. This final glacial pulse left a legacy of diverse landforms, including one high mound standing alone amidst rolling hummocks near the surging White River. Towering above the landscape, this glacial kame—composed of diverse sediments from the far north—was an enigmatic, orphaned formation. In time, the citizens of Indianapolis came to call it Crown Hill.

In 1820 the Indiana General Assembly in Corydon voted to establish a new state capital where the National Road—then inching its way west—crossed the White River, which they mistakenly thought to be navigable. While founded on a misconception, Indianapolis prospered through the pioneers' ambitious visions and hardscrabble pragmatism. Though the state capital site was little more than a scarcely populated swampy spot on the prairie, the Hoosier leaders hired Scottish-born engineer Alexander Ralston to develop a grand plan for Indianapolis. Ralston had famously assisted French architect Pierre L'Enfant in 1791 when he laid out Washington, D.C. The well-credentialed Ralston was available for the frontier commission, in part,

because he was laying low on a southern Indiana homestead after his involvement with Aaron Burr's megalomaniac conspiracy.

Ralston's plan for Indianapolis conceived of a proud city of one square mile, centered on the Governor's Circle, where the governor's mansion was to stand. Radiating diagonally out from the circular commons, broad avenues led through the imagined city to the hinterlands. Kentucky Avenue arrowed to the southwest toward the serpentine White River. Just past the intersection of South and West Streets, which delineated the edge of town, Ralston called for a five-acre city cemetery to be located near the river on high ground that was considered ill-suited for habitation—for the living, at any rate. Almost immediately after Ralston delivered his plans in 1821, construction on the new city began. It was the same year as the cemetery's first interment, a Pennsylvania Dutch merchant from Cincinnati named Daniel Shafer, who had a general store below Pogue's Run at the far southern edge of town. Struggling to the new graveyard, Shafer's burial party encountered so much tangled brush on Kentucky Avenue that it had to bushwhack along the riverbank to the burying ground.

Some of Indianapolis's most prominent early settlers were involved with the first cemetery. They included James M. Ray, a New Jersey native who conducted the city's first land sales and later had business interests that included Indianapolis's first sawmill, as well as banks, railroads, and insurance. Said to have been the secretary of nearly every city organization, Ray's civic commitments ranged from churches and bible schools to the

school for the blind to overseeing the welfare of Indiana's Civil War veterans. Ray's role in the town's cemeteries continued for many decades. In 1834 Ray and a number of other important citizens, including James Blake, Nicholas McCarty, and John G. Brown, bought an adjacent five-acre parcel of land to enlarge the cemetery, now replete with hundreds of grave markers

of Indiana limestone, slate, granite, and white New England marble that was already dissolving like granulated sugar in the rain. Divided by gravel paths, the markers stood amongst the mature native trees and pruned shrubbery along the river, which periodically devoured the cemetery's banks. The graveyard grew further in 1852, when the president of the Vandalia Railroad

laid out acreage near his tracks as a cemetery addition. The graveyard expanded again in 1862, when the combined twenty-five-acre cemetery came to be known as Greenlawn. The same year, the federal government bought a narrow strip along the Vandalia tracks to bury hundreds of Confederate prisoners who had died in the city's Camp Morton.

The Civil War overwhelmed Indianapolis's pioneer cemetery. After the Union victories in 1862 at Fort Donelson and Shiloh, Confederate prisoners began flooding into Camp Morton, located at the then State Fairgrounds just north of the city, on today's Central Avenue between Nineteenth and Twenty-second Streets. More than 12,000 prisoners came to be quartered at the camp, most housed in overcrowded wooden barracks. A Union officer stated they were "dark and close and there must be much sickness." Although considered one of the better camps, there was indeed much sickness. The camp latrines were contaminating the prisoners' drinking water, leading to rampant dysentery. A smallpox epidemic erupted. Their wounds and illnesses exacerbated by poor food, housing, and care, 1,762 prisoners eventually died at Camp Morton—14.6 percent of the prison population. Beginning with the first debilitated prisoners who arrived in February 1862, a steady stream of mortuary

*Above: The 1821 "Mile Square" plat of Indianapolis, the new capital of Indiana, on Alexander Ralston's monument.* **Right:** *Indianapolis from Williams Hill (Crown Hill), 1861. Oil painting by Christian Schrader courtesy Indiana State Museum and Historic Sites.*

wagons trundled bodies to the Greenlawn Cemetery, where the gravediggers of the undertaking firm of Weaver and Williams interred the dead side by side in long trenches. The deceased rested in plain wooden coffins that Weaver and Williams had contracted to provide for $3.50 each. Their graves marked by a plain board lettered with a number, about 1,400 Confederate prisoners eventually came to be buried in Greenlawn.

It was not just Confederates who needed burial. With its extensive railroad connections and facilities, Indianapolis had become a great Union camp. Though

many soldiers wounded in fighting farther south died in Indianapolis hospitals, it was disease that carried away most of them. Modern science further strained the little cemetery. Embalming became prevalent for the first time, allowing bodies of soldiers preserved with concoctions of arsenic, creosote, mercury, turpentine, and alcohol to be returned home for burial. Beyond the space problem, Greenlawn's location in the midst of booming industrial Indianapolis was less than ideal. One of the city's most influential citizens, attorney and banker Calvin Fletcher, wrote in his diary on July 3, 1863, "The proximity to the R. R. & pork houses makes the present cemetree not so pleasent as I once supposed it would be." Not many months later, Fletcher met with other city leaders to organize a new kind of cemetery, one that resonated with the ideals of a beautiful death.

Across urbanizing America, city fathers were organizing a new style of parklike cemeteries. The origins of these new burying grounds lay in Europe, where the aesthetics of the English romantics met the practical needs of French administrators. The result was the paradigm-changing Cimetière du Père-Lachaise, which Napoléon established in 1804 at the eastern edge of Paris. The new cemetery created a sensation. Designed as a place of repose—for both living and deceased—it replaced the medieval burying grounds that plagued the city with malodorous and pestilential air. Prior to Père-Lachaise, most burials were in churchyards—consecrated grounds. The clerics banned the burial of suicides, relegating them to walled, ungated cemeteries that necessitated the laborious hoisting of bodies by ladder and the preclusion of most visitations. When the medieval churchyard cemeteries finally ran out of room in the late eighteenth century, authorities organized Les Innocents as a huge central repository for Parisian burials. By

1775 Les Innocents no longer fit its name, as it was a seething field of escaping gases and noxious odors that caused those passing by to swoon. One section burst the foundation walls of an adjoining building, causing a cascade of bones into the basement. The civil authorities closed Les Innocents and ordered the bones neatly stacked in the ancient Parisian tunnels, which came to be known as the Catacombs. Debauched minor nobility found it a perfect place for banquets, beginning the Catacombs' second career as a tourist attraction.

But when Père-Lachaise opened in the early nineteenth century, it was a long way from Paris, causing well-to-do Parisians to be reluctant to commit to the new burial grounds. To lure them, Père-Lachaise's developer, Nicholas Frochot, wisely interred some cachet by moving the caskets of literary giants Moliere and Jean LaFontaine to the cemetery. That worked so well he relocated the bodies of the star-crossed twelfth-century lovers Heloise and Abelard to Père-Lachaise in 1817 with a fanfare of publicity. The city's upper crust followed, as did a broad spectrum of Parisian society that came to include statesmen, scholars, revolutionaries, artists, writers, musicians, actresses, dancers, courtesans, clerics, merchants, and bankers. Within a few decades, 33,000 citizens were spread across Père-Lachaise's 118 acres. The Parisians had come to stay, with typical Gallic panache. The *rues* and avenues became crowded with elaborate statuary and extravagant crypts. "To be buried in Père-Lachaise is like having mahogany furniture," wrote Victor Hugo.

Père-Lachaise was a multipurpose civic enterprise. Beyond providing a hygienic resting place for the dead, the cemetery also became a recreational destination for the living, as *tout le monde* found it a salubrious spot for saunters and spooners. Père-Lachaise quickly revolutionized cemetery design, becoming the model for *extra muros*—outside the

*Opposite: Views from Crown Hill looking south, taken in 1875 and 2012. The top photo shows the National Cemetery in the upper left and the superintendent's house in the upper right.*

walls—extraurban cemeteries. "Rural cemeteries," they came to be called. Other Paris cemeteries emerged within a few years: Montmartre and Montparnasse among them. London's Highgate Cemetery, established in 1839, copied many Père-Lachaise features: nature and art commingled along picturesque landscaped lanes, gardens chockablock with sculpture and embellished architecture, an intense focus on upkeep, and a dedication to the concept of "beautiful death."

By August 1863 the civic-minded Ray had recognized Greenlawn was rapidly filling with war dead. Ray, Fletcher, and other Indianapolis leaders realized the need to establish a larger cemetery, one that could also bring the bucolic environs of a rural cemetery to rapidly growing industrial Indianapolis. Ray encountered fellow banker Hugh McColloch, a Fort Wayne financier associated with the Bank of Indiana (and later U.S. Treasury Secretary), who was visiting Indianapolis. McColloch told Ray about Fort Wayne's new cemetery, Lindenwood, which a Pittsburgh landscape architect and cemetery superintendent named John Chislett Sr. had laid out. Within a few weeks, Ray and other civic leaders invited Chislett to speak with them.

Chislett was a remarkable Englishman. Born in 1800 in Dover, Chislett learned to paint, sculpt, and play the organ before he apprenticed with a builder working in Bath, a center of the Romanticism movement that swept England in reaction to industrialization's brutal realities. Positing a relationship between culture and nature, Romantic writers such as Samuel Taylor Coleridge, Lord Byron, and Percy Shelley rhapsodized about the spiritual beauty of sublime physical landscapes. British

 and American romantic artists, including J. M. W. Turner, John Constable, Thomas Cole, and Albert Bierstadt, depicted an idealized natural world. British landscape

architects, such as Lancelot "Capability" Brown, in turn, designed entire landscapes to fulfill these visions of nature, often executed on the estates of England's landed gentry. By the early nineteenth century, American Transcendentalists, including Ralph Waldo Emerson and Henry David Thoreau, were likewise linking spirituality with nature, calling for urbanized citizens to have a rural respite from the hurly-burly city. America was ripe for a new kind of garden cemetery.

A slender fellow with a trimmed beard fringing his chin, Chislett arrived in Pittsburgh in 1832, just a year after Boston city fathers established the parklike Mount Auburn Cemetery, based on Père-Lachaise's "domesticated landscape" aesthetic. With Mount Auburn's immediate popularity, the American rural cemetery movement took off, with six more opening in the next five years, among them Laurel Hill in Philadelphia in 1836 and Green-Wood Cemetery in Brooklyn in 1838. Influential American landscape architect Andrew Jackson Downing popularized rural cemeteries in his widely read journal, *The Horticulturist*. Downing wrote in 1849 that not even twenty years after Mount Auburn's opening, "there is scarcely a city of note in the whole country that has not its rural cemetery." Downing termed the rural cemetery, "a resting place for the dead, at once sacred from profanation, dear to the memory, and captivating to the imagination."

Soon after arriving in Pittsburgh, Chislett began making his reputation as one of the city's leading architects with designs for banks, churches, courthouses, and office buildings in *au courant* Greek Revival and Gothic Revival styles. But the romance of landscape design called to him, prompting Chislett to help organize the Allegheny Cemetery. When it opened in 1844 with Chislett as the superintendent, Allegheny was one of America's ten rural cemeteries. Chislett designed the cemetery as a bastion

*Left: Frederick W. Chislett, first superintendent of Crown Hill Cemetery.*
*Opposite: Looking west along the lane, northeast of the barn, May 14, 1902.*

*Below:* Cabin at old west entrance, 1901.
*Bottom:* Frederick Chislett's granddaughter picking flowers, June 2, 1902.

*Opposite:* The carpenter's shop, July 18, 1902.
*Top:* A Crown Hill worker with John, one of the cemetery's horses, April 11, 1902.
*Above:* A cow in the pasture, July 7, 1902.

of Gothic Revival styling, with crenellated gatehouses and grave plots delineated by forests of statuary, obelisks, and wrought-iron fencing atop precise perimeters of stone coping.

By the time Chislett arrived in Indianapolis in the fall of 1863, he was at the top of his game, having already designed other rural cemeteries in Pennsylvania, West Virginia, Indiana, and perhaps Ohio, all reflecting the picturesque romantic style of an imagined English landscape, with scenic winding roads, gazing ponds, and lush glades for the contemplation of nature and eternity. Across the country, rural cemeteries sat at the verges of dozens of cities and towns, providing citizens space for consolation and recreation. And Indianapolis had a grave need: Greenlawn was nearly full. In a decade, the city's population had more than doubled to more than 18,000 in 1860, but the Civil War was accelerating growth. By 1870 more than 48,000 people lived in the city. The time was right for the new cemetery.

Prior to their meeting with Chislett, Ray and other organizers traveled south to Cincinnati to meet with a renowned horticulturist, Adolph Strauch, a Prussian landscape architect who served as superintendent of the city's Spring Grove rural cemetery, which began in 1844. Educated in some of Europe's most prestigious imperial gardens and horticultural establishments, Strauch was a staunch advocate of a restrained style of cemetery design later called the "lawn plan," which emphasized horticulture over monuments. Spring Grove was accordingly famous for its extraordinary collection of rare trees and shrubs from around the world. Compared to Chislett's exuberant Gothic Revival architecture at Pittsburgh, Spring Grove was decidedly more austere. Ever the autocratic Prussian, Strauch had removed all of the ironwork and stone copings that defined family plots, as well as eliminating mounds, hedges, fences, tombs, cemetery furniture, and gravestones that he decreed were disturbing his harmonious landscape of slopes, greensward, ponds, and stately avenues. Strauch wanted a coherent romantic landscape, not a collection of "petty yards or pens," as historian Richard Joseph Morris termed it.

Strauch's aesthetic had an impact on the Indianapolis men, as did his warning about cemetery governance. According to an 1875 book on Crown Hill, Strauch told the visitors that Spring Grove organizers made a mistake when they established the cemetery: "A dangerous error had been committed in organizing this Cemetery Company, by allowing every lot-holder to become, by his purchase, a voter in the annual elections for Directors." In Strauch's view, this allowed "combinations" of voters who attempted to "displace the experienced originators of the company and its valued officers, and unsettled the tested policy of the company." To a Prussian, this must have looked like perilous disorder. As the Indianapolis men contemplated the organization of the new cemetery, they took Strauch's advice to heart.

On September 12, twelve Indianapolis men, including Ray, Fletcher, James Blake, Thomas A. Morris, William S. Hubbard, Theodore P. Haughey, A. L. Roache, John C. New, S. A. Fletcher Jr., Herman Lieber, and J. D. Carmichael met with Chislett at the State Bank of Indiana at the corner of Washington and Pennsylvania Streets to discuss a new cemetery. The first meeting with Chislett went well, with the Indianapolis organizers deciding to appoint committees for site selection, planning, and incorporation.

To avoid Spring Grove's "dangerous error" of governance, the Indianapolis organizers prepared the Articles of Association of Crown Hill Cemetery, which stipulated that the corporation would consist of only thirty handpicked members, "and their successors forever," as the 1875 book put it, "with the power to fill all vacancies arising amongst them by decease or otherwise, by electing the survivors, and thus the succession of the Corporators be perpetuated until the end of time." Chislett's Allegheny Cemetery likewise had a closed board, suggesting he was likely supportive of the Crown Hill decision. So from the beginning, Crown Hill was run by a self-perpetuating Board of Corporators, as the cemetery trustees came to be known, most overwhelmingly from old, prosperous, civic-minded Indianapolis families such as the Fletchers, the Ayres, the Butlers, the Liebers, and the Lillys. Decade after decade, the thirty board seats passed down through bloodlines or close associations. Over time, membership on the Board of Corporators became the "unchallenged mark of Indianapolis social prominence," as journalist Philip J. Trounstine noted.

The site committee took to its task with dispatch. After the meeting with Chislett, Fletcher recorded in his diary that he was already negotiating for land: "I have been appointed to see 2 quakers to learn if they will sell 80 acres that purpose." The committee was working with a charge that the new cemetery should be within six miles of the city limits and no more than six hundred acres in size. The two Quakers, James Trueblood and Jonathan Wilson, each owned forty acres adjacent to the nursery farm of Martin Williams. Located in the far countryside north of town, Williams's farm was surmounted by Strawberry Hill, a favorite picnicking spot that was one of the county's highest elevations. The rolling terrain of the Williams farm was perfect for the rustic cemetery that Chislett envisioned. The corporators later termed Williams's farm, "by nature, the finest scenery within ten miles of the city." Members of the search committee remembered Chislett saying, "That is the spot! Buy those grounds at whatever price you have to pay."

Just a few decades before, the Williams farm had been part of a vast wilderness, scarcely punctuated by settlers. "Here and there was a cabin home with a little spot of clearing close by. The rest of the country was jist one great big woods for miles and miles in most every direction," Indianapolis pioneer Oliver Johnson recounted. The land between the White River and Fall Creek was covered with virgin forests of towering walnut and sugar maple, interspersed with poplar, oak, ash, beech, hickory, and wild cherry trees. "There was a bigness and certain mouldy or woodsy smell to a forest that's hard to describe, but to us it was mighty sweet and satisfyin," Johnson remembered. Wild

animals prowled the countryside. Johnson recalled being worried as a boy about being "eat up by a panther," when he had to traverse what became the Williams farm. Bears denned just a short trek north. Johnson remembered standing beside their cabin with his mother, watching a great bear chase: "That old bear was lopin along throwin his front feet to one side then to the other, looking like he was pretty tired." It was cause for celebration when the dogs treed the bear, and a Hoosier marksman took it down. "Well, we skinned and dressed the bear, and the whole neighborhood had bear meat for a change," he remembered. While it was an arduous life on the Indianapolis frontier, Johnson found it to his liking: "Yet we got along purty well them days. We had our ups and downs, but nobody went hungry and nobody done much complainin. We just about lived off the land and was satisfied."

Though the cemetery committee was determined to buy the land, Williams was a reluctant seller—he liked his 166 acres and intended to develop it. The committee members moved quickly to inveigle Williams to sell the land. The day following the Chislett meeting, Fletcher was on his way to see Williams, arranging a negotiation meeting for the next morning. The deal was soon done. To pay for the farm, Fletcher's brother, Stoughton Sr., fronted the $51,500 purchase price at nominal interest. Almost immediately, the committee purchased the Quakers' two adjacent farms of forty acres each, and two other smaller plots. This acreage of farm, orchard, meadow, and marsh became the core of Crown Hill. On October 22, 1863, the *Indiana State Sentinel* announced: "The public will be gratified to learn that the arrangements for a rural cemetery in this vicinity are completed, and that, from its suitable distance from the city, the convenient access to it on a gravel way without any railroad crossing, and the appropriate features of the grounds, with the crowning beauty of including the most conspicuous elevation in this region, we may be assured that, in the hands of the citizens who

*Opposite: The Pioneer Cemetery at Crown Hill reflects a commitment to the community to provide a beautiful and permanent resting place for pioneers who were relocated to Crown Hill when their original cemeteries were closed. It is comprised of three separate cemeteries: Greenlawn Cemetery, Rhoads Cemetery, and the Wright-Whitesell-Gentry Cemetery.*

*Above and far left:* Exterior and interior of the superintendent's home. Frederick Chislett's great-granddaughter is sitting on the porch steps.
*Left:* Field northeast of Chislett's home, which is just north of the Service Yard.

have engaged in the enterprise, Crown Hill Cemetery will, in its future, rank favorably with the lovely cities of the dead, which are so pleasantly attractive in other parts of the country."

The corporators had a vision—to convert the forest and swamp into "a vast and exquisite lawn, studded with native trees and groups of shrubbery, swelling into graceful undulations or sinking into shaded and solitary dells, and everywhere shining with elegant monuments and sedulous and graceful labors of the superintendent," as an early Crown Hill writer put it.

To accomplish their task, the corporators needed a superintendent. Luckily, a qualified man was available. Although Chislett returned to his work in Pittsburgh, the Chislett family was not done with Crown Hill. John Sr.'s son, Frederick, had worked with his father at Allegheny Cemetery, but was currently pursuing a career in hardware in Dubuque, Iowa. Leaping on the opportunity, the corporators promptly offered Frederick the job as the first Crown Hill superintendent, a position he was to hold until his death in 1899, when his son, John, succeeded him.

Many years later, John Jr., Frederick's son, recalled his family's arrival at Crown Hill, then a solitary farm in the middle of the woods: "Father and mother and we three little boys landed in Indianapolis on a warm, rainy day, December 31, 1863. We went out to the old Martin Williams log cabin on the south slope of Crown Hill, and next morning the mercury was twenty-seven below zero. It was the historic cold New Year. For a time we really suffered. Though a little child then, I remember it well!" Coming at the end of a long warm fall, the bitter cold snap caused great misery, particularly in the tented army and prison camps, where many died.

"Crown Hill was then a wild, secluded place," John Jr. remembered. "Father would not open the door after dark to anyone and often had to drive some one away at the point of his revolver." There was considerable controversy about the corporators' decision to locate the cemetery so far from town. It took a good part of a day to make a round-trip. Many thought no one would bury loved ones in such a lonely place. And it was not without risk or travail to get there. Indianapolis was

thronged with encamped Union soldiers, many disaffected by the endless slaughter that had gone on year after year. They made travel out to Crown Hill complicated, as the Chisletts, workers, and visitors had to pass Camp Carrington, near the canal where Methodist Hospital now stands. "Soldiers from the camps were sometimes very troublesome, and getting things out there in any sort of shape was a pretty hard proposition," John Jr. wrote.

By the following summer, there were loads of materials heading out to Crown Hill, as Frederick began overseeing the construction of the first road that led from the entrance on Michigan Road into the cemetery. In addition, workers began draining low marshy ground and removing thickets and bramble, replacing them with specimen trees. In general, Frederick commingled his father's scenic landscape designs with Strauch's Prussian sensibilities. Early photographs show the picturesque winding lanes and vistas that are defining elements of English Romanticism, but the absence of elaborated wrought-iron cemetery fences reflected Strauch's spare *ordnung*—"no fences or railings, or obtrusive marks of individual ownership are permitted," the 1875 Crown Hill history bragged. It was as though Crown Hill was aesthetically reaching out to the diverse communities that formed the little city on the prairie: English Romanticism for the displaced New Englanders and southerners who made Indianapolis their home; a Teutonic sense of restraint for those thousands of German *auswanderers* who had migrated to the Circle City. Organized with dispatch for an eternal mission, Crown Hill was quickly becoming a reality.

On June 1, 1864, about four hundred people, most members of prominent Indianapolis families, journeyed out from town in horse and buggy to attend the cemetery dedication. Though it would soon to be a recreational destination for the city's moneyed classes, Crown Hill was pretty rough in its early stages. Fletcher visited the farm the day before the ceremony and wrote, "It looked too rude and badly fixed to hold the dedication contemplated tomorrow." In spite of the grounds' still crude condition, the dedication was a success. Four pastors gave invocations and prayers, a poet read an offering, and the attending band played several anthems. Former congressman and senator, the Honorable Albert S. White, judge of the U.S. Court of the District of Indiana, gave a lengthy speech that was acclaimed by the *Indianapolis Sentinel* as "surpassing beautiful. It appeals to every noble sentiment that animates the human heart." White, who died shortly after his dedication speech, told his audience, "You do well, friends, to leave for a day the busy pursuits of common life to plant these altars here." He concluded his remarks by saying, "Let it be the glory of Crown Hill that the rich and poor, the proud and humble, alike may enter here, . . . where the marble monument, not only, shall be preserved inviolate, but where the written records of its silent inmates shall be transmitted from generation to generation and carefully kept from moth and worm."

The oratory complete, the crowd scattered over the hills and dales to choose their final resting places. Ninety-year-old Mrs. Daniel Stewart was at the dedication, and she remembered the families' choices: "It was wonderful to note how different their taste in location for their last home proved to be. Some selected the rounded top of an elevation for the extended view it gave; others preferred the gently sloping hillside where the lengthen-

ing shadows lingered in the valleys. Some loved the western sun and the twilight, others wanted the first rays of the morning sun to rest upon their dwellings." A week later, when Crown Hill auctioned off the first plots, the Indianapolis solons again had the opportunity to display their proclivities. Ray paid $1,500 for his choice in Section 1, while the self-effacing Fletchers of old Vermont stock made do with lots that cost a third as much. The day before the sale, Calvin Fletcher noted in his diary, "Tomorrow sale of lots takes place. I feel as I did in the sale of lots in the old graveyard—no spirit of rivalry where I shall be buried—can not compeat with my neighbor in this matter. He may have any place he chooses & I will lay down where it may be quiet, if the spot can be found."

The real business of the cemetery was soon upon Crown Hill. Lucy Ann Seaton, the young wife of an army captain, was stricken with tuberculosis and died in Indianapolis on May 26, 1864. An Indianapolis newspaper announced what was to be Crown Hill's first burial and asked the community to take part: "The husband of the deceased is a gentleman of high standing, and as he is a stranger in this city we hope his invitation to the public to join in the funeral exercises will be accepted by a goodly number." Two dark horses drew undertaker Mathew Long's polished

black hearse out to Crown Hill. As the hearse passed, townspeople could see Seaton's casket behind the crepe-draped lozenge window. At the cemetery, a simple marble slab decorated with a weeping willow documented Seaton's passage from her 1831 birth in Halifax, Virginia, to her death in Indiana. At the base of the stone, an inscription perpetuated her lamenting husband's eternal hope: "Lucy, God grant I may meet you in Heaven."

GIVEN BY DENNY AND JANE SMITH
TO HONOR AND REMEMBER
TO COMFORT AND EMBRACE
2006

MY WIFE SO LOVED
MY
CHILDREN
DEAR,
SWEET TREASURES
THEY LIE
SLEEPING HERE

# 2

## MONUMENTS AND REMEMBRANCES, 1865–1875

From its humble beginnings, Crown Hill quickly began to evolve into the parklike setting the founders had envisioned. A crew of twenty-five to forty men labored through the season, laying out the seven sections, as well as roads and paths shaded by maples, elms, catalpas, and evergreens. Within a few years visitors on the summit could view the graveled roads curling precisely through the cemetery, dividing the land into discrete sections punctuated by white obelisks and low markers. Specimen trees were already growing to a healthy size. Just a few months after Lucy Ann Seaton was laid to rest in 1864 as Crown Hill's first interment, workmen completed the stone gateway at the west entrance off of Michigan Road. Built by John Pattison for $2,300, the stately main entrance was comprised of a large central gate and two narrower gates. In October of the same year, the east entrance opened with a road that wound through an allée of trees, followed a few years later by a substantial gatehouse.

The Indianapolis public began to embrace Crown Hill as a final resting place. Two years after Seaton's funeral, there were about 475 Crown Hill lot purchases. The owners included an attorney, a saw manufacturer, a saloonkeeper, a wealthy brewer, a lumberman, a cigarist, a newspaperman, a carriage maker, a cobbler, an engineer, a baker, a bookbinder, a grocer, a carpenter, a soldier, a marshal, a minister, a doctor's wife, and a jeweler. It was a shimmering partial reflection of early Indianapolis society.

Among the first interred in the new cemetery was Josephine Jones, a fourteen-year-old African American woman who died of a lung illness on February 19, 1865. A gravedigger's daughter, her father's coworkers buried Jones in Grave 1, Lot 4 of Section 4. From the beginning, Crown Hill was a place of racial and economic diversity, testifying to Albert S. White's dedicatory hope that the cemetery would honor both "the rich and poor, the proud and humble." But early in Crown Hill's history, the Crown Hill Corporators began sequestering most African Americans into segregated sections. The June 6, 1865, minutes of the Crown Hill board of directors noted, "Ordered That the Superintendent report next meeting a plan for appropriating a particular part of the Cemetery lots to be sold to the coloured people." Despite the lofty ideals expressed in White's address, the corporators clearly made distinctions between the races. The September 5, 1865, meeting minutes recorded: "It was ordered that colored persons be prohibited from riding in the omnibus except on the first & last trip each day & that they be required to enter & leave the omnibus at the out skirts of the city." There was further evidence of the founders' divided minds. The second Crown Hill annual report in 1866 stated: "Large and magnificent lots (many of them circular) valued at thousands of dollars, are joined by small plots which are within the means of the humblest citizens.

# THE CROWN HILL CEMETERY

**ORGANIZED** OCTOBER 10th 1863

Under the Laws of INDIANA.

**CONSECRATED** JUNE 1st 1864

No. 4862

### A Corporation Organized under the General Laws of the State of Indiana.

In consideration of the sum of _Twelve Hundred Twenty_ _____ Dollars
hereby gives and grants unto

_Magdalena Staub_

the exclusive right of burial for _herself_ and the persons to be named by _her_ in
event of the failure of _her_ nomination to _the_ heirs subject to all the conditions and limitations, and with the privileges specified in the Rules and Regulations of said Cemetery now in existence herewith printed on the back hereof or which may hereafter be lawfully prescribed in and upon that certain parcel of land situated in Marion County in the State of Indiana described and designated on the plat of said Cemetery as now laid out as

_North Park_ Lot No. _235_

in Section _25_ containing _1220_ superficial feet

In Testimony Whereof, The said Corporation has caused these Presents to be sealed with its Corporate Seal signed by its President and countersigned by its Secretary this _29th_ day of _October_ _1908_

Attest:

_William J Landes_ Secretary

_Geo B Yandes_ President

---

### State of Indiana, County of Marion, ss:

Before me, a Notary Public in and for the said County, the said _Geo B Yandes_ President,
and _William J Landes_ Secretary, of the Crown Hill Cemetery,
acknowledged the execution of the annexed Deed, for the uses and purposes therein expressed.

**IN TESTIMONY WHEREOF,** I have hereunto set my name and affixed my Notarial Seal, this
_29th_ day of _October_ _1908_

_Susan S Moore_ Notary Public.

My Commission Expires _Dec 9th 1911_

Wm B Burford Lith Indianapolis Ind.

. . . Every section contains its large lots, and small and cheap ones, also, and each presents attractions sufficient to all classes, so that there can never be a separation of the Cemetery into divisions for different classes, but literally:

> —Side by side, the high and low,
> And rich and poor, shall equal lie.

The first section used for burials, Section 4, included four different plots for single interments, two were reserved for white burials, two for "Persons of Color." However contradictory the thinking, African Americans and European Americans lay close to one another in the early burials. Near Jones, a fifty-five-year-old laborer named Moses Croft, who had drowned in Pogue's Run in 1865, was buried, as was Pryor Hankin, an African American who had died of typhus fever in 1865. Not far away lay Calvin Fletcher Sr., pioneer Indianapolis's great diarist. After a grand career as a lawyer, businessman, banker, public figure, and farmer, Fletcher passed away on May 26, 1866. After the funeral at Fletcher's Pennsylvania Street home, a cortege nearly a mile long stretched out to Crown Hill, where he had visited in the previous months to oversee preparations for the reinterment of his family's remains from Greenlawn. As befit the man who defined rectitude, a simple stone marked his grave in Section 7. A tall brown stepped obelisk eventually towered over the Fletcher family plot. Given the number of burials, Superintendant Frederick Chislett had reason to be pleased. He reported to the corporators in July 1866, "In comparing the amount of our sales, with the amount sold by other Cemeteries during these first two years, we have every reason to be satisfied with our success."

It was still a trek to Crown Hill. A woman who buried her mother in 1865 remembered that although the Crown Hill service began at 1:00 p.m., they did not get back to their Washington Street house until dark because the mourners had to repeatedly rest the horses exhausted from laboring down narrow, bumpy Meridian Street. But the number of burials dramatically increased in 1866, when the U.S. government authorized a National Cemetery to be established on 1.4 acres in Crown Hill. With Greenlawn filled and destined to be overrun by industrial development, the federal government wanted to move the Union dead to the new cemetery. In the spring of 1866, the Crown Hill corporators had initially offered to donate the land valued at $15,000 for the national cemetery, with the understanding that the government would improve and ornament the site. But the government representative, Brigadier General James A. Ekin, did not have the authorization to expend funds for that purpose. So an agreement was reached: the government bought the land for $5,000 and Crown Hill used the funds to ornament the burial plot.

The first reinterment was on October 19, 1866, when an honor guard moved the remains of soldier Matthew Quigley from the Statehouse Rotunda to Crown Hill, where the towered bell tolled, a military band played dirges, ministers and Governor Oliver P. Morton spoke, and a squad of soldiers fired three volleys. Quigley was the first. Soon the remains of many Union soldiers came to rest on the gentle hill—the fallen were from the infantry, the cavalry, the artillery; most were Hoosier men, most were cut down in the flower of their lives. Among them were Private Martin

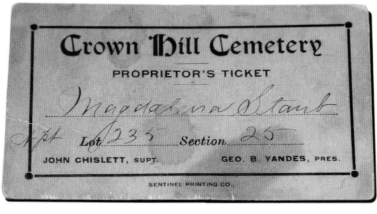

# FREDERICK KNEFLER

Frederick Knefler was a fifteen-year-old Hungarian Jewish activist when he was wounded during the Revolutions of 1848. When the czar's hussars crushed the revolution, his physician father, also a militant progressive, took Frederick and other family members to the United States, first to New York and then Indianapolis. The Kneflers were one of Indianapolis's earliest Jewish families and among those who founded the city's first synagogue, the Indianapolis Hebrew Congregation, in 1856.

Trained as a carpenter in New York, Knefler continued his trade in Indianapolis while he studied law. Working as an assistant in the Marion County Clerk's office, Knefler made the acquaintance of Lew Wallace, the governor's son. When the Civil War broke out, Governor Oliver P. Morton appointed Wallace adjutant general, charged with raising 7,500 men. Wallace recruited Knefler to be his principal assistant. Commissioned as a lieutenant, Knefler rose to the rank of brevet brigadier general. His regiment fought at Fort Henry and Fort Donelson, Shiloh, Stones River, Chickamauga, and Missionary Ridge, taking horrific losses as the price of disputed victories. During the East Tennessee winter campaign, Knefler took command of the Seventy-ninth Indiana Brigade, which played a major role in the battles of Pickett's Mill, Peach Tree Creek, Jonesboro, and Lovejoy's Station, before the unit marched into Atlanta. During the battle of Nashville, Knefler's brigade was part of a force that critically charged a Confederate unit and captured most of its armaments. When brevetted as brigadier general, Knefler was commended for "gallant and meritorious services during the war."

After the war, Knefler returned to the law in Indianapolis, where he was ap-

pointed by President Rutherford B. Hayes as head of the pension office. Knefler was the president of the Indiana Soldiers and Sailors Monument's board of regents when the cornerstone was laid in 1889, but died before the monument was completed. After his death on June 14, 1901, Knefler was interred in Crown Hill's Section 8, Lot 22.

Knefler's burial was unusual, as most members of Indianapolis's Jewish community in his day chose to be buried in the south side Hebrew cemetery on Kelly Street. Established in 1858, it predated Crown Hill. "The first thing a congregation does is set up a cemetery," said Max Nelson, longtime head of the Aaron-Ruben-Nelson Mortuary, which specializes in funeral services for the Indianapolis Jewish community. As a nonsectarian cemetery, Crown Hill had no written proscriptions against Jewish burials. Nevertheless, "Jews wanted to be buried with Jews," Nelson said.

Parrott, an Indiana cavalryman, who died on February 12, 1863; Private Silas Carr from Michigan, who died on September 16, 1864; and Private Ephrain Clarke, an Iowan soldier who died without even a record of date. Private Diamond Mendenhall and Private Dempsey Porter were both soldiers in the United States Colored Troops. Both died in the bloody spring of 1864.

Private Robert Gay was also reinterred in the National Cemetery. A Clay County schoolteacher, Gay had enlisted in the Seventy-first Regiment of the Sixth Indiana Cavalry, but not long after Confederates captured him near Richmond, Kentucky. To

> Through much of American history, "rest in peace" was a fluid concept. The practice of moving bodies, often multiple times, was common.

avoid further military service, Gay took an oath of allegiance to the Confederacy. When he returned to Indiana, he was convicted of treason and sentenced to death. On March 27, 1863, a firing squad of twenty soldiers lined up behind the Burnside Barracks just south of Camp Morton and shot the twenty-seven-year-old Gay in front of his freshly dug grave. Accounts indicated that he was "unmoved and calm." When asked if he had anything to say, he responded:

> Fellow soldiers, I am about to die for the crime of desertion. I have done wrong. I know I have done wrong; but I did it unthoughtedly. I can call God to witness, before whom I must appear in a few minutes, that I did not mean to commit a crime, if ever a man tells the truth it is when he is about to die; and I tell the truth when I say that I meant no wrong. When I took the oath of allegiance, I intended only to get home, so that I might stay; for I did not feel able for service . . . I never intended to desert my country. . . . To you who would fire at me, I would say, take your aim well. Fire at the breast; [laying his hand on his heart] that is the place. Hold on the spot firmly. I want to die quickly. Don't let me suffer. Again, I will say, I forgive everybody, and ask them to forgive me.

It was the first and only military execution in the West during the war. Many, many other soldiers with similar stories were pardoned for the same offense.

By November 1866 undertakers had moved 707 soldiers from Greenlawn to Crown Hill, reburying them in new coffins that were a regulation seven feet by twenty inches by seventeen inches, interred precisely two feet apart.

Reinterment of the Union dead was not unique. Through much of American history, "rest in peace" was a fluid concept. The practice of moving bodies, often multiple times, was common. When Fletcher chose his new family plot in Crown Hill, he intended to move the remains of his family, including his beloved wife, from Greenlawn, where he found "the original forest trees" had covered the graves settled deep into the earth. Since his wife had died in 1854, Fletcher had already moved her body at least once, relocating her to the center of his Greenlawn plot after one of his relatives had moved their dead to another graveyard. The Crown Hill organizers saw ending all this morbid mobility as a sales tool. In the first public notice of the new cemetery, the *Indiana State Sentinel* on October 22, 1863, discussed Crown Hill's promise of permanence, "The corporators trust that this selection will be approved by their fellow citizens, whose generous co-operation is solicited to secure, that the sad scattering of the dust of fore-fathers, which in the enlargement of other cities, has been disturbed in their tombs, after two hundred years of burial, may not befall the remains of those who are now among the living here, or who are dear to those among the buried." Mark Twain channeled the zeitgeist with his 1870 short story, "A Curious Dream," in which he recounted a dream of watching a skeleton carry a rotting casket and chipped grave marker down the street. Displeased with his former home in a derelict old graveyard, the skeleton was moving to a new cemetery. As a counterpoint to all the moving and shuffling, Crown Hill and other rural cemeteries promised eternal care, a place where the grieving could envision loved ones resting in perpetuity.

Caleb Blood Smith was another of those wandering souls. Lawyer, journalist, politician, and, as President Abraham Lincoln's Secretary of Interior, the first Hoosier to serve as a cabinet member, Smith died on January 7, 1864. After an initial burial in a $500 plot his widow bought in Greenlawn cemetery, Smith's remains went on the move. Fearing that the Sons of Liberty, an offshoot of the Southern-sympathizing Copperhead peace advocates, were going to desecrate Smith's body (even though Smith had resigned his cabinet post to protest the Emancipation Proclamation), his family moved his remains. Some said his wife moved him to an unauthorized hillside tomb in Crown Hill. Fearing it was unsanitary, the Crown Hill managers ordered her to remove the body. It was a "stormy time," as John Chislett Jr. remembered. Rumors had it that Smith's wife hauled him to his hometown cemetery in Connersville, others said Cincinnati, some insisted he went back to Greenlawn, but his remains were lost in the shuffle. The family theoretically intended to move his body into their elaborate Egyptian-styled limestone tomb that they built as Crown Hill's first mausoleum. While "C. B. Smith" is carved into the mausoleum frieze, no one is quite sure where Smith is interred. Though the location of Smith's body remains in dispute, records indicate his wife, daughter, and other relations are entombed there.

> Crown Hill and other rural cemeteries promised eternal care, a place where the grieving could envision loved ones resting in perpetuity.

Not many years after the Civil War ended, an effort to bind the nation's wounds began. On May 5, 1868, General John Logan, national commander of the Grand Army of the Republic, officially proclaimed the first Decoration Day, later known as Memorial Day. His General Order Number 11 proclaimed, "The 30th day of May, 1868, is designated for the purpose of strewing with flowers or otherwise decorating the graves of comrades who died in defense of their country during the late rebellion, and whose bodies now lie in almost every city, village, and hamlet church-yard in the land. In this observance no form of ceremony is prescribed, but posts and comrades will in their own way arrange such fitting services and testimonials of respect as circumstances may permit." Logan carefully picked his date. Beyond being the peak of the spring flowering, May 30 was the date the last Civil War Union soldier was mustered out, as well as not coinciding with the anniversary of any major battle. "Let us, then, at the time appointed gather around their sacred remains and garland the passionless mounds above them with the choicest flowers of spring-time; let us raise above them the dear old flag they saved from dishonor; let us in this solemn presence renew our pledges to aid and assist those whom they have left among us a sacred charge upon a nation's gratitude, the soldier's and sailor's widow and orphan," Logan proclaimed.

On May 30, 1868, just a few weeks after Logan's appeal, mourners placed flowers on the graves of Union and Confederate soldiers at Arlington National Cemetery and at 183 cemeteries in twenty-seven states—including Crown Hill. With thousands of GAR veterans in the city, Indianapolis leaders had quickly responded with pomp and ceremony. At noon on May 30, Captain Rose's Light Battery fired minute guns to signal the suspension of daily business, the first of hourly cannonades that alternated between batteries at Crown Hill and the Statehouse. At 2:00 p.m. the city's church bells began ringing as a vast processional rolled from Illinois Street toward Crown Hill. The city band, a wagon of war orphans, and mounted veterans brandishing their battle flags led the way. City and state officials, GAR soldiers and families, and a host of citizens followed in carriages and streetcars. "The procession was very large and made a fine appearance," the *Indianapolis Journal* reported. The water company also ran a fleet of canal boats to Crown Hill, the crowd embarking from the Old Yellow Bridge at Indiana Avenue and Michigan Street for a fare of ten cents, disembarking after the voyage near Golden Hill, for a slog to the cemetery.

An estimated crowd of 10,000 gathered at Crown Hill, which the *Journal* described as a "spectacle that was both a sad one, and a most gratifying one, in the indication that the fires of patriotism had been kindled anew upon the altar of every heart, and mystic chord of memory had united the people to the graves of the dead heroes." A bugler called the assembly and an adjacent general read Logan's call. Ministers read fervent prayers; choirs sang dirges and hymns; and a poet, Granville M. Ballard, read a work he had written for the event. Governor Conrad Baker gave his address, ending with the invocation, "So teach us our duty, O Lord. Amen." While a choir sang, "Peace to the Memory of the Brave," a coterie of young Indianapolis women carrying flower baskets placed an evergreen wreath on each headstone. "The scene cannot be fitly described," the *Journal* reported. Crown

Hill's first Memorial Day ended with spirited renditions of "The Star Spangled Banner," "Hail Columbia," and a final benediction.

In his order for the first Memorial Day, Logan challenged Americans to remember the fallen soldiers. He wrote, "If other eyes grow dull, other hands slack, and other hearts cold in the solemn trust, ours shall keep it well as long as the light and warmth of life remain to us." Almost a century and a half after the scarred nation celebrated its first day of memory for the fallen, Crown Hill continues the tradition of remembrance.

When Crown Hill was established, critics railed that the cemetery was too far from the city. But the city quickly reached out to Crown Hill. The 1875 history noted, "Ten years have proven that it was not too remote, and five are more likely to prove that it would have been better farther out." Though Crown Hill was

East Entrance.

West Entrance.

Above left: The first west entrance was constructed in 1864 when the cemetery opened, this photo taken in 1875.
Above right: East entrance, 1875. Below: Second west entrance built in 1901, photo taken in 1920.

almost four miles from the central city, the suburbs were just a mile from the cemetery's southern edge. By 1875 a thousand plot holders owned about a fifth of the expanded four hundred-acre cemetery. Since the initial land purchases, the corporators acquired two forty-acre plots along the northern border (just south of today's Thirty-eighth Street) in 1871, and two small trapezoidal parcels along Michigan Road in 1865 and 1875. A dozen years after opening, about fifty-five acres of Crown Hill were laid out in burial sections; thirty acres were in walks and drives. By 1871 there were 2,100 burials in the cemetery.

Omnibuses began traveling out to the cemetery in 1864. Commencing from Washington and Illinois Streets at 9:30 a.m., the omnibuses took four hours to reach Crown Hill, as the horses had to be changed at what is now Thirtieth Street because of the deep mud. The fare was considerable: fifty cents roundtrip. But the cemetery leaders wanted better, so donated $10,000 for the establishment of a streetcar line, the Crown Hill Railway Company, which formed an agreement with the Citizens Street Railway Company to run a line from Tinker Street (today's Sixteenth Street) to the Crown Hill entrance on Michigan Road, with the round-trip ticket to cost no more than twenty-five cents. The line opened in the spring of 1867, though service out to Crown Hill was on demand rather than scheduled. The mule cars generally made the trip for funerals, special gatherings, and memorial days. One woman remembered the trip was accompanied by the swishing sound on the bottom of the cars from the tall weeds growing between the tracks. Many Crown Hill visitors hired the "Crown Hill horses" and hacks from Wood and Foundray's livery stable, which had Lady Lord, a famous mare who reportedly could deduce the correct speed based on each lady's age—a decorous jog trot for more mature women and a sprightlier pace for those under forty. During the 1870s, the steam-powered *Cleopatra* also churned picnickers up the Central Canal to Crown Hill. "It is now a beautiful place, and a constant resort on fine days," W. R. Holloway reported in 1870. By 1875 the Indianapolis Street Railway Company was running the streetcars out to the cemetery, where perambulating citizens disembarked for relaxation and contemplation, joining others traversing the winding lanes in their carriages. Even as late as 1913, a two-wheeled wagonette drawn by two horses met visitors at the Crown Hill gates and conveyed them to various parts of the cemetery.

*Below: The east entrance (Thirty-fourth Street) constructed in 1885 from a design submitted by Adolph Scherrer. Photo taken in 1902.*

Beginning in the 1830s, the American rural cemeteries served as proto-parks, the models for a broad range of urban civic spaces set aside for "natural" recreation—however contrived and manufactured the natural space turned out to be. Landscape architect Andrew Jackson Downing, the influential proponent of rural cemeteries, was one of the first champions of New York's Central Park, the great touchstone of American urban parks, which was constructed in the late 1850s. Central Park's primary landscape architect, Frederick Law Olmstead, was deeply influenced by rural cemetery design. Along with his prolific work on urban parks, Olmstead designed numerous cemeteries, including Cleveland's Sunset Memorial Park, Detroit's Elmwood Cemetery, and Oakland's Mountain View. Olmstead termed the natural sanctuaries shoehorned into the American cities to be "a democratic development of the highest significance." Although through the 1860s Central Park was a less than democratic endeavor, its location was too far north for the working classes to walk or be able to afford a ticket for a tram ride. Instead, it was the playground of the wealthy, who cantered along the cemeterylike roadways in luxurious carriages.

The sinuous curves of America's cemetery roads did more than influence the carriage drives of urban parks. The cemetery roads also helped engender the entire concept of pleasure driving on byways constructed for the purpose of providing tranquil prospects and picturesque vistas. While apparently natural in their curving course through an allegorical landscape, the cemetery roads were actually highly functional, exactly segmenting the land into exquisitely surveyed sections that maximized plots and eased the way for hearses.

So Crown Hill was Indianapolis's first park. The same year Crown Hill opened, Governor Morton established the downtown Military Park on the former Union marshaling grounds, but that land was ravaged by years of bivouacking brigades. Unlike Crown Hill, Military Park was a far cry from a bucolic enclave. In contrast, the journey from city to Crown Hill was a sojourn from the industrial hubbub to a quiet retreat, a metaphor for transit and the passage of life itself. Once at Crown Hill, visitors entered a composed natural environment. Frederick Chislett had been busy. Draining, ditching, and planting, he crafted the natural contours of Crown Hill into a park that people realized was also "a very beautiful home for their dead," as author Anna Nicholas wrote. And like Central Park, Crown Hill had just enough distance from the working-class environs to soon make it "a choice resort of the better class of citizens," as the 1875 Crown Hill history noted.

*The first private mausoleum at Crown Hill was built in 1864 for the C. B. Smith family. Caleb Blood Smith, the first presidential cabinet member from Indiana, served as Secretary of the Interior for Abraham Lincoln. Caleb's body was never placed in the family mausoleum, and its whereabouts is an ongoing mystery.*

*The Kitchen–Bradley Mausoleum. John M. Kitchen, a leading Indianapolis physician, was surgeon in charge of the U. S. General Army Hospital at Indianapolis. He married Mary Bradley in 1853. Kitchen was an original Crown Hill Corporator and traveled to Tennessee to select the timber for the first cemetery fence.*

Though a place of leisure, Crown Hill was also a proper place. The cemetery rules and regulations warned, "Visitors are reminded that these grounds are sacredly devoted to the interment of the dead, and that a strict observation of the decorum which should characterize such a place will be required." Visitors were required to obtain "Special Tickets" to enter the grounds. Smoking, refreshments, and unattended children were not permitted, nor were dogs, omnibuses, or the discharge of firearms. Persons disturbing "quiet and good order," the regulations promised, "will be compelled instantly to leave the grounds." The corporators further resolved "that the police at the Cemetery be instructed to arrest any person offending any of the above rules."

Within a few years, architecture began to adorn Crown Hill's slopes, creating a conversation between art and nature that echoed Romanticism's idealized balance between art and the pastoral. By 1866 families had erected seventy-one monuments and eighty-five memorials, including the austere Kitchen Family mausoleum that masons built into a hillside. John M. Kitchen, one of the original incorporators, was a prominent Indianapolis physician, who Morton appointed to provide medical care to the military camps, including Camp Morton. Soon after Crown

Hill was established, Kitchen traveled south to Tennessee to procure lumber for the cemetery's first fence. In building Crown Hill's second mausoleum in 1866, Kitchen also pioneered "pre-planning": Though he had the foresight to build the mauso-leum within a few years of the cemetery's founding, he was not entombed there until his death in 1916.

In the spring of 1874 Chislett appointed a committee to plan a new vault to store bodies during inclement weather to replace the original built near the southeast part of the cemetery. Until the development of powered machinery, hard winter freezes often prevented burials until the spring. On January 7, 1875, the cemetery leaders voted to approach Indianapolis architect D. A. Bohlen for a "plan and estimate for a New Vault in the Hill Side with capacity to hold 50 Bodies, and also to get a cheap sketch and plan for a Greenhouse." Indianapolis architect Diedrich August Bohlen was a master of the German neo-Gothic style. Born near Hanover, Germany, Bohlen had traversed northern Germany and Poland on a *wanderjahr* architectural tour, sketching as he went. After working in Europe, he immigrated in 1852 to Indianapolis, where he worked with renowned architect Francis Costigan, but quickly went on his own. Since the founding of his firm in 1853, Bohlen had designed the Saint Mary-of-the-Woods convent and chapel, the Morris-Butler House, the Churchman House, Roberts Park Church, Saint John Catholic Church, the General German Protestant Orphans Home, and numerous other structures. The corporators already had experience with Bohlen. In 1869 he had designed a handsome house on the cemetery grounds for the Chislett family that replaced the cabin where they first lived. After additional meetings, the corporators established a budget of $30,000 for the new vault. Construction projects being what they eternally are, the building got bigger, far more elaborate, and naturally, more expensive. The vault became a vault for ninety-six bodies and chapel. Rather than a functional vault dug into the hillside, the corporators decided to build a structure that "will be both ornamental and useful and supply a much needed place for funeral services in inclement weather."

*Gothic Vault (Chapel) built in 1875.*

Bohlen did indeed design an ornamental and useful building, specifying a tall and graceful limestone paean to the Gothic-Revival style. In the summer of 1875 builder Peter Routiers began construction on the Gothic Vault, as it was then known, and by the spring of 1877 the corporators were settling up the final bills. On June 5, 1877, the corporators bragged in the minutes, "Our new Vault and Chapel has been finished at a cost of $38,922.25 and is entirely paid for. It is a beautiful and enduring structure, having capacity for storing 96 caskets and is conveniently designed for Chapel Services when desired." The corporators quickly established rental rates for the vaults: five dollars for the first month, and ten dollars for each subsequent month, most likely to expedite burial arrangements. As the architects specified, the builders sheathed the exterior in Ellettsville, Indiana, limestone and constructed the interior with two-foot-thick flat stone, with a ventilation cavity between the two walls. The ventilating shaft provided an essential advantage, as an 1875 *Journal* article explained: "It will be noticed that the arrangement of the chapel will dissipate the usual damp and foetid smell usually

a concomitant at funerals in small chapels, and will provide a great convenience to mourners in wet weather."

As the builders were working on the Gothic Vault in August 1875, a little girl, not yet six years old, passed away from a lung ailment. Mary Ella McGinnis was one of General George F. McGinnis and wife Josephine's seven children. After his Civil War service at Shiloh and Vicksburg, McGinnis had moved the family to Indianapolis, where he ran a fiduciary business and held various civic positions, including county auditor. After Mary Ella's untimely death, the undertakers buried the girl in Section 16, Lot 23.

To honor her memory, Mary Ella's heartbroken mother commissioned a celebrated Chicago sculptor, Lorado Taft, to carve a statue for the grave site. But Taft's statue did not capture the essence of Mary Ella, so the mother sent a photo of the child along with some of the girl's clothes to an Italian sculptor. Some accounts said the sculptor was in Italy, while others indicated the Italian was working in the stone mills near Bedford, Indiana. The marble statue of be-curled Mary Ella in her lace-bordered

dress and apron filled with stone flowers soon graced the cemetery. Mary Ella's mother drove her horse and buggy to Crown Hill each day to dust her daughter's statue with a whiskbroom. As the decades passed, other visitors took over for Mrs. McGinnis, leaving flowers and teddy bears for the little girl, eventually making Mary Ella the symbol of Crown Hill's tradition and enduring care.

# Cemetery Symbolism

Tom Davis

Tombstones in Puritan and Colonial times in America reflected a rather grim outlook on life. Though religion played a strong role in community life, for the most part God was seen as a remote, punishing figure. The gravestones from this era include an abundance of symbols of mortality, rather than the symbols of immortality seen so frequently at Crown Hill. The most common was the death's-head, a skull decorated with bared teeth and hungry eye sockets. Hourglasses, coffins, and scythes were also common, as were epitaphs that spoke about the brevity of life and the inevitability of death. But by the end of the 1700s, these images began to be moderated with symbols of the joy of the Resurrection. The soul effigy, a winged, disembodied head, symbolizing the soul going to heaven, replaced the death's-head.

The ninteenth century continued this trend away from a harsh, cold view of death. One expression of this trend was the rural cemetery movement, from which Crown Hill had its beginnings. The poet Emily Dickinson wrote of one rural cemetery: "It seems as if Nature had formed the spot with a distinct idea of its being a resting place for her children." W. R. Holloway, in his 1871 history of Indianapolis says this specifically of Crown Hill: "The grounds would appear to have been especially ordained by nature for the purpose of a last resting place."

People in the Victorian Era, which includes the first forty or so years of Crown Hill's existence, generously decorated their monuments to their loved ones and used symbols to express the things that words alone could not. Some of these symbols, such as angels, both those with wings and those with trumpets to announce the Resurrection, reminded the viewer of a life after death. And some, such as the stone urns that top so many columnar monuments, are a reminder of death itself. The following include symbols of both types.

The angel on the Sayles monument points to heaven with one hand, and with the other she comforts the perpetual mourner. The mourner also holds a laurel wreath. The open book has the words alpha and omega, a reference to Christ being the beginning and end, and the lighted lantern, partially hidden by the angel's wing, has a flame that represents the soul.

The Spreng family erected a monument that includes the cross, a reminder of faith in Christ and a promise of eternal life. The anchor is a symbolic reference to Hebrews 6:19 "We have this hope as an anchor for the soul, firm and secure." The poppies are a symbol of eternal sleep, and the lily of the valley often symbolizes rebirth. The urn is a reminder of death, and the ferns around the base of the monument usually symbolize humility, frankness, and sincerity. The laurel wreath is a symbol of victory and immortality.

The monument for six-year-old Lotta Lytle has a small lamb, a symbol of innocence that is typically seen on a child's grave.

Crown Hill's first private family mausoleum was built in 1864 for Caleb Blood Smith, an attorney and judge who served as President Lincoln's Secretary of the Interior. The detail of his

mausoleum shows a cobra with its tail in its mouth, an ancient symbol of eternity. The winged sun disk is a dominant symbol on Egyptian temples and is considered a symbol of divine protection. The cherub, the only non-Egyptian feature on his mausoleum, represents the soul going to heaven.

GUSTAV BOHN.
CARLSRUHE GER. INDIANAPOLIS IND.
MARCH 9 1827.      OCT. 17 1892.
MAM 20 1830.      APRIL 17 1905.
JULIE BOHN.

PATTISON

# 3

## VICTORIAN CROWN HILL, 1876–1901

Death came stately to Crown Hill in the nineteenth century, borne by the undertaker's plume-topped black hearse that regal dark horses drew through the cemetery. "The slow crunch of the gravel and the slow grind of the wheels—the slow, slow go of every woe that everybody feels," James Whitcomb Riley wrote. The occasional white hearse, the color believed to relieve some of the mourners' deep pain, announced the death of a child.

Funerals were often at home, where undertakers placed the casketed body in the darkened, be-flowered parlor. Enabled by the increasing popularity of embalming, the bereaved gathered for up to four days to lament their loved one's passing, while glorying in their release from life's burdens. The black-creped front door, the widow's somber raiment, three years of mourning, and *momento mori,* such as black mourning jewelry and photo tableaux of family members posing with the deceased, reflected death's overweening importance to Victorian-Era Americans.

In many ways, the Civil War was still alive in the mid-1870s, as Helen Willis could tragically attest. Willis's brother, Marshall Harvey Twitchell, was a staunch Republican who fought in the war. After the war, the Twitchell family moved to the defeated South to battle for a strict Reconstruction, serving as officeholders and investing in plantation land—"carpetbaggers," they were called. White southerners twice attempted to kill Twitchell, and

he eventually lost both arms in a Louisiana bomb explosion. During 1874 and 1875, members of the paramilitary White League killed Helen Willis's husband, brother, and two brothers-in-law. The killings in northern Louisiana, which became known as the Coushatta massacre, captured the nation's attention. In the summer of 1876 Twitchell and his thirty-one-year-old sister fled north under military escort, eventually reaching Indianapolis. But it was too much and too late for Willis. Twitchell wrote about himself and his sister: "As soon as they reached a region of safety, the fearful nervous tension by which Mrs. Willis had kept up gave way, and she rapidly approached her end. Chronic dread of evil from murderers became too heavy a burden for her." Though Indiana was also wracked by internecine conflict about Reconstruction, Twitchell wrote, "Indianapolis recognized this funeral as one of importance." Crown Hill had long received the victims of Southern vengeance. Doctor Samuel Fahnestock was an Indianapolis physician who white Louisianans killed in 1864. As a member of the Christian Commission, Fahnestock was caring for liberated slaves. After his death, he was interred in Section 4.

When Willis died, the *New York Times* and other newspapers across the country reported on her funeral and the sermon by Doctor Bayliss, the Methodist minister. Pallbearers carried Willis's casket—topped with a cross, crown, and wreath of im-

mortals—through an avenue of mourners, few of whom knew the woman. The hearse bore the remains to Crown Hill, where a choir sang. As the cemetery bell tolled a requiem, Bayliss gave his benediction. "Indianapolis has never witnessed a funeral occasion in which more elements of tragedy were mingled then like this; certainly none where sympathy ever was called for more imperiously or offered more freely or generously," remembered Twitchell. Willis was laid to rest in Crown Hill's Section 2. But it was a temporary resting place, as her family soon removed her remains to their home state of Vermont.

Oliver P. Morton, Indiana's formidable Civil War governor, continued to be a staunch Crown Hill supporter, becoming a Crown Hill Corporator in 1867. During his second term as governor, Morton suffered a stroke that partially paralyzed him, but was nonetheless elected as a U.S. senator. In 1873 he returned to Indianapolis to give a stirring Decoration Day speech at Crown Hill, declaring: "The nation that is ungrateful to the man who has laid down his life that it might live is unworthy of its heroes, and will go down without honor in history."

In what was considered to be the best speech Morton ever gave in Indiana, the senator channeled the deep emotions that the Civil War still roused:

We come here to-day, soldiers and fellow-citizens, to spread flowers upon the graves of these fallen heroes, to show our love for the cause for which they died, and our gratitude to them for their sacrifice. And we ought to continue to do this as long as we live. "Decoration day" is a national school; we are not only improving our own hearts, but we are instructing our children and teaching them a lesson that they will remember to their latest hour. We are telling them that these men died for a noble cause, and that they should revere and love that cause. We know there are those who now say it is time to put such things away, that we should have perfect reconciliation, and therefore that we can not strew flowers upon these graves without rekindling the feelings and animosities of the war, and that we should cease to remember with gratitude the men who died that our country might live. This is a false philosophy.

We will let by-gones be by-gones. We can not forget the past; we ought not to forget it. God has planted memory in our minds and we can not crush it out. But while we can not forget, yet we can forgive, and we will forgive all who accept the great doctrines of equal liberty and of equal rights for all and equal protection to all, and we will be reconciled to them. And while we can not forget the past, we will treat them as if the past had never occurred, and that is all that can be asked—that is true and perfect reconciliation. True reconciliation does not require us to forget these dead; does not require us to forget the living soldier and to cease to do him justice. We must remember that there is an eternal difference between right and wrong, and that we were on the right side, and that they were on the wrong side; and all that we ask of them is that hereafter they shall be on the right side. We should forever remember that we were in the right. We were grandly in the right, and they were terribly in the wrong. We want that distinction to pass down through all time; but that is entirely consistent with true reconciliation. We say to those who were on the other side of the great contest which cost us so dearly in blood and treasure; which cost us so much suffering and sacrifice—that while we shall forever cherish the lessons taught us by that struggle, and while we shall forever stand by the principles we maintained in that contest, all we ask of them is that they shall hereafter stand upon those principles; then let us go forward hand in hand, as Americans and as brethren through the future ages of our country's history.

While serving in the senate in late 1877, Morton suffered a second, fatal stroke. After thousands passed his bier in the Statehouse, cabinet members, senators, the governor, mayor, and numerous judges attended Morton's funeral at Roberts Park Church. The Reverend Bradford Cleaver said about Morton's Civil War leadership, "in that hour of darkness this man proved equal to the emergency." After a laudatory eulogy, Cleaver said, "And now bury—bury your illustrious dead—bury him to the dirge of a nation's lament." The long funeral cortege passed through a multitude of thousands before arriving at the Gothic Chapel. A newspaper account stated, "When the procession reached Crown Hill Cemetery, the military formed a hollow

square of 75 feet about the vault, and in the enclosed space the mourners and members of the Grand Lodge [Independent Order of Odd Fellows] gathered. Minute-guns were fired as the services proceeded after the form of the Odd-Fellows' burial ceremony. Owing to the lateness of the hour, the body was left in the chapel until next morning, when it was deposited in the Odd-Fellows' vault. That night it lay within a stone's throw of the place where Senator Morton delivered his address on Decoration Day—the best speech, in fact, that he ever made in Indiana." Known as "the soldier's friend," Morton became the first of eleven Indiana governors to be interred in Crown Hill.

In the decades after the Civil War, increasing numbers of soldiers were buried in Crown Hill. Some were illustrious; some less so: There are three Medal of Honor recipients in Crown Hill—Charles Brouse, Jacob (Swanson) Johnson, and John McKenzie. Brigadier General Edward Richard Sprigg Canby was a veteran of the Indian Wars, the Mexican War, and the Civil War, during which he commanded forces that checked the Confederate efforts to expand out of Texas. His 1862 victory at Glorieta is sometimes called the "Gettysburg of the West," as it marked the Confederates' farthest excursion to the West. During Reconstruction, Canby was in charge of several southern states before being reassigned to Indian affairs in the Pacific Northwest. In 1873 Canby was engaged in peace negotiations

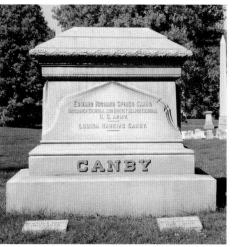

with a renegade tribe of Modocs near Tule Lake, California. During the meeting, Modoc chief Kintpuash, known as Captain Jack, said, "I want to tell you, Canby, we cannot make peace as long as these soldiers are crowding me." Soon after, Captain Jack said, "*Ut wih kutt*"—Let's do it." Pulling out a pistol, Captain Jack shot Canby in the face. Another Modoc cut his throat. Canby's death caused an uproar. He was the only general to ever be assassinated by Native Americans. The *New York Times* proclaimed, "Seldom has an event of such a character created so deep a feeling of horror and indignation." After lying in state, Canby's body was buried in Crown Hill on May 23, 1873. Four Union generals attended his funeral: William Tecumseh Sherman, Philip Sheridan, Lew Wallace, and Irvin McDowell, with Wallace and McDowell serving as pallbearers. Initially buried in the Hawkins family lot in Section 1, Canby was later moved to a place of honor adjacent to the national cemetery in Section 9, Lot 1.

*An American flag drapes the obelisk of Civil War Union General Jefferson C. Davis. The inscription on the back reads, "His memory is embalmed in the history of his country."*

Another Hoosier Civil War general, Jefferson C. Davis, coincidentally replaced Canby in the campaign against the Modocs. A veteran of the Mexican War and several Civil War battles, Davis was notable both for having the same name as the Confederate president and for having shot and killed a fellow Union general during an argument at Louisville's Galt House. Not surprisingly, the shooting clouded Davis's career, as did his racist attitudes toward freed slaves. During Sherman's March to the Sea, Davis ordered a pontoon bridge removed, causing several hundred freed slaves to be killed or captured. After the war, Davis was ordered to Alaska, where he ordered Russian settlers out of their homes to make room for Americans. After his death of pneumonia at the Palmer House in Chicago in 1879, his body was returned to his hometown of Indianapolis, and he was buried in Section 29, Lot 1.

Brigadier General Abel Streight was an Indianapolis publisher before the Civil War. Enlisting with the Fifty-first Indiana Regiment in 1861, Streight was far from the action for two years, but in 1863 he convinced the high command to let him mount a raid into the Deep South to disrupt a crucial rail line. Primarily mounted on recalcitrant Tennessee jackasses due to horse shortages, Streight's force of 1,700 men moved mulishly through Tennessee, Alabama, and Mississippi. A Southern commentator wrote: "During the raid, Confederates hurled insults toward the brigade, referring to them as the 'Jackass Cavalry.' Undoubtedly, the lack of horses had a negative effect on Union morale." At a crucial moment four hundred of the potentially seditious mules stampeded, forcing Streight to confiscate more from the surrounding countryside. Streight's demoralized and poorly mounted troops soon encountered the cavalry of legendary Confederate leader, Brigadier General Nathan Bedford Forrest. Though Streight's soldiers won the Battle of Day's Gap, the Confederates eventually captured the bulk of the Union force. After being incarcerated in Libby Prison for ten months, Streight organized a massive jailbreak of 109 prisoners, who tunneled to freedom.

After the war Streight returned to Indianapolis, where he served in the state senate and ran unsuccessfully as the Republican candidate for governor. Following his death in 1892, his formidable wife, Lovina, first had him buried in the front yard of their home on East Washington Street. Only after the neighbors strenuously objected did she relent and have him reinterred in Crown Hill. The elaborate Romanesque-arched limestone monument with a bronze bust of Streight was erected in Section 29, Lot 72, where his statue resolutely inspects the serried rows of the Union dead in the National Cemetery.

When Lovina was buried beside her husband in 1910, she was likewise afforded full military honors. Known as the "Mother of the 51st," Lovina had accompanied her husband on his campaigns in the South, where she nursed the wounded during battle. Captured three times by the Confederates, she was twice exchanged for prisoners, and according to a regimental account, once escaped by pulling a pistol (one of six) from beneath her petticoats.

On July 24, 1861, Edward Black enlisted in the Twenty-first Indiana Volunteers' First Regiment as their drummer boy. Scarcely eight years old, Black was the youngest soldier to ever enlist in the U.S. armed forces. At four feet, two inches tall, his drum was nearly half as big as he was. When the Union forces captured New Orleans in the spring of 1862, Black's band played "Pickayune" as his regiment marched into the city. At the battle of Baton Rouge in August 1862, Confederates captured the boy as a prisoner of war.

Sent in front of the advancing troops to set the pace, drummer boys were often prime targets to cause the line to lose cohesion. During one battle, an artillery blast wounded Black in the arm, according to accounts. Because of the high loss of young boys, in 1862 President Abraham Lincoln ordered that drummer boys be dismissed from the Union army.

After serving one year, two months, and five days, Black was mustered out on September 11, 1862 as a nine-year-old veteran. He returned to Indiana, but soon reenlisted with his father, and served the rest of the war. Black survived, but never fully recovered from the trauma of war, dying of battle-related causes on June 30, 1871, at the age of seventeen. He was buried in Section 16, Lot 148, where his grave marker proclaimed him to be a "Musician." Almost a hundred years later, in 1970, Black's family donated his drum to the Children's Museum of Indianapolis, where it remains a treasured object in the collection.

As the years went on, Calvin Fletcher's fellow corporators began joining him in repose at Crown Hill. James Blake was one of the town's pioneer leaders. A Pennsylvanian, Blake arrived in Indianapolis in 1821, soon after the legislature had declared it as the new capital. Blake was, according to newspaperman John Holliday, "Large and brawny, full of enthusiasm and never-flagging energy." Blake, or "Uncle Jimmy" as he was known, served as the head of numerous Indianapolis organizations, including fire departments, militias, hospitals, public libraries, Sunday Schools, and Fourth of July parades, which were predictably led by Blake's favorite bay horse pulling him in an open carriage. Blake had made his money with the city's first steam mill, real estate, railroads, and ginseng trading, but ill-starred investments later in life left him almost penniless. When Blake died in 1870, the funeral cortege out to Crown Hill was

*Edward Black*

the city's largest on record. Following behind the hearse, Blake's favorite bay horse pulled an empty carriage. Blake is buried in Section 1, Lot 69.

Almus Vinton, an energetic former druggist and paper-mill owner, also died in 1870. Vinton, a native of Cincinnati, had supervised some of the early ditching at Crown Hill. After his early death at forty-nine, he was buried in Section 13, Lot 66. Two years later, William Sheets, the temperance warrior from Virginia, passed away, followed in 1878 by Daniel Yandes, one of the town's first industrialists. Pennsylvanian Yandes arrived in Indianapolis in 1821 and soon started the first sawmill, then a tannery, a dry-goods store, a gristmill, and a cotton-spinning factory that led to railroads and other factories. He was one of Indianapolis's largest philanthropists, instrumental in the establishment of Crown Hill. But like his friend Blake, bad investments by Yandes led to penury late in life. It is said the only property he had left was his plot at Crown Hill, where he was interred in Section 6, Lot 34.

James Ray's death in 1881 signaled the end of an era. He was an Indianapolis pioneer and, like his good friend Blake, helped establish the original city cemetery and Crown Hill. It was his causal conversation about the new Fort Wayne cemetery that led to John Chislett Sr. making the momentous journey from Pittsburgh to help develop Crown Hill. A natural organizer, Ray provided managerial structure for Blake's visions. One biographer stated, "Never idle, vigilant, never careless, his word was as good as any other man's oath and his aid in any good cause was considered expected. His character brought him public trust and responsibility."

Ray was but one of several of the thirty founding corporators who died in 1881. Ovid Butler, best remembered for the eponymous university he helped found at his sprawling estate at today's Fourteenth Street and College Avenue, was an important civic leader and corporator. General John Love, a Virginian related to the famous military Lees, served in Indian Country and in Mexico during the war, before fighting in the Union army. Love was involved in railroads, a military training school, and was a partner in the Gatling Gun Company. William Morrison, banker, businessman, founder of Morrison's Opera House at Maryland and Meridian Streets, and legendary curmudgeon, died on March 15, 1881, and was buried in Section 1, Lot 68. The next year, former dry-goods and notions magnate Jacob Crossland died, and was buried in Section 1 Lot 7.

Lyman S. Ayres was a country peddler from Oswego, New York. After running general stores in New York and Ohio for more than twenty years, he agreed in 1872 to buy into an established dry-goods store in Indianapolis. Arriving by train at Union Station with his family, Ayres proceeded to found a retailing dynasty. Beginning with his Trade Palace partnership on West Washington Street, Ayres renamed it L. S. Ayres and Company two years later after buying out his partner. A few years following, Ayres moved the business across the street to 33–37 West Washington Street, an ornate Victorian structure that hummed with both manufacturing and retail. The business thrived, growing from thirty employees to over a hundred. Now an Indianapolis business leader, Ayres joined the board of corporators in 1888.

When Ayres died in 1896, there were 175 Ayres employees. But he had planned for the future. Before Ayres passed on, he purchased Hubbard's Block at the southwest corner of Meridian and Washington Streets, destined to become a lodestone of Indianapolis shopping for generations of Hoosiers. A graceful obelisk in Section 11, Lot 11 marked the Ayres plot, with a simple gravestone delineating the final resting place of Lyman S. Ayres. His son, Frederic M. Ayres, took over the business after his father's death, and in 1905 launched the great retailing emporium at Meridian and Washington Streets that his father had envisioned. In 1906 Frederic became a corporator, starting a family tradition that has endured into the twenty-first century.

Other Indianapolis leaders found their final home in Crown Hill. Colonel Eli Lilly was another Indianapolis businessman who parlayed a modest start into a fair-sized enterprise. Apprenticed into the druggist trade in Lafayette, Lilly began his own drugstore in Greencastle in 1861, just before he volunteered to join the Union army. Lilly fought at Hoover's Gap and Chickamauga. Later captured by the Confederates, Lilly was mustered out at the end of the war, after which he tried his hand at a number of Reconstruction-era businesses, including a cotton plantation in Mississippi, where his first wife died in 1866.

Upon returning to Indianapolis, Lilly filed for bankruptcy. After rebuilding his finances with a successful drugstore in Paris, Illinois, he returned to Indianapolis in 1876 and opened a pharmaceutical laboratory in a small two-story building on Pearl Street, just off Washington Street. His sign read, "Eli Lilly, Chemist." By 1880 Lilly was operating out of a large factory on McCarty Street between Delaware and Alabama Streets, where he had moved after a short sojourn on South Meridian Street. Lilly's pills and potions sold well in Indianapolis and surrounding districts, and by the late 1880s was one of the city's most prominent concerns. A workforce of more than a hundred produced pharmaceuticals that exceeded $200,000 in annual sales. Endeavoring to add rigor to what had been a haphazard

industry full of hucksters, Lilly hired the company's first scientist in 1886. The company's development of gelatin-coated capsules was an important innovation. By 1890 Lilly had turned over the business operations to his son. Josiah K. turned to civic affairs, including his leadership in the Commercial Club that championed infrastructure improvements, such as street paving, sewers, and overhead railroad crossings. When Colonel Eli died of cancer in 1898, his company had two thousand products and annual sales of $300,000. He was interred in a restrained mausoleum in Section 13, Lot 19. Lilly's civic engagement engendered a long family tradition. In 1910 Josiah became a corporator.

In 1897 former Indiana governor, congressman, and cabinet member under President Benjamin Harrison, Albert Gallatin Porter, died. Porter encapsulated a broad swath of the nineteenth-century Indiana experience. Born in 1824 in Lawrenceburg, then a major Ohio River entrepôt, Porter was the second native-born Hoosier to be elected governor. After moving to Indianapolis in 1844, he worked as an attorney, journalist, and Democratic politician before being drummed out of the party by the proslavery faction. Running as an antislavery Republican in 1858, Porter was elected to Congress. Porter returned to Indianapolis in 1863, when he joined a prestigious Indiana firm headed by Harrison. While serving in 1878 as Comptroller of the United States, the state Republican Party nominated him for governor—unbeknownst to Porter. By the time Porter found out, his campaign was in full swing. Aided by the support of the Knights of Labor, he squeaked out a victory. During his term from 1881 to 1885, Porter oversaw the development of Indiana's industrial capacity, as well as championing women's rights, public health, and the establishment of the state department that later became the Department of Natural Resources. A noted speaker, Porter nominated Harrison for president at the 1888 national convention. After serving as Harrison's Minister to Italy, Porter retired to Indianapolis to write a history of Indiana,

though he died before he could publish it. Porter is buried near his imposing pale gray monument in Section 14, Lot 92.

Another remarkable Hoosier diplomat was laid to rest in Crown Hill. Professor W. D. McCoy was an African American teacher in the Indianapolis school system. Born in Cambridge City, Indiana, McCoy was a schoolteacher in Indianapolis before spending eight years in Arkansas as a Reconstruction-era Republican officeholder. In 1879 he returned to Indianapolis. Active in the Republican Party, he was the party's unsuccessful candidate for the state legislature. A popular figure, McCoy was "ambitious and desirous of representing the country," according to George L. Knox, an influential Indianapolis African American powerbroker. McCoy's lobbying and involvement in the city's educational and civic matters ultimately led to him being nominated in 1892 as Harrison's minister to Liberia. But within a year, McCoy was dead of a tropical fever. It took several months for his body to be returned to Indiana, where he was interred in Crown Hill. His limestone tree-trunk gravestone connotes the childless McCoy's family tree coming to an end. Symbolizing sincerity and humility, carved ferns surround the base of the tree, which is entwined with a morning glory vine. A patriotic eagle stood atop the monument. An obituary of the time stated McCoy was a "man of good education and of unusual good common sense." In time, William D. McCoy Public School Number 24 was named in his honor.

Zerelda Wallace was a force of nature. A tireless temperance activist and suffragette, Wallace was the second wife of Indiana governor and congressman David Wallace, and stepmother of

the Civil War hero and author of *Ben-Hur*, Lew Wallace, who identified Zerelda as the model for his title character's engaging mother. She was also the sister-in-law of Richard Gatling, inventor of the Gatling gun. Described as

an inspirational speaker, Zerelda could present extemporaneous speeches lasting two hours. "The highest form of development is to govern one's self," she famously said. After she died on March 19, 1901, in Cataract, Indiana, she was interred in Crown Hill's Section 3, Lot 10, where a slender, pale gray obelisk marks her grave.

But Crown Hill was not just for the wealthy and powerful. A broad spectrum of Indianapolis society was interred in Crown Hill, including thousands of professionals, businessmen, and working people. So too were the artists and literati of Indianapolis. Jacob Cox was Indianapolis's first professional artist. Arriving from the East Coast in 1833 to establish a stove, tinware, and coppersmith business, Cox launched his artistic career with a banner for presidential candidate William Henry Harrison. Painting portraits was soon a profitable sideline for Cox. By 1860 he was a full-time artist, eventually painting the portraits of six Indiana governors, a host of Hoosier luminaries, and scores of landscapes. Following his death in 1892 his mourners erected a rough-hewn monument in Section 33.

Sarah T. Bolton was Indiana's first poetess—"the Pioneer Poet of Indiana," she was called. Growing up along the Ohio in southern Indiana, Bolton first published a poem at the age of thirteen. In 1831 she and her husband settled on a farm west of Indianapolis, an area that later became Central State Hospital. While juggling the disparate needs of a struggling farmwife and helpmate to her journalist-innkeeper husband, Nathaniel Bolton, Sarah penned numerous poems. After Nathaniel was named state librarian in 1851, the couple moved closer to town, where she had a greater opportunity to pursue her literary ambitions. In 1853 she wrote her most famous work, "Paddle Your Own Canoe," a multistanza poem that opened with:

Voyager upon life's sea,
To yourself be true.
And whe'er your lot may be
Paddle your own canoe.

Later set to music, and promulgated around the world, "Paddle Your Own Canoe" insured Bolton's enduring legacy.

Known for lachrymose heartstring-plucking poems, such as "The Orphan's Lament; or, I'm Standing by Your *Grave*, Mother," Bolton wrote "The Grave of Calvin Fletcher," a meditation on the Crown Hill founder and Indianapolis leader. In her poem, Bolton celebrated the connection between Fletcher's earthly gravestone and the liberation of his spirit:

Thou art not here; thou art risen
Beyond this shadowy shore,
And this monumental marble
Marks the robe thy spirit wore.

After her death in 1893, Bolton was buried in Section 5, Lot 14. Her epitaph reads, "The first singer in a new land."

Catharine Sickel began watching over the cemetery in 1884, when she was interred at the far western edge of Crown Hill in Section 18. Her German family placed Sickel's photograph in a metal frame above her gravestone's carved inscription that reads, "*Hier ruht in Gott*," (Here rests in God). Now ghostly and decaying after a hundred and twenty-nine years, Sickel's image provides a mute reminder of time's passage and the endurance of unblinking memory.

Not all the Hoosiers laid to rest in Crown Hill stayed at home. George P. McDougall was an adventurer. In 1845, when he was twenty-five years old, he traveled overland by wagon train from his home in Indianapolis to California, then still part of Mexico. California historian H. H. Bancroft wrote about McDougall (also spelled McDougal), "He was eccentric, but brave, and a favorite with the frontier population." After the Mexican-American War ended in 1848, his brother, John, who had served in Mexico as a captain in the Indiana Volunteer Company, joined him in the new town of Sacramento. (John McDougall was California's second governor.) Following the Sutter's Mill gold strike in 1848, thousands of miners rushed to California. George was at the right place at the right time. He owned a ferry and a bustling mercantile establishment in Sacramento, but political machinations and conspiracies cost him both businesses. Frustrated, he hit the road, wandering east into Utah, New Mexico, and other wild territories. Word of

George's death eventually reached his family, who considered him lost, and administered his estate.

In the 1860s Commander George Brown, another Indianapolis native, was sailing the USS *Stonewall* to Japan. A 1913 history of Sacramento related that Brown's ship made a port call in Patagonia, where a delegation of Patagonian chiefs came on board. Among the antipodeans natives was a "hirsute, squalid, weather-tanned and very tatooed man"—who proved to be none other than McDougall.

McDougall told Brown, who was a friend of his Indianapolis family, that he had analyzed some ballast dirt on a ship sailing up from Patagonia and realized there was gold to be had down there. And that is where McDougall headed, journeying through Central and South America until he hit Patagonia at the tip of the continent. When he met Brown, he was prospecting at a solitary station on the Straits of Magellan, where a Patagonian tribe called him their chief and served as his miners. The Sacramento history related that McDougall was a giant of a man, who "had always been so stately and handsome that he had been called 'Lord George McDougal.'" Brown later stated that after McDougall cleaned up and dressed in good clothes, he was "the handsomest and most distinguished man he had ever seen." When

Brown told him of his family back in Indianapolis, McDougall "sobbed and cried," but refused to return to the United States, as he was determined to develop his valuable Patagonian mine. But McDougall promised he would travel north to the seaport of Valparaiso to meet Brown. When they later met in the ancient Chilean port, Brown convinced him to return to the United States. So McDougall did—traveling back to Indiana, and eventually settling in Washington, D.C., where he lived until his death on May 16, 1872. On April 6, 1877, adventurer McDougall came home to Indianapolis, where the man they called the King of Patagonia was laid to rest in Section 25, Lot 232.

McDougall's discoverer, Brown, also came to anchor in Crown Hill. Brown distinguished himself in the Civil War with actions at Palmyra Island, where his river gunboat fought four Confederate gunboats until he was wounded and his ship was captured. Taken prisoner, Brown was incarcerated in Libby Prison before being exchanged for Confederate prisoners. Brown later helped defend Indiana against Morgan's Raid, and commanded the USS *Itasca* at the Battle of Mobile Bay. After he sailed the *Stonewall* to Japan, Brown was involved with a diplomatic kerfuffle during the Chilean Civil War in 1891 when he was accused of exceeding his orders by helping

# SUPERINTENDENTS

The inscription on the back of the monument of Crown Hill's first superintendent, Frederick W. Chislett, was written by his wife, Margaret D. E. Chislett. It states:

Frederick W. Chislett came to Indianapolis in 1863 and took charge of Crown Hill Cemetery as its first Superintendent. For 36 years he devoted himself to the development and adorn-

ment of these grounds, and by his wise and prudent management laid broad and deep the foundations of this his life work and last monument.

Margaret Chislett's words speak to the devotion of each successive superintendent to the development and adornment of the cemetery grounds. Their life work is a legacy for the generations.

Frederick W. Chislett: 1863–1899
John Chislett: 1899–1910
Walter H. Wheeler: 1910–1912
John J. Stephens: 1912–1916
Ivan H. Mann: 1916
Raymond E. Siebert: 1916–1958
John O. Teeguarden: 1958–1969
J. Robert Sutherlin: 1969–1979
Robert F. Wirsching Jr.: 1979–1992
Michael W. Dooley: 1992–2007
Robert E. Milne: 2007–present

Chilean combatants in what later came to be known as the *Itata* Incident. It must not have hurt his career, as he was named as a rear admiral two years later. Before his retirement in 1897, Brown served in the Philippines and at the Norfolk Navy Yard. After his death on July 29, 1913, he was interred in Section 6, Lot 1.

Beyond the powerful, famous, and notable, Crown Hill also served a swath of society that needed a helping hand. In Section 37 more than seven hundred unmarked graves include the remains of individuals who died in the care of Indianapolis institutions. These organizations included the Indianapolis Home for Friendless Women that former Civil War nurses Catharine

Merrill and Jane Chambers McKinney Graydon founded in the winter of 1867 to assist destitute women, such as soldiers' widows and former prostitutes. The home's constitution proclaimed its mission was to "protect unprotected women, house the homeless, save the erring, and help the tempted." Located at 1731 North Capitol Avenue, the institution, sequentially known as the Indianapolis Home for Aged and Friendless Women, the Indianapolis Home for Aged, and the Indianapolis Retirement Home, began sending its deceased to Crown Hill in 1877. By the beginning of the twentieth century, dozens of women from the Home lay in Section 37, where they were joined by hundreds of children from the Indiana Orphans Asylum, the Board of Children's Guardians, and the Indianapolis Home for Friendless Colored Children.

The children included toddler Mary Johnson, who died on July 2, 1892. The report read, "Mother is epileptic and feeble minded. Child is filthy. She died at the Orphan's Asylum." Infant James Webb was born to a mother who did not know the father or the baby's sex, nor did she have a name for him. The report read, "James Webb died November 19th of inanition [starvation]." Mary Craig's mother was dead. Her father was a vault cleaner who drank. "The home is very unsanitary," the social worker reported, before she removed Mary and her four siblings to the Marion County Orphans Asylum on November 20, 1916. "The girls' heads were covered with scars and [had] very little hair," the report read. Craig was living with a family in 1920 when they told a social worker they thought she might have tuberculosis. When the social worker admitted her to a sanitarium, the doctors quickly determined she had ad-

vanced tuberculosis. She asked to see her brother and sisters. An agent brought her a doll and some fruit. Craig died on December 9, 1920.

It was not only humans who came to rest in Crown Hill. The bereft even managed to finagle dogs into the cemetery. According to reports, one lies at the foot of Reverend Oscar C. McCullough. The dog of Doctor Sollis Runnels was reputedly also buried with his master. While not exactly a living dog, the tombstone of hardware man Charles Frese had the next best thing. When Frese died in 1887 the sculptor carved a limestone marker in the shape of a severed tree, which was installed in Section 34. A stone shotgun leaned against the tree; a hunting pouch hung from a limb. Beside the tree, a sprightly stone hunting hound waited patiently with its retrieved duck. Many years later, the hound had its own great adventure.

As the decades rolled on, increasing numbers of monuments embellished the cemetery's hillsides and dells. The early white marble slabs decorated with weeping willows and lambs gave

way to tall obelisks. Napolean Bonaparte's expeditions to Egypt early in the nineteenth century ignited a craze for things Egyptian, including obelisks. Near the Gothic Chapel, Davis's flag-draped spire spoke to the carver's delicate abilities. Lieutenant Commander George W. Armentrout was an Indiana native who graduated from the U.S. Naval Academy and served on steam frigates during the Civil War. When he died in 1872 a tall white column memorialized his service with a bas-relief of a ship and a wreath of victory encircling a sword and anchor, attached by a carved stone chain that sways gently in the stiff breeze. Anchors were a favorite symbol of Christianity. The marker of M. S. Whitehead was carved in the shape of piled boulders, surmounted with a rope and anchor that included the words, "With hope we have, both sure and steadfast."

The wife of John C. Fisher died on February 13, 1889. Though her grieving husband did not identify her by name on her monument, he clearly loved her. The carved stone statue depicts his wife's soul being carried aloft by a be-starred angel, with

the oft-quoted biblical quotation, "I am the resurrection, and the life: he that believeth in me, though he were dead, yet shall he live." Though Mrs. Fisher was unnamed, even in cemetery records, her husband demonstrated his undying affection toward his wife with a footstone that reads, "My Darling Wife," and the word "Pet," surrounded by stone flowers.

Across the cemetery, epitaphs proclaimed eternal verities. The Ackerman family monument located in Section 27 repeated the oft-inscribed message from the grave: "As you are now, so once was I. As

I am now, so you shall be. Prepare for death and follow me." But for many nineteenth-century Hoosiers, death was bittersweet. Near the Gothic Chapel, an open-faced angel overlooks the Labarth family gravestone that reads, "Mary A. Labarth and family are at rest. Thank God sweetly." One 1881 tombstone reads, "He giveth his beloved sleep."

Mausoleums increased in popularity over the years. In 1874 the Heim family constructed its mausoleum, followed by the first Claypool tomb in 1885, and the Cunningham family's in 1888. The prominent Bohn family, who included renowned Indianapolis architect Arthur Bohn, built its mausoleum in 1893. In 1896 stone carvers and masons constructed the ornate Severin mausoleum with its classical wreaths and ribbons and elaborate frieze board.

Indiana limestone and durable granite began to replace friable marble. Across the cemetery, tree stumps crafted of limestone communicated lives cut short. Near the Gothic Chapel, the Thalman family tree trunk is bedecked with carved ferns, flowers, turtledoves, and an unfurled scroll. Stone angels, eventually more than two dozen, begin to unfurl their wings, some with trumpets, some with crosses, some benign, and some stern. Tombstones perpetuated the deceased's lives and worldviews. John W. Love's grave marker includes a carved artist's palette. A lifelike statue of a boy sitting beside a stack of stone books memorializes a twelve-year-old scholar named Corliss Randle Ruckle, who died of diphtheria in 1889. The sculptor portrayed Ruckle pointing to a beginning page of a book, symbolizing his departure early in the book of life. Not far away in Section 14, a tiny stone crib memorializes baby Celia Burford, who died on April 15, 1886, just a few weeks after her birth. The monument of Arthur Jordan, whose name is honored with Butler University's Jordan Hall, includes the Victorian graves of his two children who died young, which was

common in the late nineteenth century, when more than 40 percent of all deaths were children under five. The Jordan children's epitaph reads,

A precious one from us has gone,
A voice we loved is stilled.
A place is vacant in our home,
Which never can be filled.

The corporators continued to expand Crown Hill, purchasing more than twenty acres in three parcels at the southeastern corner of the cemetery, present-day's Thirty-second and Boulevard Streets, in 1878. Eleven years later, they purchased considerable acreage north of the cemetery, across present-day's Thirty-eighth Street. They bought fifty-four acres from William Foley for $150 an acre, and eighty acres from Mary Ruddell, who appeared to bargain better, getting $305 an acre.

Superintendent Frederick Chislett continued to maintain aesthetic control of Crown Hill, prohibiting iron fences, mementos such as toys and photos, and even individual flower gardens planted in the family plots. Within the constraints of social power, ostentatious memorials were discouraged. His landscaping plan was likewise restrained. "The tendency, in so many cemeteries, to too great a profusion of shrubbery and shade trees, which excludes sunlight and makes the grounds dark and damp, is confined within judicious limits here," journalist W. R. Holloway noted about Crown Hill in his 1870 profile of Indianapolis's five cemeteries—two south-side German cemeteries (Lutheran and Catholic), the Hebrew Cemetery, and Greenlawn, which Holliday noted had lost its interment records. Lauding Crown Hill, Holloway stated, "To the natural beauties of the grounds, in their picturesque undulations and abundance of forest trees, individual taste and affection have been added (under the judicious regulations by the managers), the ornaments of evergreens and flowering plants. Enclosures of lots have been forbidden, as marring the appearance of a cemetery, and tending, with the rust and decay of time, to disfigure rather than beautify."

The corporators were also aware that a restrained cemetery was an economical cemetery. In 1881 lots sold in Crown Hill for twenty to thirty cents a square foot, while lots in more elaborate cemeteries, such as Boston's Mount Auburn and Philadelphia's Laurel Hill, cost five to eight times as much.

A cemetery inventory made July 10, 1877, gave a sense of the tools, techniques, and needs of the time. It included twenty shovels, eighteen mattocks, and a number of rakes. The horses—John, Jim, Charlie, Pink, Doctor, and Nick—ranged in value from $25 to $125. There were two spittoons in the chapel. A work schedule from the previous spring included tasks such as, "Bury Wilber C. West [1869–77] in Grave 1, Lot 109, Section 25 at 2 o'clock. Cost: $3.00," and "Bury a body [Hiram Crosby] in Grave 2, Lot 69, Section 25 at 3 o'clock. Weaver is the undertaker. Cost: $4.00."

In 1884 the corporators realized that Indianapolis development was marching up Meridian Street and the adjacent avenues. They decided the cemetery needed to turn its face to the east, so initiated plans to move Crown Hill's main entrance from Michigan Road (today's Martin Luther King Jr. Boulevard) to Thirty-fourth Street and Boulevard Place. They wanted a grand new entrance, along with an administration building to replace

*Corliss Randle Ruckle sitting in Section 12, Lot 24. His father, Nicholas R. Ruckle, served with the Indiana Zouaves commanded by Lew Wallace.*

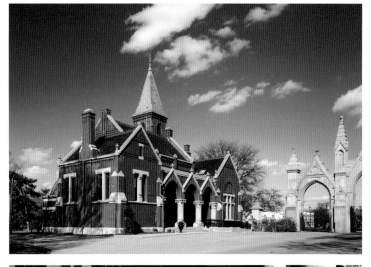

the small office at the west gate. With more than 8,000 burials by 1884, the Crown Hill managers needed more space.

After deliberations, the corporators gave the design contract to Swiss-born architect Adolph Scherrer. Before immigrating to America, Scherrer had walked across central Europe studying great architecture, including imperial Vienna, where he studied under leading architects at the Academy of Fine Arts. In 1872 he arrived in Indianapolis, where he soon became the principal architect of the Statehouse. For Crown Hill's new entrance, Scherrer designed a soaring High-Victorian Gothic gateway with three compound spired archways. Beside the entrance, Scherrer's new "gate keeper's residence and office" also provided a private redoubt for grieving families. The Victorian Gothic-styled red brick "Waiting Station," as it came to be known, included a sitting room, dining room, kitchen, and three bedrooms for the residence, as well as the office's general waiting room, ladies' waiting room, two offices, a bell tower, fireproof vault, and lavatories. Elaborately decorated with carved hardwood trim and wainscoting, and decorative tile, the structure was state of the art, with equipment from the Central Union Telephone Company. The three-arched limestone gateway and Waiting Station cost $48,000.

It was built on a tight deadline. Construction on the new gate and office building commenced in May 1885, and it was completed by late 1885. In part, the work was hastened by the death of Vice President Thomas A. Hendricks, a former governor of Indiana who was serving under President Grover Cleveland. Only a few months after taking office, Hendricks died in his sleep in Indianapolis. At the lavish funeral ceremony at Saint Paul Episcopal Cathedral, hundreds of dignitaries, including Cleveland, attended. Crown Hill was ready; its con-

tractors had rushed to finish the gateway so Hendricks's funeral cortege could be the first to pass through the new entrance. The two-mile-long cortege of military units and dignitaries passed through a line of mourners along Illinois Street that stretched all the way to downtown. "The scene at Indianapolis, where he died and was interred, was memorable in a notable degree," one writer noted. "Statesmen, publicists, officials of high and low degree, and citizens of every class and quality, poured into the city from every direction, and heartfelt grief shadowed every face as the imposing pageant moved onward to the tomb." When the funeral procession reached the eastern gate, an artillery escort atop Crown Hill fired a farewell salute. Hendricks's pallbearers carried their mournful weight to the gravesite that was heaped with roses, lilies, and enormous bouquets. A large, crepe-draped photograph of Hendricks overlooked his marble vault. His biographer emoted, "There is scarcely a suggestion of death, but rather a joyous welcome to the guest approaching." Memorialized by composer Charles Langes's "Thomas A. Hendricks Funeral March," Hendricks became the first of three U.S. vice presidents to be buried in Crown Hill, where his tall granite monument was erected in Section 29 near the Gothic Chapel.

Beyond the three vice presidents who served, four unelected nominees for the office were also buried in Crown Hill. Among them was the outspoken radical, George W. Julian. A Quaker attorney who was born in Centerville, Indiana, Julian fought against slavery while a member of the Indiana General Assembly. In 1852 the Free-Soil Party nominated Julian and New Hampshire's John P. Hale on an antislavery platform. Though vice presidential candidate Julian and his running mate Hale failed to win a single electoral vote, they kept the issue of slavery in the political arena. Julian was later elected as a Republican to five terms in the U.S. Congress. In 1872, as a Liberal Republican supporting Horace Greeley for president, Julian received five electoral votes for vice president. After a decade as the surveyor general of New Mexico, Julian retired to a literary career in Irvington. When he died in 1899, he was buried in Section 27, Lot 196.

William H. English was another prominent Hoosier who was an unsuccessful vice presidential candidate, losing a close race in 1880 as the Democratic running mate of William Scott Hancock. He died at noon on February 7, 1896, at his family's famed English Hotel, the grand turreted structure that filled the northwest quadrant of Monument Circle. His monument at Crown Hill was equally grand. Located at the peak of a sequestered hilltop circle, the imposing classical column is topped by a draped woman holding a wreath and leaning on an anchor, symbolic of eternal life and hope. Bracketed on each side of the monument with shocks of wheat and corn, the

carved text details the many accomplishments of the English family. The poignant inscription for granddaughter Rosalind, who died at twenty-one, lauded her accomplishments as an attorney and political speaker, and included the poem she wrote at eleven:

> Sleep and rest, sleep and rest
> mourned by those who loved thee best
> While holy angels guard and keep,
> Sleep my baby, sleep.

Crown Hill was a place of pride for Indianapolis residents, who included the cemetery as a must-see on city sightseeing tours. Part park, part sanctuary, part scenic drive, the trip became so obligatory one visitor remarked, "If you are thinking of taking me to Crown Hill, please don't. I have been there five times already since I came." Crown Hill, however, was far more than a rural retreat. Valorized by the honored dead entrusted to the cemetery's stewards, and the somber words spoken there by the esteemed, Crown Hill had become a holy landscape. Scholar

*Left: Fawns enjoying baskets of red geraniums.* ***Opposite:*** *Vice presidents buried at Crown Hill: Thomas A. Hendricks (1885), Charles W. Fairbanks (1905–1909), and Thomas R. Marshall (1913–1921).*

Robert Pogue Harrison wrote, "The surest way to take possession of a place and secure it as one's own is to bury one's dead on it." Exquisitely planned, laboriously tended, and watered by the tears of generations, Crown Hill became one with Indianapolis.

Frederick Chislett, Crown Hill's first superintendent, died on November 9, 1899. Over three decades Chislett had directed the growth of Crown Hill from a backwoods farm to a great cemetery. After his death, the corporators noted in the meeting minutes that "his body now rests in the grounds his intelligence and labors did much to beautify and make fitting for the repose that, sooner or later must come to the bodies of all." Chislett's gray-stone monument included the fitting invocation, "Because I Live Ye Shall Live Also." Though Frederick died, the Chisletts continued to carry on the Crown Hill tradition. Frederick's son, John Jr., took over for his father as superintendant, a position he held until his retirement in 1910.

As the new century dawned, Indiana citizens were inordinately proud of their Hoosier president, Benjamin Harrison. An Indianapolis resident for decades, Harrison had been a prominent Indiana politician and Civil War general before being elected to the presidency in 1888. While running for re-election against Cleveland, Harrison, dispirited by the untimely death of his beloved wife, Caroline, stopped campaigning in the critical last stages of the election. After losing to Cleveland, Harrison returned to Indiana, in spite of his misgivings about "the distressing prospect of resuming family life in Indianapolis," as his biographer phrased it. But after cheering thousands greeted his train in Indianapolis, he told his son, "I made no mistake in coming home at once—there are no friends like the old ones." Harrison embraced his post-political life. He played with his grandchildren, remarried and had a new baby of his own, and took on numerous legal cases, including an international boundary dispute between Britain and Venezuela, all the while keeping up a vigorous holiday schedule at his homes on the New Jersey shore and in the Adirondack Mountains.

Harrison was a frequent visitor to Crown Hill, where he buried his wife, Caroline, in 1892. Beyond her responsibilities as First Lady, Caroline was the first president-general of the Daughters of the American Revolution. She was also an early supporter of Johns Hopkins University Medical School, though her support was subject to her provision that the college admit women.

Harrison found solace at Crown Hill. In early 1893 he wrote to his niece, "During the afternoon we drove out to the Cemetery & placed some flowers on your dear Aunt's grave. Her absence made the Home coming very sad & every one seemed to be in sympathy with my feelings." In October of the year Harrison again rode out the Crown Hill, "The day was bright & the Cemetery was peaceful and beautiful beyond description." But with winter descending a month later, he wrote: "The trees are now all bare and the ground covered with leaves from which all the brightness has gone." Harrison was supervising a monument to his wife at the base of Crown Hill in Section 13. He fretted, "I have heard nothing from the contractors." By the following February, all was well. Chislett had written him that the monument was "a very satisfactory piece of work," and Harrison was soon able to confirm it for himself. On February 21, 1894, he wrote, "This afternoon I drove out to the cemetery to see the monument which has just been set up. It is apparently a good piece of work, but the lot will need to be graded to give it a better effect as the higher ground behind it hides more of the base on that side. This will be done as soon as the ground thaws & when the lot is resodded it will look very well I think."

In March 1901 Harrison's domestic tranquility was rent. He contracted influenza, which soon progressed into pneumonia. Despite the ministrations of numerous physicians, his condition rapidly deteriorated. On March 13, 1901, Harrison died with one hand in his wife's, and the other hand in his minister's.

Harrison's bier was laid in the Statehouse, where thousands of Indiana soldiers, including the survivors of his old regiment, gathered in his honor. The funeral was on March 17, 1901, a beautiful Sunday afternoon. President William McKinley and a

*Benjamin Harrison, twenty-third U.S. president (1889 to 1893).*

stand for what he believed to be right and just. . . . A fearless man inwardly commands respect, and above everything else Harrison was fearless and just." Earlier in the services, Riley had been less reverent, when he wearied of an over-long prayer by a sanctimonious clergyman. Author Frank McKinney "Kin" Hubbard, then a young newspaperman sent to cover the funeral, was sitting nearby. He noticed that the pallbearers were bent over, trying to suppress laughs by stuffing handkerchiefs in their mouths. Pallbearer Riley was giving a running commentary. As Hubbard told it, Riley explained the minister's orations to his fellow mourners: "Now he's explaining to God all about Ben so God will know how to get along with him." Stiffled snorts. "Now he's got a program laid out to keep God busy for the next couple o' years." Hubbard later recounted, "Riley nearly ruined the funeral."

host of other top-hatted dignitaries left the Harrison house on North Delaware Street, followed by pallbearers carrying Harrison's flag-draped casket. Throngs lined the avenues and Monument Circle to watch the cortege pass. At the First Presbyterian Church funeral services, speakers read tributes from all over the world. To this day, Harrison is memorialized on this birthday with a wreath-laying ceremony—a wreath given by the current U.S. president.

But poet James Whitcomb Riley perhaps best summarized the Hoosier president. He spoke of Harrison always being a "conspicuous figure on the horizon of my world." Riley said, "One of the characteristics of General Harrison always commanded my profound respect—his fearless independence and

Four dark horses pulled the black hearse with Harrison's casket toward Crown Hill. Soldiers on horseback served as the honor guard, and a long line of carriages. At the cemetery, the bareheaded pallbearers struggled across the damp ground toward Harrison's grave site, where the mountain of flowers served as floral testament to the esteem of his fellow citizens. His monument reads:

Statesman, yet friend to man:
Of soul sincere
In action faithful and
In honor clear.

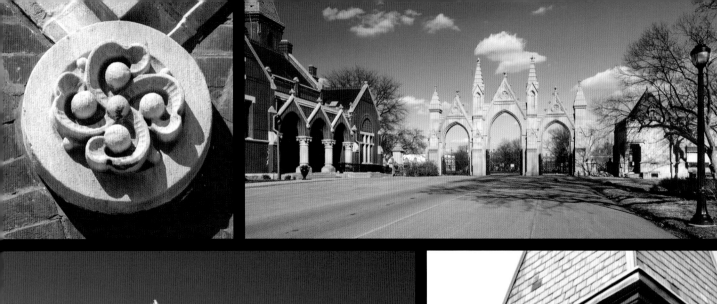

DICKSON

INDIANA AIDS MEMORIAL

# 4

## THE GOLDEN AGE, 1902–1929

Crown Hill first allowed an automobile to drive into the cemetery on November 7, 1912. Given that Indiana was the birthplace of the automobile, it was only appropriate that Crown Hill served as the final resting place for many of the automobile industry's most dynamic progenitors.

Indianapolis had been at the forefront of automobile development since local blacksmith and carriage maker Charles H. Black manipulated a Benz-powered horseless carriage around the downtown in 1891. (Black was the brother of Civil War drummer Edward Black, America's youngest soldier.) During his six-block automobile drive, Black ran into a surrey, causing the first auto accident. A few blocks away, he then ran into the Occidental Hotel show window, followed by a collision with a second window nearby. After Black's three car wrecks during the city's first automobile ride, the police encouraged him to return to his carriage factory. In spite of the inauspicious beginning, automobiles caught on in Indianapolis. Undeterred by his shaky start, Black began manufacturing autos in 1896 and three years later began producing the "Indianapolis" model.

Indianapolis entrepreneurs were soon producing two-passenger Waverly electrics and National Electromobiles. By 1902 the first Marmons were rolling out of the Indianapolis factory. In 1905 Overlands followed from their facility on Henry Street. Indianapolis-made cars proliferated, including the American

Underslung, the Indiana, the Lindsey, the Kugel, the White Steam, the Mohawk, the Cyclop, and the Comet. Within a few years, Indianapolis artisans were laboriously handcrafting luxurious Coles and Duesenbergs, as well as sleek Stutz and Cord roadsters. Until 1905 there were more auto companies in Indianapolis than any city in Michigan. From 1896 to 1937 more than sixty-five different makes of cars were manufactured in the Circle City, putting it in the top three motor cities in America.

Then in 1909 some of Indianapolis's leading lights organized a pioneering automobile test track on the western edge of town, not far from Crown Hill. Automobile industry pioneer and owner of the Prest-O-Lite company, Carl Fisher; Prest-O-Lite partner James Allison; bicycle-chain magnate and fellow automobile enthusiast Arthur Newby; and automotive parts manufacturer Frank Wheeler bought a 320-acre farm and installed a two-and-a-half-mile unpaved race track. During the first three days of automobile races held August 19–21, 1909, one driver, three riding mechanics, and four spectators were killed, and a number were injured, prompting the partners to pave the track with three million ten-pound bricks. When auto races resumed the next year, there were no further major accidents, emboldening Fisher to announce a 500-mile race to be held in May 1911. Eighty thousand spectators showed up to watch the field vie for $25,000 in prize money. A local car, the Marmon Wasp,

took first place. Fisher decided to make the 500-mile race an annual event, even though there were five deaths during the event, prompting the *New York Times* to rant that auto races, "bring out the very worst of human nature." The paper insisted, "They are an amusement congenial only to savages and should be stopped." Seldom listening to East Coast invectives anyway, Indianapolis was soon car crazy.

Even horse-drawn hearses succumbed to the automobile frenzy. The first motorized hearses were electric. The Flanner and Buchanan Funeral Home used electric cars in its Indianapolis funerals by 1903, at a time when a full Flanner and Buchanan funeral with casket, embalming, and transport cost a little more than $300 and a Crown Hill lot cost $160, with burial an additional $6. In early 1909 innovative Chicago undertaker H. Durward Ludlow directed America's first "automobile funeral" that used the internal combustion engine. Ludlow carried Wilfrid A. Pruyn to his grave in a bus retrofitted with the carriage from a horse-drawn hearse. Ludlow's wealthier clients embraced the modern conveyance, prompting Ludlow to replace his auto hearse with a larger model. The same year Pruyn made his last journey in a motorized hearse, Cincinnati's Crane and Breed Company began manufacturing hearses that sped along at thirty miles per hour, a fast clip for those days. Competing models began to emerge. In 1912 another Cincinnati firm, Sayers and Scovill, which was destined to dominate the hearse industry for decades, introduced its first motorized funeral car, somewhat based on a motorized ambulance it had introduced in 1907. Powered by a six-cylinder engine, the hearse was superior to most of its competition. Sayers and Scovill initially produced a twelve-column, carved-panel hearse that mimicked the horse-drawn aesthetic. But within a few years the company began featuring a more restrained carved-panel hearse painted pale gray that fashion-conscious urban funeral

directors increasingly favored over the traditional black coach. While the public liked motorized hearses, funeral directors found the $6,000 price tag to be onerous, especially when horse-drawn hearses cost three-quarters less. As prices on motorized hearses dropped and speeds increased, undertakers realized that faster hearses meant more funerals per day. By 1920 motorized hearses were the industry standard.

Change came slowly to tradition-rich Crown Hill. In 1917 the superintendent was still making his rounds in a horse and buggy. The cemetery did not buy its first automobile until 1918, when long lines of cars were already snaking into the cemetery for burials and memorial events. By then the cemetery's former farm and paddock had been transformed into Section 53's grave sites—there just was not the need for pastures. But Crown Hill's last workhorse, a perennial Memorial Day favorite, was not sold until February 1933.

When the automobile revolution was still in its early days, some of Indianapolis's automotive pioneers passed away, becoming the first of dozens of automobile giants to be buried in Crown Hill. Daniel Marmon was a gifted mechanic and engineer who made his first fortune in milling equipment. As a principal of the Nordyke and Marmon Company, he helped the firm move from Richmond to Indianapolis in 1875. Marmon's son, Howard, inherited his father's engineering prowess. After graduating from the University of California at Berkeley in 1899 during the dawn of the horseless carriages, Howard soon added automobiles to the company's offerings. When Daniel died in 1909, automobiles were already a major part of the company's business. Daniel was buried in Section 31, Lot 285, where his automotive family eventually surrounded him.

David McLean Parry was first a carriage maker. In the 1890s Parry oversaw a mammoth operation that employed 2,400 workers to produce up to a thousand carriages a day, more

*Opposite: The four founders of the Indianapolis Motor Speedway—Frank Wheeler, Arthur Newby, Carl Fisher, and James Allison—all rest at Crown Hill.*

than the nation's next five largest carriage makers combined. Parry tinkered with electric cars as early as 1892, but it was not until 1909 that he founded the Parry Auto Company, which included the Overland Automobile Company. After Overland was sold, Parry reorganized to build the New Parry, then the Pathfinder, though those companies also sank under the weight of overcapitalized and underutilized equipment. Ensconced on Golden Hill, his one hundred-acre manorial estate across from Crown Hill, Parry promulgated an antilabor gospel that decried unions and socialism. When Parry died in 1915 he was buried in Section 14, Lot 6. Parry's fellow carriage maker Black, Indianapolis's first driver and automobile manufacturer, died in 1918 and was buried in Section 25, Lot 185.

From the beginning, Indiana had cast its lot with expensive, craft-made automobiles. Its primary rival, Michigan, had opted to manufacture less-expensive cars using mass-production methods. Typified by Henry Ford's assembly line, standardized vehicles began to dominate the market. Ford's Model T debuted in 1908, the same year Michigan capitalists organized General Motors. The impact on auto production was almost immediate. In 1910 a total of 10 percent of the autos sold cost less than a thousand dollars. By 1916 the figure had climbed to 82 percent.

Before World War I there was a market for both inexpensive, mass-produced cars and high-end, craft-built cars, especially if the generally smaller Hoosier factories consolidated into larger

concerns. But a postwar economic recession prompted sharp price cutting that capital-starved Hoosier manufacturers were unprepared to match. In 1910 there were sixty-seven Indiana car manufacturers. After four years of winnowing, there were only thirty-eight survivors. Just twenty-seven Hoosier manufacturers remained in 1919, the year after the war ended. By 1921 only ten Indiana automobile companies were still in business.

Wheeler, the auto magnate and Speedway partner, died in 1921. Wheeler had parlayed a successful carburetor company into presidency of the Langenskamp-Wheeler Brass Works and directorship of the Stutz Fire Engine Company. But depressed by declining health and business setbacks that caused him to sell Allison his share of the Speedway, Wheeler killed himself with a shotgun on May 27, 1921, just three days before the Indianapolis 500. Wheeler was buried in Section 46, Lot 24 under a small granite marker.

Barnstorming racecar driver Howdy Wilcox drove in the first eleven Indianapolis 500s. After a series of middling finishes, Wilcox won the race in 1919. His victory set off an immense celebration, as he was the first American to win the 500 since 1912, when another Indianapolis racer, Joe Dawson, won. Inspired by Wilcox's victory, the Speedway band struck up "Back Home Again in Indiana," beginning the song's long association with the 500. Wilcox was the first 500 driver to break 100 miles per hour. After his September 4, 1923, death in a race in Altoona, Pennsylvania, Wilcox was interred in the family lot in Section 56, Lot 240, where a rusticated granite marker memorialized him, as well as his wife and baby daughter.

The owner of Wilcox's winning 1919 car, Allison, was the next Speedway founder to pass away. A longtime friend and partner with Fisher in Prest-O-Lite, the Speedway, and Miami Beach development, Allison formed the Indianapolis Speedway Team Company to engineer racecars for the Indianapolis 500, includ-

*Doctor John Klein visits Crown Hill with his 1931 Duesenberg Model J Rollston Convertible Victoria originally built for Ralph Pulitzer of the New York City publishing family.*

ing Wilcox's winner. During World War I the company became a major defense contractor as Allison Experimental Company, which was renamed Allison Engineering Company in the 1920s.

Allison died on August 11, 1928, at Riverdale, his $2 million-dollar Cold Springs Road estate. Prone to lung infections, Allison contracted bronchial pneumonia while honeymooning with his new bride, Lucille, whom he married after scandalously divorcing Sarah, his wife of twenty years. His death unleashed a court battle between the two wives and Allison's mother that lasted for years. General Motors purchased the Allison Engineering Company in 1929, the year after Allison's death. Marked

> "No matter where I may be, Indianapolis is my home, the place where my heart is," he wrote a friend.

by an ornately carved, urn-topped monument, Allison was buried in Section 23, Lot 2, where he eventually rested with his parents, siblings, and nephews and nieces. His wives were buried elsewhere.

Indiana's post-Civil War emergence as an industrial and political power also fueled a golden age of arts and literature. "In 1900 perhaps no other place on earth displayed more native charm or held out greater promise than Indiana," wrote journalist John Bartlow Martin. With the railroads funneling the region's economic wealth through the capital city, Indianapolis blossomed into a thriving commercial entrepôt, where affluent families patronized the arts. In 1891 painters T. C. Steele and William Forsyth established the Indiana School of Art in a church on the Monument Circle. Just three years later, influential Chicago critic Hamlin Garland proclaimed Indiana impressionist painters to be the "Hoosier Group," which came to include Steele, Forsyth, Otto Stark, J. Ottis Adams, and Richard Gruelle. The five were soon garnering national acclaim for their impressionist art that expressed an unabashed affection for the heartland's rural beauty.

The members of the Hoosier Group knew Crown Hill. When Steele's beloved wife, Libbie, died in 1899 after a long fight with rheumatoid arthritis, he buried her under a plain granite marker in Section 38. The marker reads, "Elizabeth Lakin Steele, 1850–1899." Born in Rushville, Libbie was a great help to her husband. He told his friends, "My wife is my most helpful critic. She brings to me a clearer eye, a more poetic vision."

Gruelle was a self-taught artist who weathered one economic downturn by painting scenes on metal safes. In 1882 he moved to Indianapolis. Though Gruelle had previously focused on portraiture, he began painting the landscape around Indianapolis. In the late 1880s the city art scene was crackling with the return of Steele, Forsythe, Stark, and Adams from studies abroad. Though Gruelle moved to several East Coast locales, he always maintained a connection to Indianapolis, including illustrating some of James Whitcomb Riley's most beloved poems and holding annual exhibitions in the city during his long visits. "No matter where I may be, Indianapolis is my home, the place where my heart is," he wrote a friend. In 1912 a stroke ended his artistry. During a trip to Indianapolis on November 8, 1914, Gruelle died, the first of the Hoosier Group to pass on. He was buried in Crown Hill in Section 35, Lot 213.

Stark was the next member of the illustrious Hoosier Group to enter Crown Hill. Born in Indianapolis in 1859, he served an early apprenticeship as a lithographer in Cincinnati, and then continued his art training first in New York and then Paris, where he married his French wife, Marie. Stark and his family returned to New York, where his wife died. With four children to raise alone, Stark returned to Indianapolis to be closer to his family. By 1894 Stark was operating an art studio, where he painted and offered art classes. En plein air paintings soon absorbed him, yielding the art that he exhibited with the other Hoosier Group painters at the fateful *Five Hoosier Painters* show in Chicago that grabbed Garland's attention. "We thought we had made a great discovery," crowed noted Chicago sculptor

Lorado Taft, and we gloated with my rejoicing over the Hoosier paintings." (Luckily, Taft did not hold a grudge against Indianapolis. Mary Ella McGinnis's mother had rejected his statue of her daughter back in 1875.)

Wearying of the pace of exhibition painting, Stark took a position as an art teacher at Manual Training High School in 1899, and later at the John Herron Art Institute, which began in 1902. While he remained a dedicated teacher, Stark also showed his paintings in numerous galleries in the United States and abroad. For many years he painted public murals in schools and hospitals, including a large mural in the City Hospital's (Wishard Hospital and soon Eskenazi Health) children's dining room, where he painted "all the toys known to childhood in one great circus frolic," according to author Mary Q. Burnet. On April 26, 1926, Stark passed away following a stroke. Up to his final days, he painted his family and Indiana landscapes. As befitted the self-effacing painter, Stark's grave in Section 62, Lot 1083 was memorialized with a small, restrained granite marker.

William Forsyth married Alice Atkinson, one of his stu-

dents at the second Indiana School of Art. Their eldest daughter, Constance, became an artist and teacher whose watercolors were exhibited in England, Scotland, France, and Indiana. William Forsyth, the last surviving member of the Hoosier Group, died at his home in Irvington located on the east side of Indianapolis on March 29, 1935. He was buried in Section 39, Lot 298, as were Alice and Constance. A bronze bas-relief portrait of Forsyth graces his monument.

From the 1880s to the beginning of World War II, Indiana authors were perennially on the best-seller charts. The best-selling book of the nineteenth century was *Ben-Hur,* written by Lew Wallace, who had strong ties to Indianapolis. With royalties from his best-selling *The Prince of India,* Wallace built Indianapolis's first major apartment building, the seven-story Blacherne at Meridian and Vermont Streets. Wallace's best sellers were not flukes. Using a Purdue librarian's elaborate scoring system based on sales from 1900 to 1940, Indiana authors ranked at 215, right behind New York's 216, while Pennsylvania was a distant third at 125.

Through the early twentieth century, the focus of America's literary limelight was on Indianapolis, where authors Riley, Booth Tarkington, Meredith Nicholson, and Frank McKinney "Kin" Hubbard episodically lived. Through the 1880s, Riley had built his career with long tours on the Lyceum circuit, but by the 1890s he was a wealthy man with several best-selling books, including *Rhymes of Childhood,* which sold millions of copies. Tarkington's *Gentleman from Indiana,* published in 1899, followed by *Penrod, The Magnificent Ambersons,* and *Alice Adams,* brought him fame and wealth, while also drawing attention to Indianapolis as a literary destination. Nicholson was another hometown boy who made good. His book, *The Hoosiers,* helped solidify the distinct midwestern identity formulated by Wallace, Riley, and other Indiana writers. Akin to Scotland's Robert Burns and New England's Robert Frost, the Hoosier writers used Indiana's common language and mores to frame—for better or worse—their homeland's cultural identity. The writers "revealed the Hoosiers to themselves," as George Ade wrote about Riley. Using Indiana locales and themes, Nicholson's *The House of a Thousand Candles* and *A Hoosier Chronicle* both climbed the best-seller lists. Nationally syndicated cartoonist and author Hubbard used a wry wit in his character Abe Martin to portray

nostalgic but worldwise Hoosiers, wary of change but nonetheless resigned to its inevitability. "An optimist is a fellow who believes what's going to be will be postponed," Hubbard wrote.

To add to the literary ferment, the Bobbs-Merrill Company, an Indianapolis publishing firm that dated back to 1850, cranked out dozens of best sellers, including books by Riley, Nicholson, and L. Frank Baum, author of the *Wizard of Oz* series. From 1899 through 1909, the company published sixteen novels that ranked among the year's top ten best-selling books. When William Conrad Bobbs, the longtime director and guiding light of the company, died in 1926, he was interred in Section 25, Lot 252.

The early twentieth century was a time of immense economic and social change for Indianapolis. The essentially conservative midwestern town "became a city almost against its will," as Nicholson wrote in 1904. Unabashedly affectionate toward the structured order and civility that he perceived in post-Civil War Indianapolis, Nicholson joined the Crown Hill Board

of Corporators in 1916. Tarkington, who shared Nicholson's concerns about the rapidly changing social order, wrote about the city, "It was heaving up in the middle incredibly; it was spreading incredibly; and as it heaved and spread, it befouled itself and darkened the sky. Its boundary was mere shapelessness on the run."

Social change was impacting literature too. Even as America hurtled toward its internationalist involvement with World War I, Americans' taste for sentimental fiction was waning. Hard-edged fiction, as later typified by authors such as Theodore Dreiser, Sinclair Lewis, Ernest Hemingway, and F. Scott Fitzgerald, spoke to the complicated world of modern midwesterners increasingly adrift from nineteenth-century verities. While the golden age of Indiana literature still glowed through the 1920s, the glimmer diminished.

In 1916 the colossus of Indiana literature, Riley, died. There was an outpouring of appreciation and grief after news of his death chattered out of the nation's teletypes on July 23, 1916.

*Opposite and Above, left: James Whitcomb Riley's body is taken from his Lockerbie residence for its journey to Crown Hill as crowds line the streets. Right: Riley tells the story of Indiana for a film commissioned as part of Indiana's centennial celebration.*

The *Philadelphia Inquirer* called him "the most popular poet of his generation." Writing that Riley was the first "American poet" since Henry Wadsworth Longfellow, the *New York Sun* averred, "In his verses, Indiana spoke to the world." President Woodrow Wilson telegraphed the Riley family: "With his departure a notable figure passes out of the nation's life; a man who imparted joyful pleasures and a thoughtful view of many things that other men would have missed. I am sure I am speaking the feeling of the whole country in expressing my own sense of loss."

Riley's health had been in decline since 1901 when his doctor diagnosed him with neurasthenia, the catch-all chronic fatigue disease of the late nineteenth and early twentieth centuries. Relying on nursing from friends and family, as well as alcohol and patent medicines, Riley spent much of the next decade in light convalescence, particularly after a stroke in 1910, which ended most of his writing. In 1911 he donated the land where the new central library was built on Pennsylvania Avenue. Still famously indulgent with children, bachelor Riley continued to dote on the young people who gathered to hear him read his poetry. Though his writing was essentially over, Riley's poems were still hot sellers, perennially repackaged by Bobbs-Merrill. Honors flowed his way: the universities of Yale, Indiana, and Pennsylvania bestowed honorary doctorates on him. He was elected to the National Institute of Arts and Letters in 1908 and received the poetry medal from the National Academy of Arts and Letters. In 1912 the governor of Indiana proclaimed October 7, Riley's birthday, to be Riley Day. By 1916, after U.S. Secretary of the Interior Franklin Lane called for the observance to be held in schools across the country, the commemoration went national. The *Indianapolis Star* claimed that a million schoolchildren paid homage to the Hoosier poet. On Saturday July 22, 1916, Riley suffered a second stroke. He recovered enough during the day to joke with his friends, but died before dawn the following morning.

The same day the Crown Hill Corporators convened a special meeting to discuss a proper home for Riley. Following the meeting, Volney T. Malott, president of the Crown Hill Cemetery Association, offered the Riley family "one of the most beautiful sites in the cemetery." There was some concern that Riley's hometown of Greenfield might supplant Indianapolis as Riley's final resting place, as the Greenfield mayor had also telegraphed an offer. But Indianapolis had put together a better package. So Hoosiers could pay their respects, Governor Samuel Ralston arranged for Riley's remains to lie in state in the capitol rotunda on Monday, July 24. Mayor Joseph Bell had declared the city's flags would be at half-mast for a week, and that city offices would be closed on Tuesday, July 25, 1916, the day of the funeral.

The afternoon following Riley's death, the governor and mayor came to his Lockerbie Street home, where Riley lay in his bronze casket. Watched by a crowd that gathered on Lockerbie Street, thirteen burly policemen wrestled the 1,200-pound coffin down the steps to the large white motor hearse, typically used for children's funerals. The hearse, accompanied by an honor guard of sixteen mounted policemen and forty police drill team members, led a long funeral cortege of motorcars to the Statehouse. A huge throng was already clustered on the steps as the policemen hefted Riley's coffin into the building. As many as 35,000 people passed by the poet's coffin to view Riley in his pristine white suit, before the viewing ended at 10 p.m. The next afternoon, a small group of family and close friends gathered at the Lockerbie Street house for the funeral. Reverend Joseph Milburn, a Presbyterian minister and close friend, read Riley's poem, "Away," which opened with the lines: "I cannot say, and I will not say / That he is dead.—He is just away!"

Riley went away to Crown Hill. As the hearse slowly motored his body through Crown Hill, thousands of mourners lined the lanes. Sheltered under their umbrellas in the threatening weather, mothers waited with their children. An enormous crowd

*Opposite: A nighttime view of the memorial for James Whitcomb Riley, the Hoosier Poet.*

surrounded the ivy-covered Gothic Chapel, which a committee of prominent citizens had transformed into "a flower-bedecked and decorated crypt." Palms, boxwoods, bay trees, and flowers lined the walls; marble urns filled with ferns and pink gladiolus stood in niches near the ceiling; Turkish rugs adorned the marble floors. "When the funeral cortege swept into view down the curving path leading from the great gates of the cemetery to the vault, the crowd fell back," the *Indianapolis Star* reported. "And it is a curious thing that, just as the flag draped hearse came to a stop outside the chapel the rain began to fall—while the sun shone. Down came the rain, flashing like diamonds in the sun, while a rainbow spread its gorgeous arc across the sky for the briefest space of time. It was not a gloomy shower, but half smiles and half tears."

While Riley's body lay ensconced in a Crown Hill vault, a tug of war was still going on between Greenfield and Indianapolis. In public meetings and political proclamations, Greenfield vehemently laid claim to their native son's remains. The *Greenfield Republican* argued, "It would be wrong to bury him anywhere but in Greenfield. Here is where he, without doubt, wanted to be buried. Here people will come to see his birthplace. Here is where they will come to see the 'Old Swimmin' Hole' and here is where they should come to see his tomb." The paper reported that a local citizen contended that "certain Indianapolis influences" had made an effort to grab Riley's body for Crown Hill. Adding to the furor, former Greenfield mayor, John Eagan, sneered at the "selfish commercial spirit of Indianapolis people who sought interment at Crown Hill for merely cold-blooded mercenary purposes."

Crown Hill supporter Nicholson rejoined that Riley had chosen to live for many decades in Indianapolis, where he had actually written many of those Greenfield poems, as well as poems entitled "At Lockerbie" and "At Crown Hill." Despite deputations of protesting Greenfield citizens, plans for Riley's permanent burial at Crown Hill progressed while he lay in his temporary vault. When the wrangling and political positioning finally died

down, Crown Hill came through on its promise to provide "one of the most beautiful sites in the cemetery." On October 6, 1917, the Hoosier Poet was laid to rest at the summit of Crown Hill, the first burial on the site.

Riley had visited the cemetery many times, and perhaps the view from the summit had inspired his poem, "At Crown Hill," which opens with the stanza:

> Leave him here in the fresh greening grasses and trees
> And the symbols of love, and the solace of these—
> The saintly white lilies and blossoms he keeps
> In endless caress as he breathlessly sleeps.
> The tears of our eyes wrong the scene of his rest,
> For the sky's at its clearest—the sun's at its best—
> The earth at its greenest—its wild bud and bloom
> At its sweetest—and sweetest its honey'd perfume.
> Home! Home!—Leave him here in his lordly estate,
> And with never a tear as we turn from the gate!

It took a few more years for Riley's supporters to arrange for the open-canopied monument to be erected. And then in 1927 the cemetery contracted for the curbs and stairways up to the memorial, providing access to the aerie where generations of visitors have taken in the great defining vista of Indianapolis.

As the twentieth century unfurled, many Civil War survivors began joining their brothers in arms at Crown Hill. Congressional Medal of Honor recipient Captain Charles W. Brouse died in 1904, forty-one years after the momentous Battle of Missionary Ridge, where Brouse courageously strode the battlements after ordering his men to take cover from the horrific fire. To keep up his men's morale, he continued to walk the earthworks until severely wounded. When Brouse died in 1904 at age sixty-five, the Grand Army of the Republic, the forerunner of the American Legion, buried him in the National Cemetery with full military honors.

Ivan N. Walker was another long-lived Civil War veteran interred in Crown Hill. A lieutenant colonel of the Seventy-third Indiana Volunteer Infantry, Walker was captured and imprisoned in Richmond, Virginia's Libby Prison with General

Abel Streight, held as leverage for John Hunt Morgan and his Confederate raiders, who were incarcerated in Ohio. In February 1864 Walker tunneled to freedom with more than a hundred other Union prisoners, but was recaptured just short of the Union lines. After a career as a public and railroad official, Walker served in 1895 as the GAR's commander in chief.

> The advertisements claimed, "It restores the natural colors, arrests decomposition, and effectually eradicates all infection, leaving the corpse free from the slightest unpleasant odor, and in a fit condition for home funerals."

When Walker died in November 1905, the pernicious illness he contracted in Libby Prison was listed as the cause. Walker was buried in Section 13, Lot 1, under a simple white headstone.

Civil War mortician Daniel H. Prunk passed away in 1923. He was not the first of the Civil war undertakers to be interred in Crown Hill. William W. Weaver, the pioneer Indianapolis undertaker who moved Union dead from Greenlawn to Crown Hill, was reinterred after his death on April 3, 1866. Weaver was Indianapolis's first undertaker, beginning his work in 1840. In 1866 he had his office in the Exchange Building on North Illinois Street. Each day he advertised, "Persons wishing to purchase lots at Crown Hill Cemetery will be taken to the grounds on application to the undersigned. W. W. Weaver." After he died, Weaver was buried in a $125 grave in Section 1, Lot 39, but was reinterred in 1875 after seven members of the Weaver family died of disease.

Prunk was a Virginia native who had graduated from Cincinnati's Eclectic Medical Institute and worked as a doctor before the war. During the war, he served as a surgeon for various Indiana units before being dismissed in March 1863 for falsifying soldiers' disability discharges in exchange for payoffs. But Prunk was soon back in service, where he freelanced as an embalmer—who established a reputation for getting soldiers' bodies back home. Prunk advertised his "improved mode of embalming bodies." The advertisements claimed, "It restores the natural colors, arrests decomposition, and effectually eradicates all infection, leaving the corpse free from the slightest unpleasant odor, and in a fit condition for home funerals." After the war, Prunk again switched sides, practicing as a south-side Indianapolis physician. When he died at age ninety-four, he was buried in Section 35, Lot 1.

Wallace, the author of *Ben-Hur,* was also the commander of the Eleventh Indiana Regiment, a Zouave unit famous for its red kepis and formidable fighting skills. After Wallace's death in 1905, he was buried in his hometown of Crawfordsville, but his family inscribed his name on their Crown Hill cenotaph. It was appropriate: Wallace knew Crown Hill well. In 1896 he spoke to thousands of people gathered at the cemetery for Memorial Day. He said, "Under our feet, in final rest, sleep thousands of men. Who they were, and how they came to be here, are memories too sacred to be forgotten in this generation; and that they may not be forgotten in the generations to come, behold these preparations—this part of the earth set apart and consecrated, these tablets erected by a grateful government at the bidding of a grateful people."

Wallace had another connection to the capital city: During 1877 he had reactivated his fearsome Zouaves to suppress the city's "Bread or Blood" labor strife.

The "Bread or Blood" incident happened in the summer of 1877, when labor agitation and hunger swept the city during the nadir of a depression that had begun four years before. A crowd of Indianapolis workingmen had petitioned the City Council on June 1 to "most respectfully ask and pray that you give us work or devise some means by which we can relieve our suffering families." The city fathers offered little: one committee of prominent Indianapolis leaders suggesting the labor surplus could be relieved by "the withdrawal of a reasonable number of laborers from this field." The *Indianapolis Journal* fulminated about the workmen's "considerable communistic feeling." On the evening of June 6, a crowd of five hundred unemployed workers gathered on the Statehouse lawn. Firebrands, such as William Dreythaler, L. P. McCormick, and W. H. "Tip" Ballard, threatened violence if they did not get some relief. The cry of "Bread or Blood" filled the air. The memory of the violent Paris Commune of 1871, when socialist and anarchist workers formed the first working-class government, traumatized Indianapolis's comfortable classes. The police and fire departments were already on the alert.

Mayor John Caven, a Scotch-Irishman who had been born in Pennsylvania, had been elected in 1863 with the political support of Irish immigrant working-class voters. Speaking to the crowd on the Statehouse lawn, Caven defused tension by first announcing that the halted Belt Line Railroad construction project would soon be resumed and provide six hundred jobs. Caven then addressed the most urgent issue: hunger. Some workers' families had not eaten for two days. Caven called for the crowd to follow him to Sampson's Bakery, south of the Statehouse. There he began handing out six loaves of bread to each person who queued up. When they exhausted Sampson's supply,

# ANNA NICHOLAS

Anna Nicholas, the author of *The Story of Crown Hill,* which was published in 1928, was a cherished Indianapolis journalist, author, and literary figure. Born in

Pennsylvania, she came late in the nineteenth century to Indianapolis, where she worked for the *Indianapolis Journal* and then the *Indianapolis Star* when the two papers merged in 1904. For decades, she worked as an editorial writer, serving as a bemused observer of the Circle City's triumphs and digressions.

In her first book, a collection of short stories titled *An Idyl of the Wabash and Other Stories,* Nicholas portrayed a prim, young, and stern schoolteacher coming to Indiana with "a sense of an almost perilous adventure." After arriving in

Indiana, her character concluded, "the people were queer, but that they seemed friendly, and she thought she'd get along real well." And Nicholas did get along real well. She was a colleague of James Whitcomb Riley, Lew Wallace, Booth Tarkington, and many other Hoosier literary figures, and coached Charles Major, later famous for his book *When Knighthood Was in Flower.* Beyond her own writing, which included another volume of short stories titled *The Making of Thomas Barton,* Nicholas served as a literary adviser for the Bowen-Merrill Publishing Company. In his paradigm-shifting book, *The Hoosiers,* Meredith Nicholson praised her literary abilities, writing that Nicholas's stories were "distinguished by the evident sincerity of their purpose to reflect life honestly." He later noted "her poise and serenity." A founder of the Women's Rotary Club, Nicholas was active in both the

Indianapolis Women's Press Club and the Woman's Club of Indiana, which she joined in 1888.

After Nicholas's death on January 29, 1929, at the age of seventy-nine, her colleagues, friends, and family testified to their loss. They characterized her as a gracious woman and a graceful writer, who could absorb the grit of humanity without being tainted by it. Nicholas was laid to rest in Section 15, Lot 33, in the cemetery she knew so well. As Nichoals wrote in the *Story of Crown Hill*, "The history of a cemetery can never be complete any more than the history of a city of the living. After all has been done, after we have made this place as beautiful as human hands may, bending nature and art to our purpose, the place where we lay our dead is consecrated not only by the use to which it is put, but by the tears, the broken hearts, the bitter anguish of the living as they murmur the last farewells."

Caven and the crowd moved on Bryce's Bakery on South Street, where the mayor again handed out bread until everyone got at least a few loaves. Caven later wrote, "As soon as I had paid Mr. Bryce his bill I went out in the street, and where a few minutes before was that hungry crowd was as still as the grave, not a human being in sight."

As violent strikes spread across the country, Indianapolis solons were increasingly edgy, and workers were increasingly militant. On July 23, 1877, 2,000 people assembled on the Statehouse lawn. Flyers circulated that read, "We Are Striking for Our Bread and Butter." The railway workers struck the next day, idling 1,100 miles of Indiana tracks. Virtually no freight moved. The city shut down—even the newsboys went on strike. As rumors of class war swept the city, Caven called for a public meeting in front of city hall. As many as 3,000 heard Caven announce the formation of Committees of Safety, composed of citizens who were to "put down any perpetrators of violence."

The Indiana Guard mobilized thousands of troops armed with new breech-loading Springfield rifles, Gatling guns, and cannons. Wallace telegraphed the core of his Zouaves to hurry to Indianapolis: "the crisis has come here this afternoon. . . . Don't fail in this." Indianapolis was soon an armed camp, with the Indiana Guard, five companies of regular army troops, and several hundred deputized citizens patrolling the city. Wallace's former Zouaves patrolled with fixed bayonets. Dirt flew at the Circle as soldiers dug entrenchments. Cavalrymen cantered through the eerily empty streets. Caven had given the police orders to "shoot down any man found burning or robbing and send for the dead animal car to cart away the

> On July 23, 1877, 2,000 people assembled on the Statehouse lawn. Flyers circulated that read, "We Are Striking for Our Bread and Butter."

# JACOB PIATT DUNN JR.

Jacob Piatt Dunn Jr. was a busy fellow: attorney, historian, reforming journalist, politico, ethnologist, and prospector in an era when Indiana was an important political state. "His willpower was strong and he was slow to admit that he could not accomplish anything he undertook," former governor and U.S. senator Samuel Ralston said about Dunn. The son of a man of Protestant rectitude, Dunn

was born in Lawrenceburg, Indiana, in 1855. The family moved to Indianapolis in 1861, but young Dunn was off for degrees from Earlham College and the University of Michigan, where he earned a law degree. After practicing law for a few years in Indianapolis, Dunn journeyed to Colorado, where he worked his family's silver interests and cultivated an interest in Native Americans. In 1884 he permanently returned to Indianapolis. Two years later, Dunn made his mark as a historian with the publication of his groundbreaking book *Massacres of the*

*Mountains: A History of the Indian Wars of the Far West, 1815–1875,* which used government publications to document the subject. It was considered a minor classic.

The same year, Dunn began serving as the executive secretary of the Indiana Historical Society, and he was instrumental in reviving the moribund organization. He went on to write extensively for the IHS and other historical and political publications, while also producing the two-volume *Greater Indianapolis* that was published in 1910. Nine years later, his five-volume carcass." The combined military, civil militia, and law enforcement officials totaled in the thousands—almost one in four of the men in Indianapolis were actively engaged in suppressing a feared labor uprising.

But in the face of military might, Indianapolis's working class was quiescent. The railroad men were soon compromising and had the trains running again within a few days. On July 28, the *Indianapolis News* reported, "Meridian Street smiles again. The Strike. Ha ha ha! Ho ho ho." Wallace's warriors went home. Work continued on the Belt Line railway loop that supporters claimed would bring new heights of civic prosperity to Indianapolis. Caven thundered with biblical color, "our city will be girt about with a cordon of industries like the pillar of cloud by day and the pillar of fire by night telling us the angel of prosperity is going before us and leading us on." The belt line did employ hundreds of workers during its construction, and industry did boom along the rail route. But when the

construction projects of 1877 ended, Indianapolis workers were again mired in an economic morass that persisted for years.

Some of the principal Bread or Blood actors were memorialized at Crown Hill. After his death on February 15, 1905, Wallace's family erected a cenotaph topped with a statue of a sorrowful woman in Section 36, Lot 3. Caven died of senile debility a few weeks later on March 9, 1905, at the age of eighty. He was buried in a Masonic area in Section 13, Lot 46. When labor advocate Ballard died of heart failure on March 28, 1900, he was buried on May 14 in Section 35, Lot 67.

Though he did not serve in the Civil War, the conflict between the states ignited inventor Richard Jordan Gatling's obsession with machine guns. Devised and tested in Indianapolis, Gatling's "terrible marvel" changed battle forever. While Gatling was born in North Carolina and spent much of his business career elsewhere, his enduring Indianapolis connections drew him back when he died in 1903.

*Indiana and Indianans* covered the state exhaustively. He served as state librarian and as the Indianapolis city controller. Through work with Miami tribal descendants of Chief Little Turtle and Francis Godfroy, Dunn wrote a dictionary of the Miami language and published other books about native Indianans.

Dunn made his most lasting impact through his work as a reforming journalist and politician. In Dunn's era Indiana was a cesspool of electoral corruption. Through the reforms he championed, such as the Australian secret ballot and constitutional reform, Indiana's reputation began to improve. Similar to many Progressives, Dunn's views included an embedded bias against immigrants and African Americans. Notwithstanding that bias, Dunn was a leading light in the Hoosier Progressives' drive for "good government"—"goo-goos," their detractors called them. Historian Ray E. Boomhower, author of Dunn's definitive biography, stated that "one man, Jacob Piatt Dunn, Jr., an attorney, journalist, Indiana historian, and Democrat, was in the vanguard of a reform endeavor

stretching from the late nineteenth century to the early twentieth century and dedicated to cleansing the sordid reputation Indiana had earned for itself through election chicanery."

In 1921 Dunn embarked on a two-month prospecting expedition to Haiti, where he was searching for manganese. When he returned, he joined Ralston's staff as chief aide. Dunn's death in Washington, D.C., on June 6, 1924, was front-page news in Indianapolis. Three days later, the multitalented Dunn was interred in Crown Hill's Section 13, Lot 9.

When Gatling first arrived in Indianapolis in 1850, he was already a successful young entrepreneur, holding a number of patents, including one for a mechanical seed planter that he had parlayed into a considerable fortune. As a wealthy businessman, he invested in Indiana real estate and railroads. In 1854 he married a well-connected local beauty, Jemima Sanders, the youngest daughter of prominent physician Doctor John Sanders. Jemima was a sister of Zerelda Wallace, the wife of Governor David Wallace and stepmother to Lew Wallace. With his marriage, Gatling sealed his position in the Indianapolis hierarchy.

In the summer of 1861 as the nation was careening into carnage, the inveterate tinkerer Gatling (he had filed five patents in 1860 alone) had a conversation with Benjamin Harrison, the rising Indianapolis attorney in charge of the Indiana volunteers. The trainloads of war casualties already arriving at Union Station appalled both men—and the conflict was increasingly looking to be a long, bloody one. Harrison told Gatling that his men needed superior weaponry to survive. Harkening to his mechanical seed drill's basic design, Gatling realized he could use the same principles to design a gun that would fire quickly and continuously. The Gatling Gun was born.

With the support of important Indianapolis men, including Governor Oliver P. Morton, Gatling engineered and prototyped the first reliable machine gun, which he thought would shorten wars. Thousands attended demonstrations of his gun in India-

napolis. "It occurred to me that if I could invent a machine—a gun—which could be its rapidity of fire, enable one to do as much battle duty as a hundred, that it would, to a great

*Richard Jordan Gatling*

extent, supersede the necessity of large armies, and consequently exposure to battle and disease would be greatly diminished," Gatling later wrote. With a ready market and financial resources from his midwestern backers, Gatling had a production run of guns made at a Cincinnati-type foundry. In an advertisement, Gatling bragged his gun would produce "a great revolution in the art of warfare," and "can perform the work of a regiment." He specified, "The gun can be discharged at the rate of *two hundred shots per minute,* and it bears the same relation to other fire arms that McCormack's Reaper does to a sickle or the sewing machine to the common needle." But Gatling soon hit the intransigence of the U.S. military, which looked askance at radical new weaponry. Though an army ordnance officer who tested the gun in 1863 termed it "admirable," and concluded it was "well-executed" and "not likely to get out of working order," the army refused to give Gatling an order. One notorious Union officer, General Benjamin Butler, did purchase a dozen Gatling Guns for his troops, but they had negligible effect in the battles where they were used. Admiral David Dixon Porter bought one to affix on a steamboat, in hopes of suppressing the guerrillas who peppered the boats from southern riverbanks. But the gun again had little impact. It was not until 1866, that the army finally gave Gatling an order for a hundred of his guns.

As the bloody nineteenth century wound on, the Gatling Gun found its market, particularly after 1866, when Gatling sold his invention to the Colt Patent Firearms Company in Hartford, Connecticut, and moved there himself. Police departments and militia found the guns ideal to face down striking laborers. The *New York Times* had famously used them to protect its building from protestors during the New York City draft riots of 1863. Indianapolis authorities had deployed them during the 1877 labor unrest. The U.S. Army sent Gatling Guns west during the

Indian Wars (though George Armstrong Custer notoriously declined to take any to Little Bighorn). Teddy Roosevelt lauded the Gatlings in his charge up San Juan Hill. Dozens of nations around the globe snapped up Gatling's gun, which played an important imperial role in Britain's colonial wars in Africa and the Middle East. Russia, Germany, France, and Turkey contracted for Gatling Guns, then Argentina, China, Denmark, Egypt, Holland, Italy, Japan, Korea, Mexico, Morocco, Romania, Spain, Sweden, Switzerland, and Tunisia. An Afghan warlord organized a corps of Gatling-equipped camels, which carried the machine gun mounted high on the front hump.

At the age of eighty-five, Gatling was still inventing. In his later years he had refocused on agriculture, inventing a steam-powered plow that he was promoting when he died in New York on February 26, 1903. The family shipped his body back to Indianapolis, where it arrived midday on March 2, 1903. At the funeral at a family friend's house at 1308 Central Avenue, Reverend A. R. Benton noted Gatling's local family and business connections, as well as the contradictions of Gatling's work: "Paradoxical as it may seem, it was his contention that the more destructive the weapons of war, the fewer are its casualties. In his earnest and convincing way, he maintained his aim to invent such a weapon was humane, beneficent and philanthropic."

Surrounded by the gray obelisk pickets of the Sanford and Wallace clans, Gatling was interred in Crown Hill's Section 3, where the classical Gatling memorial now stands. Mercifully for him, Gatling, "The Father of the Machine Gun," was laid to rest before the mechanized slaughter of World War I ended forever the argument that machine guns reduced casualties.

World War I brought its own harvest of fallen heroes to Crown Hill. Hilton U. Brown Jr. was the son of Hilton U. Brown Sr., a longtime *Indianapolis News* editor. In November 1918 the young Brown was a second lieutenant fighting on the Argonne front. Just eight days before the armistice, an artillery shell landed near him. His brother, Paul, wrote, "He died the way all soldiers would want to die—quickly on the far advanced battle line of a great drive." Like so many American soldiers who fell during the Great War, Brown's remains were first hastily buried on the battlefield and then later removed to one of the sprawling U.S. military graveyards that punctuated France with rows of white crosses. France postumously awarded Brown the Croix de Guerre. As a war correspondant, his newspaperman father was able to visit his son's grave in the American-Sedan Cemetery near Beaumont, but honored his wish that he remain buried in the country he was defending. His parents instead memorialized their son with a cenotaph that eventually stood beside their own graves in Section 2 Lot 32.

Not all of Crown Hill's World War I interments fell in Europe. On September 22, 1918, Captain Joseph Hammond, a New Zealander who was a Royal Air Force pilot and member of the British Aviation Mission, was in Indianapolis on a tour to promote the Fourth Liberty Loan War Bond Drive. Hammond was an adventurer, who besides being a raffish test pilot had worked as a prospector and trapper in Alaska and as a cowboy in Buffalo Bill's circus. Returning to Indianapolis by plane from an air show in Greenfield, Indiana, Hammond's aircraft went into a right-hand spin, causing the left wing to hit a tree and crash into a cornfield on the Marion County

Poor Farm that abutted the Speedway. Hammond's next of kin were a long way off, however, and something needed to be done. Carl Fisher stepped in. In 1916 Fisher had purchased a lot in Crown Hill's Section 13, where workmen had crafted his granite mausoleum with Egyptian-styled columns and art-deco bronze doors. Fisher arranged for Hammond's body to be temporarily interred in his own niche in the family mausoleum. But temporary turned out to be for a very long time, as Hammond's family never removed his remains.

Another of the four apocalyptic horsemen, pestilence, also brought the fallen to Crown Hill. The Spanish Flu epidemic began raging in 1917. Fifty million to one hundred million people eventually died during the worldwide pandemic, including more than 675,000 Americans—43,000 servicemen among them. Lieutenant John Hampton Holliday was the son of banker, newspaperman and Crown Hill corporator John H. Holliday and his wife, Evaline. After graduating from the Massachusetts Institute of Technology, young Holliday had earned a master's degree from Columbia University. He was among the first Indianapolis soldiers to fall to the influenza, dying in late 1917 in Georgetown Hospital in Washington, D.C. He was interred in the family plot in Section 7, Lot 39. Two American sailors, Jesse Felts and Walter Hensley, were at the Great Lakes Naval Hospital in Illinois when the flu hit them. Tennessee-born Felts was an Indianapolis accountant when he enlisted on August 24, 1918, and less than a month later, on September 21, he was dead, leaving a young widow. Hensley was a clerk at the Van Camp Packing Company and died of pneumonia two days after Felts. They were among the first flu victims to be interred in Crown Hill, where both were laid to rest in Section 59 during September 1918. From September through November 1918, almost half of the 747 burials in Crown Hill resulted from flu-related illnesses. Captain Eugene

> "I will face all things unafraid, both physical and abstract, as I have always tried to do in the past."

Kothe, a graduate of Culver Military Academy and Purdue University, died of the flu in Washington, D.C. on October 14, 1918. Sergeant Frederick Larsen died of pneumonia in England five days after Kothe. Osric Mills Watkins was another military flu victim. A Shortridge High School, Wabash College, and Harvard University student before volunteering to become an aircraft pilot, twenty-one-year-old Watkins died of flu-related pneumonia in France on October 23, 1918. In a letter to his parents written just prior to his death, he wrote, "I will face all things unafraid, both physical and abstract, as I have always tried to do in the past." Watkins was buried in Section 58, Lot 80.

The first quarter of the twentieth century was a busy time for Crown Hill. In 1901 the corporators ordered the original 1864 entrance at the cemetery's west edge to be torn down. In its place, architect Herbert Foltz designed a formidable limestone bastion with an arched Romanesque gate and crenellated gatehouse to be erected at the southwest corner of Crown Hill. When automobiles were permitted to enter the cemetery, the new gate facilitated a scenic east-west alternative to the increasingly crowded Thirty-eighth Street, or Maple Road, as it was then known. In 1904 Crown Hill added a Gothic-styled sentry house that was known as Porter's Lodge at the eastern gate. Designed by Indianapolis architects Vonnegut and Bohn, the small copper-roofed building had a first-floor reception area and a second-floor garret that served as residential space. In 1911 the corporators purchased forty acres at the northwest corner of the cemetery from Fred and Bernie Cline, making Crown Hill's 550 acres the third-largest nongovernment cemetery in the country.

In 1913 the three-story Victorian superintendent's house, built in 1868, at the southwestern corner of the cemetery burned. Luckily the corporators had embarked on a replacement, which was under construction near the east entrance and Waiting Station. The handsome brick three-story structure served as the superintendent's home until 1950.

The same year the corporators decided to build a new superintendent's house, they also decided to replace the cemetery's wooden and wire fencing with something more fitting. In the spring of 1914 famous Saint Louis-based architect and city planner George Kessler provided a fence design, which the board immediately approved. Kessler, after building a sterling reputation with numerous municipal and private projects around the country, had resolved a politically charged Indianapolis parks controversy in 1909, and went on to lead the city's parks commission until 1915. To replace Crown Hill's utilitarian fencing, Kessler designed an elegant brick and wrought-iron fence that eventually extended approximately three miles and cost almost $138,000. Standing on a four-foot-thick concrete foundation, the main brick supports rose more than twelve feet high at

**When completed, Kessler's graceful brick and wrought-iron fence wrapped the cemetery in harmonious twenty-five-foot sections that framed Crown Hill's interplay of landscape and monument.**

the entrances and corners, with intervening eight-foot-high fence columns. When completed, Kessler's graceful brick and wrought-iron fence wrapped the cemetery in harmonious twenty-five-foot sections that framed Crown Hill's interplay of landscape and monument.

In 1917 the architectural firm of D. A. Bohlen and Son returned to Crown Hill to design an addition to the Gothic Chapel that their founder had wrought four decades before. The original architect, Dietrich Bohlen, died in 1890 and was buried in the family plot near the chapel in Section 25, Lot 175. During the 1917 renovation the firm added a polygonal apse to the structure, with three leaded-glass windows piercing the limestone walls, as well as a restroom and boiler heat system that mourners came to appreciate.

In the 1920s the architectural firm of Latham and Walters began designing the service buildings, barns, and workshops that were constructed in the southeast corner of the cemetery. The brick-and-wood structures blended together in a compound that resembled the aesthetic of a working country estate. On February 13, 1925, architect Adolph Scherrer died, and three

days later his funeral cortege passed though the soaring stone gates that he designed. He was buried in Section 53, Lot 201.

There was both change and continuity in the management. Superintendent John Chislett Jr. retired in 1910, though continued his service to Crown Hill as a consulting engineer until he joined the board of corporators in 1915. Under Chislett, the workforce grew to about seventy men during the summer, and dropped to forty in the winter. At the time of Chislett's retirement, about a quarter of the cemetery had been laid off into lots on forty-eight sections, where 45,047 people were buried. Chislett ended on a high note. During his last year, burials averaged more than five a day. Walter H. Wheeler took over as superintendent in 1910, but had a short tenure, leaving in 1912. Son of Walter V. Wheeler, the temperance worker and founder of the Wheeler Mission Ministries, Walter H. went on to found Memorial Park Cemetery on Washington Street and Post Road. John J. Stephens replaced Wheeler and served for four years before Raymond E. Siebert took the helm in 1916. In the mold of Frederick and John Chislett, Siebert was destined to be another long-lived Crown Hill superintendent: Siebert's Crown Hill administration lasted from 1916 to 1958. In 1923 he also began serving as secretary of Crown Hill, a position he held until his retirement.

The Crown Hill superintendents continued their determined stewardship. In 1923 writer M. M. Scott noted, "The grounds had been admirably handled and developed and landscaped until the result is sylvan growth which affords many lovely vistas and artistic skylines and which grows increasingly beautiful as the years go on." Journalist Anna Nicholas wrote in her 1928 book, *The Story of Crown Hill*, "So it has come about that the decorative effects are chiefly these controlled by the cemetery management and are comprised in the landscape gardening—the grouping of trees and shrubs, the occasional masses of color, the vistas, the smoothness and greenness of the sward, the winding driveways." It was, she concluded, "more harmonious and artistic."

The Chisletts' dictums regarding extraneous grave decoration also continued, as Scott noted: "Wise regulations prescribing a uniform height to and sodding of all graves, and prohibiting the using of trellises, toys, boxes, cases, globes, shells, cans, jugs, bottles and bric-a-brac." According to Scott, the Crown Hill virtues envisioned by the original corporators had endured a half century after the cemetery's founding: "Here is a hallowed spot where a money-making, pleasure-seeking, 'getting-and-spending' world may not enter."

The Crown Hill corporators, superintendents, and staff eternally labored to maintain an image of permanence and stability that reflected an idealized world, where man and nature benignly coexisted. But it was a manufactured, tightly tended wildness, a landscape aesthetic and built environment that reflected encoded social strata in a matrix of egalitarian order. The spires and tombs of prominence that picketed the expensive sections of the grounds stood in contrast to the low, modest markers and unmarked graves of the less-affluent areas.

Established in December 1874, Section CG, "Colored Grounds" was a segregated, single-interment area for African American burials just north of the cemetery's west entrance. By 1890 Crown Hill was selling lots in the adjacent segregated Section NG, "Negro Grounds," later known as "New Grounds." Crown Hill also established segregated single-interment areas

for African Americans in Sections C, D, E, F, 43, and 71, which were located south of Thirty-eighth Street in the northwest corner of the original cemetery grounds. African American families who purchased lots for multiple burials were not segregated, and their lots were scattered across the cemetery.

Lillian Thomas Fox was a crusading African American journalist and activist. Writing and editing the *Indianapolis Freeman* beginning in 1891, Fox was Indianapolis's first African American female journalist. In 1900 when she started writing for the *Indianapolis News*, Fox became the first African American woman to report for a white-owned city paper. She later founded the Woman's Improvement Club that funded tuberculosis care and scholarships for indigent African Americans, and organized the Indiana State Federation of Colored Women's Clubs. When Fox died on August 29, 1917, she was interred in Section F, Lot 5906 under a white stone marker contributed by the Federation of Colored Women's Clubs in her honor.

In 1922 African American policeman William Whitfield was buried in Section F, Lot 7056. Whitfield was Indiana's first African American officer to die in the line of duty. While patrolling his beat in a white neighborhood south of the fairgrounds, Whitfield was shot in the stomach on June 18, 1922. After being refused by the City Hospital, Whitfield was shuttled to the segre-

## NETTIE RANSFORD'S GRAVESTONE

A phantasmagoria of carved symbols embellish Nettie Ransford's gravestone, which was installed in Section 27, Lot 146 after her death in 1928. One side of the marker displays a large clock stopped at 6:01. The other side includes a pentacle,

a cross, crown, chalice, candle, sword, and gavel, all surrounded by the letters "FATAL." A Masonic acronym associated with the Order of the Eastern Star, "FATAL" was short for "Fairest among Thousands Altogether Lovely."

gated Ward's Sanitarium, where he suffered from his wound until his death on November 27, 1922. After his death, Whitfield was interred without ceremony in Crown Hill, though a few months later an unexceptional white officer who died of a ruptured appendix received a lavish send-off with a twenty-one-gun salute and playing of "Taps." The city of Indianapolis refused to pay Whifield's $362.15 medical bills or his funeral expenses. They had to come out of his meager estate of $468.76. For seventy-five years, Whitfield lay in an unmarked grave, but on November 30, 1998, the League of Indianapolis Police honored Whitfield with a memorial headstone and dedication ceremony that was attended by several hundred officers, the police chief, the mayor, and other city officials.

By the early 1920s, nearly 76,000 people were interred in Crown Hill. In just over a decade, the cemetery had buried an additional 30,000 bodies, which included another 1,161 reinterments from Greenlawn. (Because Greenlawn had lost its records, only thirty-five of the pioneer dead were identified.) Recognizing the demand for burials was growing, the corporators voted in 1925 to begin developing the cemetery land north of Thirty-eighth Street. Much of what came to be known as the north grounds were cleared, graded, and drainage tiled the same year. Crown Hill's growth was in spite of increased cemetery competition in Indianapolis. In 1900 New Crown Cemetery opened on the southeast side. Woodland Cemetery (soon to be renamed Memorial Park) opened in 1917 on East Washington

Street, followed two years later by two Floral Park cemeteries, one on West Twenty-first Street and one on Cossell Road. A Masonic cemetery opened in 1926 near east side Cumberland on what had been the farm of the Buchanan undertaking family. The cemetery was later known as Washington Park Cemetery. In 1927 Glenn Haven Memorial Park began on Kessler Boulevard, a year before adjacent Rest Haven, later renamed Washington Park North, opened. To facilitate easy access to Crown Hill's new northern sections, the corporators also authorized a Thirty-eighth Street (then Maple Road) bridge and underpass, which was known as the Subway. A classical structure designed by Bohlen and built by Edward Strathman and Company, the Subway cost about $170,000 when it opened after two years of construction.

Crown Hill mausoleum construction spiked in the first decade of the twentieth century, when masons erected twenty-two new mausoleums, more than tripling the number built in the nineteenth century. In addition to Fisher's mausoleum, prominent Indianapolis families displayed their wealth with splendid final homes. The elegant Rhodius family mausoleum, built in 1906, included elaborate bronze doors, monogrammed bronze urns, and a bronze bust of millionaire George Rhodius in the interior, watched over by a stained-glass dragon-slaying Saint George.

In 1908 the Staub family built its mausoleum in Section 25, Lot 180. Constructed by the Goth Monument Company, the

massive structure was made of rusticated stone with polished pillars and urns and a marble interior. Enormous slabs of stone formed the peaked roof. One of the entombments was Joseph Staub, an Alsatian who owned the city's first merchant tailor shop at 59 East Washington Street in an upright Federal-style house. When he

died in 1896 the *Indianapolis Journal* stated, "In all his business dealings Mr. Staub was honest and upright, and had a fair name in the business world that falls to few." Staub was probably first buried in the plot he purchased in Section 5, Lot 57, which cost $170 in 1863. It was Deed No. 2 for the new cemetery. Staub's business continued through his son John W. Staub, who, when he died in 1927, was likewise interred in the tomb. In place of tailoring, John W. had embraced oil as a business of the future, purchasing an interest in Crescent Oil and Indianapolis Oil companies, as well as serving as a director of Diamond Chain. A Thirty-third Degree Mason, Staub was memorialized by a Masonic officer, who wrote, "A splendid type of man and Mason has been laid to rest."

But families did not just build new tombs. In 1910 the hotelier Claypool family enlarged its mausoleum that had been built in 1885 in Section 29, Lot 7. The Claypools expanded the tomb, redecorating it in a modern style. The sleek new exterior featured a carved frieze that depicted an angel hovering over a

mourning family, with a stained-glass angel gracing the interior. Through the early twentieth century, stained-glass windows done in the studios of American masters, such as Louis Comfort Tiffany and John LaFarge, decorated many of the Crown Hill tombs.

The mausoleum-building pace slowed considerably after 1910, with only five constructed in the next decade. During the Roaring Twenties, just seven were built, including the domed Lilly mausoleum in Section 13 that was finished in 1928. Retailing magnate George J. Marott's family tomb was built in 1924 in the full Egyptian-Revival style, with carved papyrus columns, cobras, and winged sun disks, along with stained-glass camels and pyramids. Two lions, one roaring and one in repose, flanked the entry steps.

As the level of artistry blossomed in Indianapolis, so did the level of the memorials in Crown Hill. Viennese sculptor Rudolf Schwarz moved to Indianapolis in 1897 when he was commissioned to do carvings for the Soldiers and Sailors Monument statuary groups. Schwarz, who also taught at Herron Art Institute, used the lost art of wax casting to craft many of his bronze works, the first to do so in Indiana. His work included numerous war memorials, statues of politicians, and castings for Crown Hill mausoleums and memorials.

Schwarz's masterpiece was the magnificent bronze statue that Butler University professor and later Citizens Gas general manager Jacob Dorrsey Forrest commissioned for the monument to his wife, Albertina. Also a Butler professor, Albertina died in 1904 at the age of twenty-eight while vacationing with her husband in Florida. Rudoph Schwarz's poignant statue, *Woman in Repose*, depicted a kneeling woman wracked with mourning beneath a couplet from Alfred Lord Tennyson's poem, *In Memoriam*. The grieving woman clutched a palm branch, a symbol of victory, and on the monument bench Schwarz included a wreath, another symbol of victory. The Tennyson inscription read:

> A Loss Forever New.
> A Void Where Heart On Heart Reposed,
> And, Where Warm Hands Have Prest And Closed,
> Silence.

After he died in 1930, Jacob was buried beside his wife's glorious monument in an unmarked grave.

Teutonic Schwarz channeled the German propensity to express profound loss with grave markers depicting lamenta-

# CHARLES GOTH

Late in the nineteenth century, Charles Goth founded his monument company near the corner of Michigan and Illinois Streets. There were nearby competitors: J. R. Cowie and Company, a marble and granite monument manufacturer, was at Ohio and Delaware Streets, and August Diener's monument works was on East Washington Street, where artisans hand-crafted ornate statuary and monuments. Within a few decades, both the Goth and Diener companies moved close to Crown Hill. Early on, Crown Hill also got into the monument business. On March 27, 1865, the cemetery board authorized the super-intendent to purchase a derrick, heavy wagon, and other equipment to sell and install monuments "at reasonable rates for

the purpose of preventing extortion."

The Goth Monument Company, which included Charles and his brother, John, moved to Thirty-fourth Street and Graceland Avenue, near the cemetery's Thirty-fourth Street gate. The Goths were responsible for many of the elaborate nineteenth- and early-twentieth-century memorial structures in Crown Hill, including the Staub family mausoleum. In 1929 the price of Goth markers started at thirty-five dollars; monuments began at $150. A mausoleum could be ordered for $7,000. The Goth firm kept up with changing modes, shifting from muscling out limestone monuments with hammer and chisel to using pneumatic tools to incise durable granite. The Goths eventu-ally evolved into monument designers, as Vermont quarries fabricated the monuments to the Goths' specifications.

Charles's work influenced his two daughters, Marie and Genevieve, who both became noted painters. When he

traveled east to the quarries, he took his daughters with him. Making a stop in New York, they would visit the Metropoli-tan Museum of Art and other museums. Marie later studied at the Art Students League in New York for a decade, before returning to Indiana to become a pillar of the Brown County artist colony as a portraitist. Her sister, Genevieve, studied at John Herron School of Art and the Cin-cinnati Academy of Art, and also received recognition for her still-life paintings.

Charles had a stroke when he was sixty-five, but carried on his work for another dozen years despite his drag-ging foot. On May 14, 1938, Charles died after a yearlong illness. He was seventy-nine. After a service at Hisey and Titus Funeral Home, he was interred two days later in Section 44, Lot 311. Charles has a nice, restrained raised-letter monument, near the grave of one of his his two artist daughters.

cious female figures, wreaths, inverted torches, urns, crosses, and grieving angels. At the Duden family monument, a stone statue of a woman holding roses mourns beside a finely wrought bronze plate reading: "*Machtiger als der tod die liebe*," roughly translating to, "Stronger than death is love." The inscription continued in English:

> Far from the cares and hopes and fears,
> Out where the silence is deeper than tears,
> Glad as the solitude, deep as the night,
> Lost in God's light.

Schwarz's artistic talents were unfortunately not matched with business acumen. Though Schwarz's important Indiana-German supporters Carl Lieber and Theodore Stempfel provided a studio, secured commissions, and managed Schwarz's business affairs, he typically lost money on his work due to under bidding, especially on the war monuments. Crown Hill pieces were often Schwarz's only moneymakers. After some years, Schwarz's patrons realized they could not mend his unbusinesslike ways and withdrew their support. When Schwarz died on April 4, 1912, he was in penury, and his family had lived for weeks on coffee and bread. Stempfel later wrote that "worry, loneliness, disappointment and undernourishment had caused his fatal illness." Schwarz's friends and supporters gathered at Flanner and Buchanan for a memorial service, during which banker Evans Woollen, as the president of the Art Association of Indianapolis, summarized the sculptor's artistic but tragic life: "That was Mr. Schwarz's life—struggling on the one

hand for the ideal, the while he struggled with the other against adversity." Following the service, Schwarz was cremated.

Germans were an important part of Indianapolis society, dating back to the 1840s. By 1852 the city's population of 18,000 included about 2,000 Germans, including many progressives who had fled Europe after the suppression of the Revolution of 1848. They were to have an important cultural impact on Indianapolis. Herman Lieber, Carl's father, was both a pioneering art impressario and an original Crown Hill Corporator. In 1854 Herman established Lieber's Art Emporium on Washington Street. As a great patron of the arts, Lieber established the Indianapolis Art Society. He later financed Steele's and Stark's Munich stud-

# Forrest Memorial at Crown Hill puts grief on display

WILL HIGGINS

Cemeteries are sad, graves are sad, death is sad.

But this particular final resting place, Albertina Allen Forrest's, in the old, Gothic-rich section of Crown Hill Cemetery, is beyond sad.

It's anguished, it's raw, it's actually shocking. The onlooker is pole-axed even if he/she did not know Albertina Forrest, which he/she did not because Albertina Forrest has been dead since April 27, 1904.

Cerebral hemorrhage, said the newspaper. It hit while she was recuperating in Daytona, Florida., after suffering "fainting spells."

She was thirty-one.

Her husband, Jacob Dorrsey Forrest, obviously was in tremendous pain, and he was not shy about expressing it. He erected a large and costly monument to his wife at her grave site that radiates classical beauty: Ionic columns, a cornice of granite, broad steps—basically, it's a mini-Greek temple.

More than classical beauty, though, it radiates despair, forlornness, hopelessness—heartbreak in the extreme.

"I became fascinated with (Albertina Forrest) in the 1960s," said Wayne Sanford, a retired cemetery historian who has seen thousands of graves in cemeteries all over the country. "I looked at (the Forrest monument) and thought, 'What on earth?' It's totally unique."

It bears none of the comforting "R.I.P."-style sentiment—"Gone to a greater reward," "Called home," and so forth.

The monument instead has an inscription from Tennyson: "A loss forever new, a void where heart on heart reposed, and where warm hands have prest and closed, silence."

The most striking thing is the bronze figure of a woman, life-size, designed by the sculptor Rudolph Schwarz (who also did some of the bronzes on the Soldiers and Sailors Monument), curled up in a heap, prostrate between the columns, her head buried in her hands.

There's a term for her/it: perpetual mourner. PM's were not representative of a particular person (Albertina Forrest's main mourner, after all, was male, her husband) but rather of grief in general. The figures were expensive, but not uncommon in the Victorian Era, when mourning was practically competitive.

"It was the style of the period," Sanford said. "You mourned, and you mourned well."

Crown Hill has about one hundred perpetual mourners, but Albertina Forrest's is different. The bronze figure "has thrown herself on the grave as if she can't let go," Sanford observed, "and I have never seen anything like that."

"There was a tendency in the Victorian Age," said Tom Davis, Crown Hill's resident historian, "to romanticize death, to see hope in it. . . . 'We'll meet again.' But this one is just: overwhelming loss."

The one bright note is the PM holds a palm leaf, which back in the day symbolized victory over death. But when you consider the figure's body language, it does not seem like much of a win.

The monument fronts one of the cemetery's roads, so you can see it from your car. Many people have noticed it. It's one of Crown Hill's more asked-about graves, even though Albertina Forrest was not a celebrity.

Albertina Forrest was an intellectual. She taught at Butler, when Butler was in Irvington and was still a college. Today it's in Meridian-Kessler and is a university. It's not clear what subject Forrest taught, but she is known to have written a treatise called "The Cry 'Back to Christ': Its Implication."

"Mrs. Forrest was a brilliant woman, endowed with a high mentality, strong character and many lovable graces," said the *Indianapolis Star* in a three-paragraph obit under the headline: "DEATH OF MRS. FORREST."

She and her husband did not have children, nor are there any known descendants.

For Jacob Forrest, life post-Albertina went on. Davis discovered while doing research that twelve years after Albertina's death, Jacob married a woman named Cordelia Cox, the daughter of a wealthy Kokomo man. He had taught at Butler alongside his first wife but later left teaching and went into business. He prospered, became an executive with Citizen's Gas.

But when he died, in 1930, Jacob Forrest returned to his first wife. He was buried next to Albertina in the shadow of the mini-Greek temple in a grave that, for reason (or reasons) no one alive knows, is unmarked.

*Originally published October 22, 2012 in the* Indianapolis Star.

MÄCHTIGER ALS DER TOD
DIE LIEBE

FAR FROM THE CARES AND HOPES AND FEARS
OUT WHERE THE SILENCE IS DEEPER THAN TEARS
GLAD AS THE SOLITUDE, DEEP AS THE NIGHT,
LOST, IN GOD'S LIGHT.

DUDEN

his father, John C., who was a Crown Hill founder. In 1908 William L. Elder replaced his father John R., only later to be followed by Bowman Elder and then William L. Elder in 1955, joined by his son, William L., in 1994. Stoughton A. Fletcher was elected corporator in 1911, adding to the Fletcher presence on the board, which eventually included Calvin Fletcher, and his son, grandson, nephew, and nephew's son. Charles Martindale took the seat of his father, Elijah, in 1922, the same year Alex R. Holliday took over for his father, John H., who had begun serving in 1880. Frederic M. Ayres replaced his father, Lyman S., in 1926. Some superannuated corporators soldiered on. Harry Bates was elected to the board in 1881, but in 1927 at the age of ninety-three was still serving from his home in Pasadena, California. A. A. Barnes, who was born in 1839 and became a corporator in 1901, was still serving in 1927. The board added rising members of the community. Automotive scion Walter C. Marmon was elected in 1911. Banker and political leader Evans Woollen came on the board in 1912. Harvard-educated George C. Hume, heir to the Mansur fortune, joined

ies, and was instrumental in the development of the Hoosier Group. Lieber was an ardent freethinker, part of the progressive, antireligious Association of Free-Thinkers that flourished in Indianapolis's intellectual German community to the end of the 1880s. Lieber was thirty-one years old when he joined the other august corporators, and he served on the Crown Hill board until his death in March 22, 1908. Given Lieber's artistic and intellectual bent, it was fitting that his monument in Section 5, Lot 70 included a large bronze quill, probably cast by Schwarz. After his death, Lieber's son, Otto, took his seat as corporator. From 1863 to 1986, five generations of Liebers served on the Crown Hill Board of Corporators.

By the late 1920s there were other multigenerational corporators. Newspaperman Harry S. New took over in 1906 for

the board in 1914. Corporators added movie-theater magnate and banker Fred Dickson in 1915.

Illustrious Indiana politicians continued to make Crown Hill their final home. Charles Warren Fairbanks served as U.S. senator from Indiana from 1897 to 1905, when he became vice president under President Theodore Roosevelt. After a celebrated decades-long public career, Fairbanks returned to Indianapolis to practice law. When he died on June 4, 1918, his family interred him in Section 24, where a large memorial with classical fluted columns marked his grave. Thomas Riley Marshall was the next former vice president from Indiana to pass away. After serving as Indiana governor from 1909 to 1913, Marshall was nominated as Woodrow Wilson's running mate. Marshall served from 1913 to 1921, best known for his *bon mot,* "What this country needs is a really good five-cent cigar," which Marshall said as a rejoinder during a senatorial debate when a senator ponderously orated, "What this country needs." The phrase was actually coined by Hubbard, who had stated it in an Abe Martin cartoon. After his vice presidential terms, Marshall also returned to Indianapolis to practice law. While visiting Washington, D.C., Marshall died on June 1, 1925, and was later interred in the stark stone mausoleum located in a discrete triangle of land adjacent to Section 46.

U.S. Senator Albert J. Beveridge was buried nearby. Serving as senator from 1899 to 1911, Beveridge was a progressive who authored legislation that reformed the meat-packing industry. A noted biographer in the years after his political career, Beveridge penned *The Life of Marshall*, about U.S. Supreme Court Justice John Marshall, and had finished two of the planned four volumes on Abraham Lincoln when he was stricken by a heart attack. The cortege to Crown Hill took Beveridge to familiar ground. After returning to his literary life in Indianapolis, Beveridge began each day with a perambulation along the canal from Butler University to Michigan Road near Crown Hill. In the 1940s a large marble monument with allegorical Greek figures carved by sculptor John Gregory was installed to honor Beveridge's career as a politician, orator, and author.

Some less illustrious politicians also came to their final rest in Crown Hill. Former Indianapolis mayor John Duvall was part of Indiana's infamous political fling with the Ku Klux Klan during the mid-1920s, when Grand Dragon D. C. Stephenson, later convicted of murder, boasted, "I am the law in Indiana." Governor Edward L. Jackson, later indicted for bribery, was a klansman who Stephenson controlled. In 1925 the Klan also gained control of the Republican Party in Indianapolis, and made a clean sweep of the municipal elections. A week after the election, the anti-Klan *Indianapolis Times* wrote, "The city hall will be turned over to the Ku Klux Klan on January 1. Mayor-elect John L. Duvall has rewarded his friends." Numerous klansmen soon sat in positions of power in Duvall's administration. It was not until Stephenson's conviction of second-degree murder in late 1925 that the tide began to turn on the Klan in Indianapolis. Led by attorney, saloonkeeper, slot-machine king, and Republican political boss William H. Armitage, the Republican Old Guard launched an attack on Duvall and his Klan henchmen. The *Times* unleashed a salvo of investigative articles on crooked Klan politicians, which garnered the paper a Pulitzer Prize. In 1927 Duvall and the Klan-led council dissolved in scandals over corruption. Duvall was convicted of accepting illegal campaign

*Opposite: Final resting place of Herman Lieber who came to Indianapolis from Cincinnati in 1854 to celebrate the "consecration of the colors" with the local Turnverein. Miss Mary Metzger, the future Mrs. Lieber, presented the flag at the Turner ball flag unfurling ceremony. In 1892 Lieber was elected a director of the stock company founded to fund Das Deutsche Haus, renamed the Athenaeum in response to the anti-German sentiment during World War I.*

contributions, forced to resign, sentenced to thirty days in jail, fined a thousand dollars, and barred from political activity for four years. When he died in 1962, Duvall was buried in Crown Hill's Section 98, Lot 722. Armitage died in 1948 and was interred in a vault-like tomb in Crown Hill's Section 104, Lot 1. Because the statute of limitations had expired, indicted klansman governor Jackson escaped bribery conviction but finished out his term in disgrace. He later bought a cattle farm near Orleans, Indiana, where he died and was buried in 1954. After serving decades in prison, Stephenson died in 1966 in Tennessee, where he was interred.

Indianapolis Democratic political boss Thomas Taggart was distinctly anti-Klan. In the 1880s Irish-born Taggart began parlaying his warm personality, organizational skills, and successful ownership of Union Depot into a skyrocketing Marion County political career that went statewide and then national. Taggart's political posts included stints as county auditor, county Democratic chair, mayor, U.S. senator, and Democratic national chair. Through the early decades of the twentieth century when Indiana was a crucial political state, Taggart was a national kingmaker.

Taggart also had a gift for seizing business opportunities: After selling the Union Depot, he gained controlling interests in the Grand and Denison Hotels, and invested profitably in cop-

per, gas, and oil industries. In 1901, after serving as Indianapolis mayor, Taggart or-ganized a consortium to develop the French Lick Springs Hotel into the posh gambling resort that sparkled through the Roaring Twenties. All of it made him a wealthy man, with mansions in Indianapolis, French Lick, and Hyannis Port, Massachusetts (next to the Joseph Kennedy compound).

Taggart's health declined through the 1920s, with serious nasal and stomach aliments taking their toll. He was seventy-two when the end came on March 6, 1929. After Taggart died at his Delaware Street mansion, his funeral was in the dining room, where flowers surrounded his casket. Ten pallbearers and twenty-seven honorary ones were among those gathered for the brief service. Episcopal bishop Reverend Joseph M. Francis eulogized Taggart, concluding, "A valient fighter and yet a more valient loser, who harbored no grudges and bore no malice, he has left behind him a heritage which will endure." After the funeral, the cortege proceeded to Crown Hill. Taggart was laid to rest in the family plot near his eldest daughter, Florence, who had died in a tragic yatching accident in 1899. A soaring gray obelisk in Section 3 near the slope of Crown Hill marked the spot.

When Taggart died in 1929, it was as though an era died with him. Not many months later, the stock market crashed, taking with it the fortunes of the French Lick clientele and the playgrounds where they flocked. In the years after Taggart's death, Indiana lost its prominence in the national political arena, and the Great Depression devastated the state's industrial base. After a vast florescence, an age of austerity had commenced.

*Opposite: Senator Albert J. Beveridge monument. Classical figures were carved on each side of the marble block by New York artist John Gregory to depict Beveridge's life as a politician, author, and orator. **Left:** Thomas Taggart.*

# 5

## HOLDING ON, 1930–1945

The 1930s were a time of just holding on. Dispirited Hoosiers watched banks fold, industries shut down, payrolls shrink, and breadlines lengthen—Wheeler Mission volunteers served more meals in one month of 1930 than they did in all of 1928. As industrial and construction jobs evaporated and Indianapolis's unemployment rate climbed toward 30 percent, freshly urbanized Hoosiers began to migrate out of the city. From the turn of the century to 1930, Indianapolis's population had more than doubled from 169,164 to 364,161—up 16 percent just since 1920. But with the economy struggling in the 1930s, the city's rate of increase flattened.

But death endured through the Great Depression, and the number of Crown Hill burials continued to climb. By the late 1930s, there were more than 100,000 people buried in the cemetery. The American way of death had changed since Crown Hill began. Undertakers evolved into certified funeral directors, offering professionalized mortuary services. Ornate metal and polished wood caskets replaced the old six-sided wooden coffins. The bereaved increasingly declined viewings in the family living room, preferring services take place in the funeral home's "parlor." The curried black funeral horses were long gone, replaced by shiny motor hearses. Using rationalized business and public relations strategies, cemeteries likewise adapted to the scientific century, emphasizing efficient, sanitary services that spoke to the modern mourner's desire for an insulating distance from death's realities.

The social values and rituals around death may have changed, but citizens of all stripes continued to come to Crown Hill. The families of Indianapolis's celebrated automotive pioneers buried them in the cemetery's familiar grounds, where so many of their contemporaries already lay. Owner of the Pope Motor Car Company and driver in the first Indianapolis 500, Frank P. Fox, died in 1931 and was buried in Section 104, Lot 293. Frederick S. Duesenberg, who developed the engine that won the 1924, 1925, and 1927 Indianapolis 500 races, died in July 1932, and was interred adjacent to Fox in Section 104, Lot 294. Speedway founder Arthur Newby died in 1933 and was buried near the large granite family monument in Section 23, Lot 39. Walter C. Marmon, partner in the automobile company whose entry won the first 500 and later president of Indianapolis Light and Heating, passed away in 1940, and was interred in Section 29, Lot 44, the same plot where his innovative brother and auto company partner, Howard, who died on April 4, 1943, was interred. Eddie Edenburn was an Indianapolis 500 riding mechanic from the early days of racing. Born in 1885, Edenburn died in 1934, and was buried in Section 60, Lot 713. After driv-

ing in six Indianapolis 500s and winning the 1931 race, Louis F. Schneider was laid to rest in Section 42, Lot 124 after his death in September 1942.

When automobile industry giant Carl Fisher died in Miami Beach on May 11, 1939, his remains came to an unexpected end. Fisher had built an expensive Crown Hill mausoleum in 1916, when he was awash with cash after selling his Prest-O-Lite Company. After the sale, the peripatetic Fisher focused on developing his south Florida holdings and championing cross-country highways, such as the ten-million-dollar Lincoln Highway and the north-south Dixie Highway, both long-distance roads that helped spark America's great auto industry expansion. A devastating hurricane in 1926 destroyed Fisher's Florida development. As the Florida property was pledged as security, the storm damage also cost him his Montauk development on Long Island. The Great Depression ate away at his remaining fortune, and by the time of his death in 1939, he was financially wiped out. It took four years for Fisher's ashes to be brought back to Indianapolis. On a snowy January 12, 1943, the anniversary of Fisher's sixty-third birthday, Indianapolis mayor Robert Tyndall and six other friends honored him with yellow roses and evergreens at Crown Hill as the small bronze urn was placed in the mausoleum. But Fisher's niche was still filled with the remains of the World War I pilot who had been "temporarily" entombed there in 1918. With the niches all filled, his friends decided the best alternative was to place Fisher's cremains on a table inside the tomb, where the urn remained. When Fisher died, the only Indianapolis property he still owned was his plot in Crown Hill.

Other Indianapolis leaders joined their forebears. John Chislett Jr., former Crown Hill superintendent and corporator, died in 1938. After he resigned his Crown Hill corporator position in 1920, he returned to Pittsburgh and then relocated to the sunny climes of La Jolla, California. On March 5, 1938, Chislett was interred in Section 14, Lot 14, adjacent to his superintendent father, Frederick. When retailer Lyman S. Ayres died in 1896, his son Frederic inherited his mantle of leadership. Frederic died

on June 20, 1940, and he was buried in the Ayres family plot in Section 11, Lot 19. Banker, presidential candidate, and football coach Evans Woollen Sr. died in 1942. He had served as a Crown Hill Corporator from 1922 until his death in 1942, when his son, Evans Jr., was named as the cemetery's hundredth corporator.

Indianapolis businessman and philanthropist Arthur Jordan died in September 1934. Jordan was a small-town boy made good. He built a regional conglomerate with companies handling wholesale poultry, keys, and ice and coal, as well as his Meridian Insurance. In 1926 he gave Butler University a million dollars to build Jordan Hall, as well as helping to organize the

consolidation of the city's four music conservatories into the Arthur Jordan Conservatory of Music, the forerunner to Butler's Jordan College of Fine Arts. Beyond his generous support of the Young Men's Christian Association and Young Women's Christian Association, he also established the Arthur Jordan Foundation that supported local institutions. When he died, the elaborations on Jordan's canopied monument in Section 25, Lot 228 spoke to his love of the arts.

Thomas Carr Howe, who served as president of Butler from 1908 to 1920, also died in 1934. Active in local affairs, Howe served in the Indiana General Assembly, on numerous municipal and church boards, as well as leading the organization of the Indianapolis Boy Scouts. Three years after his death, Thomas Carr Howe High School was named in his honor. He was interred in Section 36.

Famous artists and authors continued to come to Crown Hill. Cartoonist-writer Frank McKinney "Kin" Hubbard died in 1930 and was eventually interred in Crown Hill's Community Mausoleum. Author Booth Tarkington died on May 19, 1946, and was entombed in the family mausoleum in Section 13. Hoosier stalwart and Crown Hill corporator Meredith Nicholson died the next year on December 20. He was buried in Section 4, Lot 6 under a modest raised headstone. Celebrity palmist Nellie Simmons Meier called herself "a professional reader of character through scientific palmistry," and contended she had read approximately 20,000 pairs of hands over thirty-five years. Her book, *Lions' Paws: The Story of Famous Hands*, a palmistry study of one hundred famous people who included Walt Disney, Margaret Sanger, Booker T. Washington, Amelia Earhart, and George Gershwin, was published in the 1930s to wide acclaim. Indianapolis booster Nicholson wrote in the introduction: "She has made of palmistry something more than a fad, and I venture to say that no one has ever carried the study of it further or to a higher plane." Meier and her couture-designer husband, George Philip Meier, owned Tuckaway in Meridian Park, which was one of the few private residences ever put on the National Register of Historic Places. President Franklin Delano Roosevelt asked her to donate her palm prints and readings to the Library of Congress, which she did. In October 1944 Nellie died and was buried in Section 39, Lot 470. She probably saw it coming.

Actor James Baskett won renown for his role as Uncle Remus in Walt Disney's now-suppressed 1946 movie, *Song of the South*, based on the stories of Joel Chandler Harris. Because of segregation, Baskett did not attend the film's premier in Atlanta, Georgia. Baskett won a special Academy Award for his "zippity-do-da, zippity-ey" Uncle Remus portrayal, the first African American man to win an Oscar. He died of heart disease in 1948 at age forty-four. When he died, the Indianapolis native was buried in Section 37, where his gravestone read, "Not in your day, nor yet in my day, says Uncle Remus, but once upon a time."

While Jordan and Howe labored to bring fine music and culture to the Circle City, Indianapolis ragtime celebrities were en-tertaining the nation during the century's first decades. Emerging from minstrel-show music, ragtime went international after Scott Joplin's "Maple Leaf Rag" took hold. In Indianapolis, the ragtime energy emanated from the J. H. Aufdereide and Company. A well-regarded loan broker, Aufdereide initially organized the company to produce sheet music for songs written by his daughter, noted ragtime composer, May Frances Aufdereide. As Aufdereide's company pumped out the happy, syncopated music, Indianapolis became a major ragtime center, along with New York, Chicago, and Kansas City. May's first big hit was "Dusty Rag," followed by others such as "Richmond Rag," "Thriller Rag," and "Buzzer Rag." The company was soon producing other Indianapolis ragtime composers, including Julia Niebergall, Paul Pratt, Cecil Duane Crabb, J. Russel Robinson, Will B. Morrison, and Gladys Yelvington. When Aufdereide died in August 1947, he was buried in Crown Hill's Section 42, Lot 107.

Other Indianapolis ragtime greats joined him. Crabb, a former sign painter from Centerville, produced the blackface minstrel engraving for the cover of May's "Dusty Rag," and also wrote well-received ragtime hits, including "Fluffy Ruffles." When he died in 1953 he was buried in Section 3, Lot 51. Niebergall penned the sprightly tunes, "Horseshoe Rag,"

"Hoosier Rag," and "Red Rambler Rag." As ragtime music lost favor in the ensuing years, Niebergall remained a mainstay of the city's musical community, playing gigs around the city for many decades. After her death in October 1968, Niebergall was

*Booth Tarkington.*

buried in Section 38, Lot 146. Indianapolis musician Glenn C. Leap composed the New York-published ragtime hits "Stewed Chicken" and "Ragtime Mephisto." When Leap died in January 1956 he was buried in Section 62, Lot 218.

Beginning in the 1930s, Indiana Avenue was the epicenter of the Indianapolis jazz scene that over the next few decades produced such international stars as Wes Montgomery, Slide Hampton, Freddie Hubbard, J. J. Johnson, Leroy Vinnegar, Jimmy Coe, Leroy Carr, Scrapper Blackwell, and David Baker. Compressed by segregation into the Indiana Avenue neighborhood and nurtured by the extraordinary Crispus Attucks High School faculty, Indianapolis African American musicians played in the dozens of small clubs, such as the Paradise, Sunset Terrace, Missile Room, and Henri's that lined the avenue and adjacent streets. In the process of collaboration and competition, they developed a distinctive Indianapolis jazz sound that pulsed with a powerful, relaxed style of swing.

Beloved local piano player Erroll Grandy was called "the godfather of Indianapolis jazz," because of his mentorship of musicians that included Montgomery, Hubbard, and Johnson. The son of a Norfolk, Virginia, minister who moved the family to Indianapolis in 1936, Grandy had worked his way through the Jordan Conservatory of Music by playing at the Boulevard Kitchen at Twenty-first and Boulevard Streets. A vibrant and accomplished piano player, Grandy accompanied touring luminaries, including Count Basie, Lionel Hampton, and Billie Holiday. After decades as an Indianapolis jazz legend, Grandy was honored by Indianapolis with an Erroll Grandy Day on May 6, 1984, which was celebrated with a mammoth benefit concert featuring fourteen Indianapolis jazz groups. After Grandy died on June 12, 1991, the pianist and mentor was buried in Section 98, Lot 986, where a small gravestone flush with the ground marked his final rest.

In the depths of the Great Depression, a mausoleum construction boom unexpectedly erupted at Crown Hill. After twenty-two tombs were built from 1901 to 1910, wealthy families only commissioned twelve mausoleums in the next twenty years, suggesting the expensive structures were going out of fashion. But during the economic downturn of the 1930s, well-to-do families in Indianapolis unexpectedly commissioned nine mausoleums, including the Schwitzer, Malott, and Tutweiler tombs. They were fashionable. The exterior of the Dollman Mausoleum, built in 1938 in Section 46, Lot 15, reflected the *au courant* streamlined Art Moderne look, though a conservative ecclesiastic stained-glass motif decorated the interior. The Fortune mausoleum, built a few years later in Section 61, Lot 2, likewise was a modernist design.

Some of the zest for mausoleum construction probably had to do with canny shopping. Eight of the nine were commissioned in the last half of the 1930s, when construction costs were still close to their nadir, but the reviving Indianapolis economy portended higher prices. Moneyed folks could get a lot of mausoleum for their bucks. But it also appeared the tomb boom might have represented a subconscious drive to perpetuate social position in a time of wild cultural upheaval. In the early 1930s architects designed banker James Weldon Lynch's imposing columned mausoleum in the image of a bank, including a lobby-like interior clad in marble with a long table at the rear. Built at the zenith of Prohibition-era gangsters and gun molls, Lynch's banker tomb would no doubt have caught the attention of another Crown Hill inhabitant, who famously arrived in the 1930s.

Bank robber John Dillinger came back to Crown Hill on Wednesday July 25, 1934, three days after he had died in a rain of bullets outside Chicago's Biograph Theater. His killing ended a nearly yearlong escapade that had captured America's imagination. During his rampage, he and his gang had stolen $300,000 in multiple bank robberies, including $21,000 from Indianapolis's Massachusetts Avenue Bank on September 6, 1933. When casing banks and jails, Dillinger's gang had been wily. They posed as Indiana State Police, bank security alarm salesmen, and movie executives scouting for locations. Dillinger

had escaped supposedly impregnable jails, once with a carved wooden gun. "See what I locked all of you monkeys up with," he laughed at his disarmed jailers as he turned the key on them. For months Dillinger led hundreds of police officers and federal agents on a wild chase across four states. To some Depression-ravaged Americans who had lost farms and homes to voracious banks and felt abandoned by an uncaring government, Dillinger looked like a Hoosier Robin Hood. To the authorities who counted as many as twenty-three people killed by the gang, Dillinger was Public Enemy Number 1.

The night Dillinger died, people dipped handkerchiefs, newspapers, even dress hems in his drying blood in the alley beside the Biograph. The next day thousands of morbid Chicagoans filed through the Cook County morgue to see his bullet-riddled body, while Dillinger's father, stepbrother, and Mooresville mortician E. F. Harvey drove north in an old hearse to retrieve the remains. When his family arrived at the Chicago funeral home then storing Dillinger's body, journalists questioned his father, who told them, "They shot him down in cold blood." John Dillinger Sr. asked why federal agents shot his son when they had so many guns trained on him, then conjectured maybe it was better he was not captured alive. Led in to see his dead son, Dillinger's father said, "My boy!" before being led away.

The Dillinger family arrived back in Mooresville on Tuesday, July 24, to be greeted by another line of curiosity seekers that filed into the funeral home until 2:00 a.m. The next day there was a simple family funeral at the home of Dillinger's sister in the southwestern Indianapolis neighborhood of Maywood, where a mob of 2,500 gawkers gathered. A minister gave a short invocation and the family sang the hymn of spiritual encouragement, "God Will Take Care of You," which began with, "Be not dismayed whate'er betide, God will take care of you." After the

*Above left:* John Dillinger strikes a pose with a pistol and a tommy gun. *Above right:* Coins left by visitors on Dillinger's grave marker are donated to the Riley Children's Foundation.

service, a cortege of five cars and the hearse slowly drove toward Crown Hill, but had to repeatedly stop for police to clear crowds from the route.

So John Jr. was coming back to Crown Hill. In February 1907, when he was three years old, his mother, Mollie, had died. During the funeral, young Johnnie had stood on a chair by the casket, shaking his mother as if trying to wake her. Dillinger's mother was laid to rest in the sixteen-by twenty-foot family plot that his father had bought in Section 44, Lot 94, located near the Boulevard Street fence. Less than three decades later, as the small cortege accompanying Dillinger's body approached the cemetery, a huge throng of 5,000 people surged near the gate and along the fence. The police struggled to maintain order in the stifling 104-degree heat. That morning the newspaper had blared a front-page story about Dillinger's upcoming Crown Hill interment, leading with, "Through the triple gateway of Crown Hill cemetery, with its slender gothic towers of carved Indiana limestone covered with Virginia creeper, the body of John Dillinger, public enemy No. 1, will pass to its last resting place." The family was relieved to learn the crowd would not be allowed to enter the cemetery during the burial ceremony.

The Crown Hill staff began preparing for the hoopla when they learned of Dillinger's death. When some Crown Hill plot owners complained about Dillinger's upcoming interment, superintendant Raymond E. Siebert stated the cemetery had to do its duty. He told reporters, "The cemetery has no legal right to object to the burial of Dillinger in the family lot. John Sr. has owned the lot for several years and his wife is buried there. He is a man who bought property from us, and as owner of that property, has a legal right to bury the body of his son there." In the twenty-seven years since he bought the plot, John Sr. had already buried his parents, two wives, and two grandchildren in Crown Hill. It was the place to bury his boy.

The Dillinger family huddled under the tent erected at the burial site, trying to ignore the crowd pressing against the Boulevard Street fence. As the minister began to give the final invocation, the skies opened, drowning his words in cleans-

ing rain and claps of thunder. Lightning flashed as undertakers lowered Dillinger's wooden casket into his grave. As the family motored away from Crown Hill, the police unleashed the mob of onlookers, who raced for the gravesite to snatch flowers and even handfuls of mud. After the police restored order, the cemetery authorities established a round-the-clock watch over the burial site to protect against grave robbers and the ghoulish general public.

But the senior Dillinger was still concerned about his son. According to Crown Hill executive Howard T. Wood, interested parties offered the Dillinger family ten thousand dollars for the body, which they wanted to exhibit in a sideshow. A few days after the funeral, Dillinger's father returned to Crown Hill to arrange for the casket to be reburied under a protective cap of concrete and scrap iron that was then topped with four immense reinforced-concrete slabs placed in stepped gradations above Dillinger's body. Because of their fears of grave robbery and desecration, the family waited two years before they erected a tombstone in Dillinger's memory.

They were right to be concerned. Almost immediately after the monument company installed the low rectangular marker, people began chipping off pieces. The gravestone was soon reduced to an oval, as the Dillinger grave became a pilgrimage site. Almost a decade after Dillinger's burial, a newspaper story reported, "there has been no grass growing on the plot of ground," because of the thousands of people tromping around the grave. It all took its toll. In 1959 Dillinger's surviving sister, Audrey Hancock, gave her permission to the Blakely Granite Company to replace Dillinger's headstone. The permission stipulated, "The new stone will be exactly like the old one (with the exception of the damage now evident on the old marker.)" The original gravestone eventually became a museum piece at the John Dillinger Museum in Lake County, Indiana, where the bank robber made his famous wooden-gun escape. But the new gravestone did not last either. There were thefts. A motorcycle gang stole Dillinger's tombstone in 1980, intending to mount it on the wall of their clubhouse—but authorities got the marker back. In 1990 workers replaced the now battered and chipped Dillinger marker with a third headstone. With the 2009 release of the movie *Public Enemies*, which starred Johnny Depp as Dillinger, thousands of visitors from around the world made the pilgrimage to Dillinger's gravesite at Crown Hill.

Beyond crime and violence, the Great Depression also brought labor strife to Indiana. Workers struck with picket lines

> After exhuming the soldiers from the trenches, the undertakers reinterred the remains in Crown Hill's Section 32, Lot 285, which came to be known as the Confederate Mound.

and agitation. Management fought back with lockouts, strike-breakers, and police protection. In early 1939 there were seven labor disputes in Indianapolis. The unrest spread to Crown Hill when the Congress of Industrial Organization's Cemetery Workers Local 322 protested the dismissal of two union workers. Already tense about pay negotiations, the eighty Crown Hill workers declared a graveyard strike. The *Indianapolis News* wryly headlined: "Here's the Latest in Picketing—Crown Hill Cemetery," carrying a photo of disputatious grounds workers walking a picket line near the gate. The dispute went on for two months, with police escorting nonstriking workers through the picket lines, while striking workers shared their feelings about failed labor solidarity. However riled, the striking cemetery workers maintained appropriate decorum. The *News* reported, "A funeral, scheduled for 8 a.m. today was not disturbed. A police department squad car, however, remained outside the cemetery to assure order."

More of the Civil War came to rest in Crown Hill in 1931 when undertakers moved twenty-five wooden boxes that contained the remains of 1,616 Confederates from Greenlawn Cemetery. The soldiers' remains had already been moved in 1870, when the owners of the Vandalia Railroad wanted the soldiers' plot for more tracks and a new engine house. The dictates of commerce being declared paramount, gravediggers exhumed

the soldiers and reburied them in two long trenches in another section of Greenlawn.

In 1912 a concerned U.S. government dispatched an officer to locate the bodies and provide a proper memorial inscribed with the soldiers' names—if the remains could be found. After some investigation, he located the mass graves in a weedy plot surrounded by an iron fence. The government's twenty-seven-foot high stone monument included an inscription that read, "Erected by the United States to mark the burial place of 1616 Confederate soldiers and sailors who died here while prisoners of war and whose graves cannot now be identified." By 1928 the monument was so defaced and blackened with locomotive soot that the city's Southern Club arranged for it to be temporarily moved to the south side of Garfield Park, anticipating that it would eventually grace the Confederates' final resting place in Crown Hill. The monument, however, remained in Garfield Park, and the fallen Confederates remained nameless for another six decades.

By 1931, when the undertakers began their work, the city administrators had not only allowed surrounding factories and railroads to encroach on derelict Greenlawn, they had also turned the city cemetery into an unsupervised public park, where amidst the untended tombstones, "nightly orgies were frequent," according to a *News* article of the time. So the Confederate dead were going to a quieter place. After exhuming the soldiers from the trenches, the undertakers reinterred the remains in Crown Hill's Section 32, Lot 285, which came to be known as the Confederate Mound. The 1,616 soldiers were overwhelmingly Confederate Army privates who had succumbed to disease at Camp Morton. Among the men was Mississippian John Bruner, who died in August 1862, and Tennessean Anderson McConnell, who died March 10, 1862. Arthur McConnell, also from Tennessee, died five months to the day later. John Brown from Louisiana passed on in April 1863; A. E. Abercrombie from South Carolina died in January 1864; Alabama's Johnson Hamner died on November 17, 1863;

CONFEDERATE MOUND

THESE CONFEDERATE
SOLDIERS AND SAILORS DIED
AT INDIANAPOLIS WHILE
PRISONERS OF WAR.
THEY WERE TRANSFERRED
HERE FROM GREENLAWN
CEMETERY IN 1933
TO REST ETERNAL.
A LARGE MONUMENT TO
THESE DEAD NOW STANDS IN
GARFIELD PARK,
INDIANAPOLIS, INDIANA.

PAX

M. T. K. Gill from Georgia died in September 1863; Texan W. I. Cunningham died in August 1864; and Virginian Levi Spracher died in February 1865. The deceased included twenty-six African Americans, who the records typically identified as "Negro Servant," primarily slaves who chose to stay with their Confederate masters. Among them were Henry Mayo, a Virginian who died on April 23, 1862; C. L. Mathews from Mississippi, who died on January 18, 1862; and Kentuckian C. Christian, who passed away on November 22, 1863. From across the Confederate South there were ten Kings who died in Camp Morton, twelve Martins, nine Johnsons, seventeen Jones, a dozen Taylors, thirteen Williams, and twenty-six Smiths.

> When World War II began raging, Crown Hill again volunteered to help. In October 1942 more than 2,600 soldiers were bivouacked at the north end of the cemetery in a well-policed tent ground.

From 1862 to 1865 they just died and died and died, yet, Camp Morton was considered one of the better Union prison camps.

Even after the undertakers finished their work in 1931, bodies surfaced at Greenlawn. One Confederate was reinterred in 1945 when his remains were unearthed at the Diamond Chain Company. In 1965, and again in 1980, bulldozers encountered bodies during construction projects at the firm, and both times boxes of clay-encrusted bones were sent to Crown Hill for reburial.

Alexander Ralston, who surveyed and platted Indianapolis in 1821, was another citizen who moved from Greenlawn. He died six years after designing the Indianapolis city plan. After being buried in Greenlawn, he was reinterred in 1874 in an unmarked Crown Hill grave located in a plot for "destitute teachers." It was not until 1937 that Ralston got some recognition. The Indianapolis Teachers' Federation commissioned a tombstone in Section 3, Lot 30 for him, using funds donated by "Indianapolis citizens prior to 1895." The federation commissioned a perfect tombstone for the civil engineer: a rusticated granite marker

that depicted his plan for Indianapolis, the precise checkerboard of streets with diagonal avenues radiating out from the Circle. The plan's mile-square symmetry reflected his belief that a mile was as big as Indianapolis could possibly grow.

When World War II began raging, Crown Hill again volunteered to help. In October 1942 more than 2,600 soldiers were bivouacked at the north end of the cemetery in a well-policed tent ground. The soldiers were part of the Army War Show task force. Organized as a recruitment event, the Army War Show was held in the Butler Bowl, where thousands attended the three performances of the "dramatic military spectacle," as the *Indianapolis Star* termed the event. The show included marching formations, mass calisthenics, Signal Corps demonstrations, and flamethrowers. A tank roared up a ramp to crush a car parked below. The soldiers fired hundreds of thousands of blank rifle, machine gun, and cannon rounds at each performance. The show climaxed with a mock battle "with all the din and smoke until the enemy flag has been hauled down and the prisoners herded together." And then the soldiers went back to the cemetery.

With the military draft vacuuming up men, Crown Hill struggled with labor shortages. By 1943 the cemetery workforce was short twenty-five laborers, requiring supervisors to choose between grass mowing and burial preparation. Soon they enlisted high school boys to help with the maintenance and digging. And there was more burial ground to maintain: Crown Hill had made its first family interment north of Thirty-eighth Street in 1935—vindicating the prescient land purchases made by earlier generations of corporators. With more than a 100,000 people buried in Crown Hill by the early 1940s, and more coming in at a rate of 1,400 per year, there was a call for new facilities. Responding to the demand, in 1945 the corporators announced plans for a lavish new Community Mausoleum to be built on the north grounds.

But cemetery competition was getting fierce. Crown Hill was forced to respond with modern business tactics. In the mid-

# WILLIAM F. LAW

In the 1930s William F. Law was a bondsman, a regular figure around the Indianapolis police department and municipal courts. He was an active Mason, a Zoave, a founder of the Gatling Gun Club, and loved to study the works of Confucius. A dapper guy who sported a snap-brim fedora, Law carried bonds on some risky men, including Charles Geisking of the notorious Brady Gang, another Indiana-born group of Great Depression-era desperados who specialized in knocking off grocery stores. Federal Bureau of Investigation agents gunned down most of the gang in an ambush in downtown Bangor, Maine, on October 12, 1937, an epochal event still reenacted there. While the historical record does not show whether Law lost bond money on that one, it does show the now former bondsman died on Saturday, October 12, 1940.

A few days later, a workman was cleaning out Law's house at 611 North Delaware Street. The workman had labored all day in the cluttered basement when he moved a pile of lumber and doors. Underneath he found a dusty metal coffin. When he opened it, he discovered a human body, reduced to bones, hair, and teeth.

Law's wife, Ruth Phares, was a Shortridge High graduate who had married over the objections of her family. Law remained estranged from his wife's family. Ruth died of tuberculosis on June 30, 1929, and her husband placed her remains in Crown Hill's Gothic Chapel vault. The casket lay in an open vault that Law often visited. He was clearly distressed, obsessively speaking of his dead wife. For three years she lay in the Crown Hill vault, with Law meticulously paying the mounting vault-storage fees. At one point, Law had snapped at his wife's family: "My wife will never be buried, and you will never find her body." Well, they did not for a long time.

On February 6, 1933, Law showed up at the Gothic Chapel brandishing a legal release for the body. After three years of holding the body in a temporary vault, the Crown Hill officials had earlier sent Law a registered letter informing him that his wife would be buried if he did not deal with the matter. He did, telling the Crown Hill officials that he was going to bury his wife in Illinois. Law had been so weird for so long that the Crown Hill superintendent told the cemetery's attorneys to prepare a legal document about the removal. The attendants loaded Ruth's casket into Law's truck. But rather than going to Illinois, Ruth Law went to Delaware—Delaware Street, that is.

After the coffin was discovered, Ruth's mother identified the body by remnants of the dress still on the skeleton. The mother was sure about the dress, because she had made it. No one could puzzle out how Law had managed to get the casket weighing hundreds of pounds into his basement. Law's friends did say that they had noticed "a change" in Law after his wife died, and, "It was with great difficulty that anyone could gain admittance to his home, and it was impossible to enter the basement of the home." After her long hiatus in the Delaware Street basement, Ruth was at last buried in Crown Hill, interred in Section 37, Lot 630 on October 25, 1940, almost eleven years after she died.

# WALT WALTERS

With his blue bandanna, earring, and handlebar moustache, Walt Walters looks a bit like a pirate. But he is really more of a cemetery buccaneer, a freebooter who comes to make a clean sweep of time-worn graveyards. For the last fifteen years, Walters has dedicated himself to restoring vintage gravestones, from humble markers in country graveyards to towering monuments in grand urban cemeteries such as Crown Hill. With a rotary wheel, nylon brushes, ammonia and water, epoxy glue, and a load of expertise, Walters and his merry crew transform filthy and decrepit gravestones into pristine monuments.

One sweltering day in August 2011, Walters and his crew were busy in Section 6, one of Crown Hill's most historic areas. The sound of whirring rotary brushes and

a tall tripod to straighten tilting obelisks marked their work site. Pitted, lichen-covered gravestones with illegible inscriptions were the "befores." Walters proudly pointed out the restored "afters": blinding white monuments with crisp lettering that memorialized the passage of a human life.

Walters got his start when he worked on a county highway crew. He saw all of the dilapidated pioneer cemeteries and found his calling. Now working in the Midwest and upper South, Walters fixes what he called "all the bad cemeteries." He estimates that he has restored more than 10,000 gravestones. "It don't take a rocket scientist to do this, but it does take a heart," he said. "And I got one of them." Standing beneath a soaring, damaged, red-stone obelisk, Walters described his quest to find exactly the right adhesive to make the correct repair. "It's detective work, mainly," he said. A member of the Association of Gravestone Studies, Walters gives workshops for the Indiana Historical Society. "I don't like public speaking," he said, "but I believe in my work." After a short tour of some of his Crown Hill restoration triumphs, he turned to go back to his work. Gravestones were calling. But before he left, Walters glanced around the historic old cemetery with its thickets of monuments, and said, "It's an honor to work in Crown Hill."

*Before and after photos of the Pattison memorial, tracing roots back to Colonial times. Historic monument restoration is supported by tax-deductible contributions to the Crown Hill Heritage Foundation.*

1940s the corporators approved Crown Hill's first sales force. Corporators later told an *Indianapolis Star* reporter, "the decision was one over which the board agonized." Howard T. Wood, who served as the cemetery's executive vice president for thirty years, told the reporter, "Until then, people came to Crown Hill—Crown Hill didn't go to them."

Thousands of Indianapolis soldiers served in World War II. Many of those killed in the conflict were interred in sprawling American military cemeteries in the former war zones. But some soldiers' remains made it back home. One was Lieutenant David W. Foster, who died just after Christmas on December 29, 1944. Foster was a bomber pilot on a mission against a communications center in Prum, Germany. His formation of four bombers took off in a dense fog from Britain's Wroxham air base. But it was a disastrous departure, as the planes hit trees soon after takeoff. Fifteen men were killed, including Foster. His tombstone in Section 66, Lot 166, where he was interred in 1948, reads, "Killed in action in the performance of his duty as pilot of a B-24 bomber."

Others returned home after enduring the war's travails. One was Henry Clay Conner Jr., who served in the Pacific as a lieutenant in the U.S. Army Air Corps. When the Japanese attacked Bataan in the Philippines, Conner aided in the defense. After the American surrender, Conner evaded capture, taking refuge in the Zambales Mountains above Clark Field, where he organized the Negrito tribesmen into a guerrilla force armed with bows and spears. Conner and his men gathered information crucial to the recapture of the island in 1945. After his death in 1983, Conner was buried in Section 223, Lot 1009.

On Memorial Day 1943 more than 75,000 thousand people descended on Crown Hill to decorate graves with more than twenty tons of flowers. For the second straight year, the Memorial Day traffic to Crown Hill was not jockeying with the lines of race fans heading to the Speedway. Beginning in 1942, the Indianapolis 500 mile race was canceled, first by the owners and then by the federal government, which banned auto racing for the duration of the war. So with patriotism at its peak, and

holiday competition in abeyance, the Memorial Day crowds at Crown Hill reached record levels. And the day of remembrance was not just for war veterans as it had been in the years after the Civil War, when it was known as Decoration Day. In the 1880s, the term Memorial Day began to be used, reflecting the desire to honor all of the deceased, and by World War II it was the common name for the holiday.

Just before Memorial Day 1943 Governor Henry F. Schricker urged workers to maintain the war production schedules through the holiday. But there was a solemn downtown memorial parade and services at Crown Hill, where marines in full-dress uniform placed a wreath on the Section 212, Lot 545 grave of Lieutenant Dallas F. Shadinger, who had died in a plane crash. With war concerns paramount in people's minds, the Crown Hill Memorial Day speaker was Lieutenant George T. Stewart, Fort Benjamin Harrison's chief of intelligence and internal security.

In 1944, as the soldiers in Great Britain prepared for the invasion of the continent, their loved ones on the Indiana home front steeled themselves for the worst. Susanah Jameson Mayberry, Booth Tarkington's great-niece, was one of them. She had married her husband, Francis Mayberry, in Tarkington's North Meridian Street home on January 3, 1944, just before Mayberry deployed overseas. She and her sister war brides waited anxiously for the postman, dreaded the ring of the telephone, or the unannounced visitor who might bear heartbreaking news. She later wrote in her memoir, *On Love and Leland,* "Ask any woman of any age what her husband's serial number is and she'll reel it off instantly. I am as sure of this as I am of anything in the world." Back in Indiana, when word came that the great allied invasion of France had begun, women began spontaneously gathering in churches around the city. As the bells tolled hymns such as "Onward, Christian Soldiers," "The Battle Hymn of the Republic," and "Rock of Ages," the women

grasped each other's hands in silent harmony. Susanah wrote, "Prayers were almost palpable in the air. Terror is a great leveler. I still remember thinking then, I guess it was for the first time, that a lot of women who were kneeling here, would not have their prayers answered. Every prayer I think must have been the same. 'God, please keep him safe.'"

Captain Mayberry fought in the Battle of the Bulge, but survived to return home to Susanah. They are buried beside one another in Section 13 Lot 56, near the Tarkington mausoleum. Francis died in 1997, Susanah, two years later.

SUSANAH J. MAYBERRY
1921 — 1999
FRANCIS T. MAYBERRY
1914 — 1997

CHARLES WARREN FAIRBANKS
U. S. SENATE 1897 — 1905
VICE PRESIDENT THE
UNITED STATES 1905 — 1909

CORNELIA COLE FAIRBANKS
PRESIDENT GENERAL
D A R
1901 — 1905

FAIRBANKS

# 6

## CONTINUITY AND RENEWAL, 1946–1979

Indianapolis emerged from World War II with a brash confidence. Defense contracts had stimulated manufacturing and construction and after the war the pent-up demand for consumer goods further fueled the city's factories, now retooled for such durable goods as automobiles and appliances. "The future is bright—bright beyond our feeble imaginations," crowed a major study of Indiana's economic potential. Flush with industrial and commercial success, Indianapolis leaders encouraged major civic growth. With the improving economy, the population again began to climb and construction exploded. Soon tens of thousands of Indianapolis breadwinners were driving their new American cars to their new suburban homes at the city's periphery.

But there was the eternal tension between change and tradition. While proud of the growth, the conservative city fathers were also wary of transformation and diversity. Intent on maintaining Indianapolis's small-town ethos, postwar city leaders focused on low tax rates, small government, and a modulated arts-and-culture scene. Indianapolis, though, was definitely changing. The trend lines led out to suburbs, where shopping centers and commercial strips were draining the retail vitality out of downtown. As Indianapolis's moneyed class left formerly posh neighborhoods north of the downtown, the large houses were subdivided into apartments, where increasing numbers of

African American citizens, many relocated from the South, took up residence. From 1930 to 1980 the African American population in Indianapolis more than tripled, increasing from 10.6 percent of the city's population to 20.3 percent. From 1950 to 1960 the African American population in Indianapolis's Center Township, the central city area that includes part of Crown Hill, grew 54 percent, while the white population only increased 23 percent. The next decade, the number of white residents of Center Township plummeted almost 18 percent, while African American residency continued to rise. After a century as a fairly homogenous small city, Indianapolis was becoming a diverse metropolis.

Some of the labor issues that bedeviled the Crown Hill superintendent and board in the late 1930s continued in the postwar era, when manpower shortages were pumping up demand for able-bodied workers. Meredith Nicholson, the author and a Crown Hill Corporator, penned a newspaper column about Crown Hill in the 1940s that concluded: "I venture the information that it is no fault of Mr. [Raymond E.] Siebert that the grounds have not saluted June with their usual orderliness and charm because of the impossibility of obtaining labor." Soon the cemetery workers were petitioning the superintendent for higher wages—much higher wages. The board responded with study committees and eventually a labor consultant, who reconfigured the wage schedules to bring some momentary peace to the cemetery. In the midst of the ongoing labor issues, there was one bright spot. A well-qualified man had returned from serving as a U.S. Navy officer to join the Crown Hill management staff. The corporators were pleased. On June 4, 1946, the board minutes recorded, "About five months ago we employed Mr. Howard Wood as assistant superintendent and assistant secretary." The minutes went on to discuss Wood's work in the Far East during the war, handling large amounts of government property, and "discharging his duties with efficiency and ability." The board anticipated that Wood's ability to take some of the cemetery responsibilities from superintendent Siebert would allow him to focus on new development. As the labor issues continued to boil into 1949, the corporators voted to elect Wood to be the executive manager in charge of all operations in the cemetery. Siebert remained secretary to the board of managers, and was charged with directing new development.

In what became a perennial refrain at the board meetings, the corporators continued to show concern in 1946 about low returns on cemetery investments, rising costs, increased com-

petition, and the need to boost sales. In 1946 there were 1,547 interments, raising the number of buried in Crown Hill to more than 110,000. Almost 24 percent of the 5,784 deaths in Marion County in 1946 were buried in Crown Hill. By 1947 the proportion jumped to almost 28 percent. While it was a big drop from the 1920s, when about 45 percent of the Marion County interments were buried in Crown Hill, it was still a lot of burials.

At last freed from the wartime shortages, in 1946 the corporators launched the long-discussed Community Mausoleum project on the north grounds. "Plans Resumed," a February 1946 *Indianapolis Star* article headlined, reporting that the war held up construction "because of the shortage of materials vital to this type of building." The corporators realized that few families had the means for private mausoleums, yet many preferred aboveground interments. So the idea of a shared entombment building was born. "The crypt embodies all the advantages of mausoleum entombment at a moderate cost comparable to in-the-ground interment," a Crown Hill brochure read. The board contracted with D. A. Bohlen and Company to draw up plans for the structure that would include hundreds of crypts and niches, along with private memorial rooms for the entombment of up to ten family members. "These distinguished memorial rooms compare favorably with the construction of private mausoleums, and have the added advantage of daily care, and assured comfort during visitation," the brochure copy

*Right: Cornerstone dedication with (left to right) Bowman Elder, Benjamin D. Hitz, Robert Bohlen, Garvin M. Brown, Howard T. Wood, Francis A. Wilhelm, Edward J. Bennett, Arthur Leonard, and Raymond E. Siebert.*

read. With presales vital to the project, the new sales force had a mission that the corporators avidly followed. By October 1946 the sales staff had already presold 140 crypts in the yet unbuilt mausoleum. By June 1947 the number of presold crypts was up to 405.

There was increased emphasis on advertising and public relations. The brightly lit new Crown Hill sign at the corner of Thirty-eighth Street touted the cemetery in a way that seemed unimaginable just a few decades before, although the corporators were still discussing the sign years later. Newspaper advertisements helped sell the mausoleum idea. "A Magnificent Fulfillment of a Community Need," read one large Crown Hill ad that ran in May 1946 in the *Indianapolis Times*. In 1948 the corporators laid the cornerstone of the new building. By 1951 construction was complete on the Community Mausoleum. Costing about $1.25 million, the handsome art deco-styled building was clad in fine Indiana limestone. Elegant Italian and Vermont Light Cloud marbles embellished the interior. Indianapolis families quickly snapped up the thousand crypt spaces and fifty niches for cremains. With the Community Mausoleum a grand success, the corporators began planning a north addition to more than double the crypt spaces. By 1961 the north building was complete.

Demographic and racial changes in the neighborhood surrounding Crown Hill reflected the challenges the cemetery, and the community, faced at the beginning of the 1950s. Like much of Indiana, Indianapolis had a long history of racial discrimination. In the 1920s local groups, including the Chamber of Commerce and Federation of Civic Clubs, pressured the Indianapolis Board of School Commissioners to racially segregate the city's students, whom up to that time had been integrated in the schools. A separate high school for black students, Crispus Attucks, opened. The segregation also included social outings, with the popular Riverside Amusement Park barring African Americans except on specific days. When the Crispus Attucks basketball team led by Oscar Robertson won the state championships in 1955 and 1956, it was only a decade after the Indiana

High School Athletic Association allowed the school to finally compete.

Change came slowly. Indianapolis did not begin desegregating its schools until 1949, when the Indiana General Assembly passed an antisegregation law, with the city school's desegregation program finally completed in 1953, just a year before the U.S. Supreme Court's landmark *Brown v. Board of Education of Topeka* decision declaring separate schools unconstitutional. Civil rights activists picketed Riverside, causing the park to remove its "whites only patronage" signs. Crown Hill also responded. In 1949 the board took action to remove language from its mausoleum sales contract restricting entombment to "members of the Caucasian race."

By the mid-1950s the corporators were increasingly nervous about competition. There were many new cemeteries in Marion County and the surrounding areas, all vying for business. The board was particularly disturbed by what it termed "promotional-type" cemeteries—those that utilized direct door-to-door sales companies, a number of which were headquartered in Indianapolis. The sales companies used door-to-door salesmen to push preneed funeral and burial packages that were financed with long-term payment plans.

By the late 1950s Crown Hill's competitors were making great gains with a new type of mausoleum: the garden crypt. Originally sold in warm-weather states, the garden crypts typically included a central chapel with adjacent rows of stacked tombs. Because of the open-air arrangement and the density of interment, the garden crypts provided an economical alternative to burials and entombments in lavish heated and cooled mausoleums. The corporators were initially aghast at the idea—calling them "schemes" designed for a "different income group." A corporator committee organized to investigate the new product archly reported that they "would not recommend the building of garden crypts in Crown Hill." But by the late 1950s the cost of enclosed mausoleums and the lost sales to competitors pushing the less expensive garden crypts forced the board to come to terms with the new idea. The Crown Hill Mausoleum Plan-

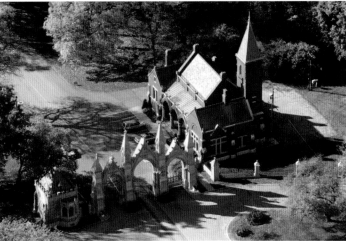

ning Committee was making numerous field trips to research the concept, and in early 1960 authorized D. A. Bohlen to draw up plans for Crown Hill's first garden crypts. Bohlen soon had plans for 13,000 garden crypts that would be constructed in the northeast section of the north grounds. With some concern, the board signed off on the project. In the minutes, the corporators noted that the garden crypts would be far from the original sections, where their plots were located, so the new tombs would not change "to any large degree the appearance of the cemetery as we know it."

On April 9, 1963, the corporators met for their annual meeting. It was Crown Hill's centennial year. The board of corporators continued to be an organization comprised of the men from Indianapolis's leading families, with new members chosen as much for pedigree as experience and capacity. At the centennial meeting, the minutes quoted a section of Anna Nichols's 1928 Crown Hill book: "While Indianapolis has grown rapidly in the last third of its century of life, the pioneer element has long remained in the lead, is still felt; the early families have scattered less perhaps than is usual in growing towns, and sons and sons' sons have carried on to an uncommon degree, what their father's began. There has been a remarkable continuity of purpose and action, taking the history throughout—a strong and honorable purpose of high class men behind all progress, even though progress might seem to lag."

The reference to lagging progress was telling, as business news was troubling in the hundredth year: interments in Crown Hill dropped to 19.7 percent of the county deaths, and sales were not keeping pace with the large outlays for mausoleum construction. Facing an excess capacity of unsold crypt spaces, the board cast about for increased revenues to right things. By 1964 a committee was investigating the possibility of adding a funeral home to the cemetery, but the board soon learned a mortuary would cost Crown Hill its tax-exempt status. The corporators were also in discussions with the Indiana State Highway Commission, which canceled Crown Hill's planned entrance off of Thirty-eighth Street just west of the Subway. After extensive

negotiations, the cemetery agreed to place the entrance off of Clarendon Avenue. And there was Jessica Mitford's best-selling exposé on the funeral industry, *The American Way of Death*, which left some public relations problems in its wake. The 1965 board minutes include a fulmination about "well-organized efforts by a few to sell the American people on the idea that their traditions of burial and respect for the dead should be abandoned."

In 1967 sales improved, reversing a three-year trend of declining crypt purchases. Lot sales set new records. The promotion plan and three-person sales force were making a difference. The manager reported "good relations" with the forty-seven employees. By 1967 there were 138,000 interments in Crown Hill; 2,200 were entombed or inurned in the mausoleum. On the other hand, the Crown Hill percentage of the county's interments continued to drop. Wood's executive vice president report indicated the burials were down to 19 percent. He cited two reasons. First, while Indianapolis's burgeoning regional medical centers were attracting patients from all over the state, the dead returned home for burial. The second, and the biggest problem was increased competition—more cemeteries with more aggressive sales strategies.

In the 1960s and 1970s urban renewal, the catchall development phrase that included inner-city expressway construction and massive projects such as the Indiana University–Purdue University at Indianapolis campus, precipitated widespread demolition, including Crown Hill's Romanesque-style gates that had stood at the cemetery's southwest corner since 1901. With ramps for Interstate 65 being built just adjacent to the entrance, the corporators judged it prudent to close the gates in 1965. As the ramps opened a year later, workmen tore the gates down. In the mid-1960s urban development also impacted the magnificent maple trees that lined Maple Road, the appropriately named street bisecting Crown Hill. The opening of the six-lane West Thirty-eighth Street bridge in 1962 hastened the widening of Maple Road, which was then renamed Thirty-eighth Street. The new name was just as well. When the construction was completed, half the maples were gone, dramatically altering the cemetery's historic streetscape.

The Crown Hill staff moved into a new office building on the north grounds in 1968. At that year's annual meeting, the executive vice president discouraged the board from maintaining the Waiting Station, noting the high costs of renovation. With the go-go 1960s modernism ascendant, it appeared the wrecking ball was headed for the Waiting Station. But the Waiting Station survived. Industrialist, philanthropist, and Crown Hill corporator Eli Lilly stepped forward to save it. In 1970 the corporators signed a long-term lease with Historic Landmarks Foundation of Indiana. The group could use the building for a dollar a year if they restored it.

It was still the nascent days of historic preservation in Indianapolis. In the early 1960s the demolition of important city structures, including the English Opera House and Hotel, the grand turreted Second-Empire Marion County Courthouse, and the original Second Presbyterian Church at Vermont and Pennsylvania Streets, had alarmed Lilly and other Indianapolis leaders. In response, they organized HLFI to help preserve historic structures. During one of the first workshops, Lilly met a young architect named H. Roll McLaughlin, who became smitten with historic preservation while on a European sabbatical from his position with James Associates. Lilly sat in on McLaughlin's slide presentation and realized he had found a kindred spirit. Supported by Lilly, HLFI's first foray into historic preservation was the Morris-Butler House, an imposing Civil War-era mansion on the near north side that McLaughlin and HLFI transformed into a Victorian house museum. Lilly must have liked what the young HLFI wrought. Not long after the completion of the project, he called McLaughlin into his office and handed him an envelope. Lilly had already made contributions to HLFI totaling about $200,000. When McLaughlin opened the envelope, he noted the philanthropist had generously donated 40,000 shares of Lilly stock to HLFI. Doing a quick calculation, McLaughlin was pleased to learn the gifted stock was worth about $250,000.

Later, when an associate joined him, they refigured the value, and the two men realized Lilly had given HLFI more than $3 million worth of stock. "I nearly died," McLaughlin later said.

By the time Lilly and the energetic HLFI staff got involved with Crown Hill's Waiting Station, they were in the midst of a neighborhood-sized transformation of the Lockerbie Square area around the Riley Home. The Lockerbie project eventually involved purchasing and facilitating the restoration of dozens of structures. So the Waiting Station, unappreciated and in need of some help, was a good project for the well-led and well-funded HLFI. The collaboration among Lilly, Crown Hill, and HLFI proved to be a vital one for the historic cemetery threatened by the postwar enthusiasm for modernism.

HLFI began to renovate the structure for use as an office. At the time, the Waiting Station was in rough condition—the exterior was overgrown with ivy and the interior was grungy and down at the heels from deferred maintenance. Florescent lights hung from the ceiling, and the grand entry was chopped up with helter-skelter partitions. By February 1971 the restoration was complete. The exterior was restored to historic standards, and the interior was renovated to the needs of the 1970s office, while carefully refinishing the glorious vintage woodwork that helped make the building so spectacular.

Other historic cemetery structures were also in poor shape and underutilized. With the completion of the Community Mausoleum in the early 1950s, the historic Gothic Chapel was no longer needed, and over the next few decades became little more than a storage shed for the cemetery lawn mowers. After HLFI finished work on the Waiting Station, it began work on the Gothic Chapel. A 1972 *Indianapolis Star* article trumpeted, "Crown Hill's Old Chapel Redone," noting the new Ludiwici tile roof and quincunx landscape design. HLFI directed the $120,000 project that also included removal of the old vaults, installation of new mechanical systems and restrooms, and a contemporary sound system. An $18,000 decorating project made the chapel ready for committal services, which again

became a regular event. HLFI's work at Crown Hill reached a new peak on February 28, 1973, when the cemetery was added to the prestigious National Register of Historic Places.

While history was being preserved, new forms were embellishing the cemetery. The tombstone trade sadly reported in the 1970s that the obelisks and large monuments of the nineteenth and early twentieth centuries had given way to smaller markers. A spokesperson for the Blakely Granite Company on East New York Street stated it had not sold a tower monument "for years." One journalist reported, "Flat markers are now the vogue." The cemeteries loved the flush grave markers' low maintenance costs because mowers could run right over them. Families liked the smaller stones' economical price.

Despite the popularity of the new Community Mausoleum, families ordered two magnificent private mausoleums in the 1950s. The Holcomb family contracted with Amick and Wearley Monuments in 1952 to construct an austere modernist tomb in Section 73, Lot 36. Inside a portal of curved and striated granite, a bronze casting of a classical-style grieving woman with a bowed head graced the mausoleum door. In 1959 monument fabricators erected the Rhoads family mausoleum in Section

> Beyond its role as a sacred ground for the city's dead, Crown Hill remained a multifaceted community resource, a place for remembrance, for learning, and for celebration.

45. It was not until 1971 that another private mausoleum was built, when the Voight family mausoleum was completed. The popularity of private mausoleums that took off in 1890 with Louis Sullivan's Getty mausoleum in Chicago's Graceland cemetery was running its course, a victim of changing tastes and high costs. By the end of the 1970s a family tomb could cost more than $500,000.

The corporators spotted a good deal in 1962 when the old Marion County Courthouse was being torn down. For a few hundred dollars each, the board bought three classical limestone statues of Greek goddesses Themis, Demeter, and Persephone, and installed them in the cemetery. The statues were part of a set of twelve sculpted and painted figures that had stood atop the courthouse since 1873. Eight of the other statues went to Holliday Park, and the last to a private collection. Another monumental sculpture salvaged from a demolition came to Crown Hill about the same time. When the old Indianapolis Public Library was torn down in 1967, a grouping of classical figures by sculptor Richard Bock was taken down and stored in the cemetery service yard. The figures sat somewhat ignored until the early 1970s, when the sculpture was moved back to the grounds of the Indianapolis–Marion County Public Library.

Beyond its role as a sacred ground for the city's dead, Crown Hill remained a multifaceted community resource, a place for remembrance, for learning, and for celebration. Each school year Shortridge High School biology classes traipsed over to Crown Hill on field trips to collect leaves from the cemetery's more than a hundred species. Generations of students learned to differentiate maples from oaks at Crown Hill. As family cars became prevalent in the 1950s, the cemetery's winding lanes became the place for high schoolers to learn to drive. It is said the boulders at the section corners have prevented more than one novice from plowing into the midst of the gravestones. When the late 1960s began to heat up, Crown Hill also served as a clandestine nighttime party place for north-side teenagers. "Oh, there were *lots* of ways to get into Crown Hill," one now gray-haired former partier laughed. "It was creepy." But as it had been from its beginnings, Crown Hill also provided generations a place to retreat from the hurly-burly, to ponder meaning, and to reach an equipoise of understanding and acceptance.

Ultimately, however, Crown Hill was a final resting place. By 1977 there were more than 155,000 people interred in the cemetery—though the percentage of county deaths buried in Crown Hill continued to drop. In 1976 as competition sharpened, it was down to 15 percent. The aggressive Indianapolis-based sales contractors were causing Crown Hill problems, claiming that the cemetery was in a bad neighborhood, out of the way, run-down, and mismanaged. But the corporators had a resounding retort: "We are the best and most beautiful cemetery in the area." By 1978, the same year a massive blizzard trapped cemetery staff in the offices for days, the sales efforts were paying off—sales were up 60 percent. Crown Hill had started a monument busi-ness, adding an additional revenue stream. Most reassuring, more than 22 percent of the county dead were being interred in Crown Hill, reversing an alarming trend.

Among the thousands interred, Indianapolis Speedway luminaries kept coming to Crown Hill. Gaylord, "Snappy" Ford, one of the riding mechanics from the early days of the Indianapolis 500, died in 1953 and was entombed in the new garden crypts. After World War II a number of Indianapolis 500 drivers were buried in the cemetery. They included Chet Miller, who also died in 1953; four-time starter and pole winner Jerry Hoyt, who died in 1955; and "Little George" Amick, who survived a multicar crash in the first lap of the 1958 Indianapolis race to finish second. He died in 1959 in a sprint car race. Motorcycle and race car driver Erwin "Cannon Ball" Baker died in 1960 after setting cross-country speed records and winning innumerable races, including the first one held at the new Speedway in 1909, when he rode an Indian motorcycle to victory. Ronnie Duman died in a race in 1968 in Wisconsin. He had raced in the 500 five times, including surviving burns in the deadly 1964 race when Eddie Sachs and Dave MacDonald died. Paul Russo raced in fourteen Indianapolis 500s, including his 1957 fourth-place finish with a Novi Special.

Roscoe Turner was a legendary Indianapolis 500 official who died in 1970. He had won a Distinguished Flying Cross, organized the barnstorming Roscoe Turner Flying Circus, and worked with Howard Hughes on his *Hell's Angels* movie. Turner had set transcontinental speed records and won important races. Later he organized flying schools and the Roscoe Turner Aeronautical Corporation in Indianapolis. As a celebrity sponsor of the Gilmore Oil Company, Turner flew with a lion

cub named Gilmore, who traveled with a cub-sized parachute. When Gilmore died, Turner kept the stuffed and mounted lion in his home. After Turner's death, Gilmore went to the Smithsonian Institution, where he was kept in cold storage. Turner, on the other hand, was entombed in Crown Hill's garden crypt D-10-K.

Charles C. "Charlie" Wiggins was a topnotch mechanic and race driver, but racial barriers prevented the talented African American from competing in the Indianapolis 500 and other big-prize races. But Wiggins was determined and resourceful. Disguised as a janitor so he could work incognito as a mechanic, Wiggins helped Bill Cummings win the 500 in 1934. Wiggins also was an organizer of an African American national racing league, the Colored Speedway Association, which held races at the Indiana State Fairgrounds from 1924 to 1936. The league competed in the "Gold and Glory Sweepstakes," which attracted thousands of spectators. "Men of grease and grit," a Chicago journalist called the drivers. Wiggins was a four-time champion, earning him the title of "the Negro Speed King." A horrendous thirteen-car pile-up at the 1936 Gold and Glory Sweepstakes race at the fairgrounds created a "mountain of rending, dis-torted metal and buried men," as the *Recorder* reported. One of the men was Wiggins, who was pinned under his car. The crash cost Wiggins his leg, which he later replaced with a wooden one he turned on his workshop lathe. Until he died at the age of eighty-one, Wiggins served as a mechanic and trainer for

race drivers and continued to push for equal rights. Recurring infections from his injured leg eventually cost Wiggins and his former fashion-model wife, Roberta, all of their money. They died broke. After Wiggins's death in 1979 he was buried in an unmarked grave in Section 100, Lot 244. But the story was not over. In 2003 a Public Broadcasting Service documentary and companion book, *For Gold and Glory*, celebrated Wiggins's

*Charlie and Roberta Wiggins's polished black-granite marker included a photo of Charlie in his racecar and the inscription: "For Gold and Glory."*

career, as did an exhibition at the Indiana State Library. In June 2003 anonymous donors arranged for a memorial to be installed on his grave. Charlie and Roberta Wiggins's polished black-granite marker included a photo of Charlie in his racecar and the inscription: "For Gold and Glory."

The automotive industrialists also came to Crown Hill. After his death in 1945 Indianapolis 500 sponsor Robert M. Bowes of Bowes Seal-Fast was buried in Section 67, Lot 12. Another 500 sponsor, Charles C. Merz, of Merz Engineering, died in 1952. Arthur B. Lathrop, who owned several race cars that competed in the 500, passed away in 1970 and was buried in Section 67, Lot 91. The auto industrialist August Duesenberg died on January 18, 1955, and was laid to rest in the mausoleum, D-2-NN. Frederick "Fritz" Duesenberg died in 1974 and was entombed in crypt E-9-IV.

Other Indianapolis leaders took their rest in Crown Hill. In 1958 influential newspaper editor and civic leader Hilton U. Brown died. Brown had spent seventy years with the *Indianapolis News* and served as a longtime Butler University trustee and supporter. On September 24, 1958, Brown was interred in Section 2, Lot 32 near the cenotaph for his son, Hilton U. Brown Jr., who had died in France in the last days of World War I.

On New Year's Day 1948 Josiah K. Lilly Sr. died. The son of pharmaceutical company founder Colonel Eli Lilly, Josiah began

working in the family firm in 1876 at the age of fourteen. Four years later with the young company booming, his father asked him to go to college to obtain the technical expertise that the firm needed to grow. In 1890 Colonel Eli retired and turned the firm over to his son, who ran the company until 1922. After retiring, Josiah continued his far-reaching civic and philanthropic work, which included serving as a Crown Hill corporator from 1910 until his death. In 1938 Lilly and his two sons, Eli Lilly and J. (Josiah) K. Lilly Jr., established the Lilly Endowment, an organization that proved to have an immeasurable impact on Indianapolis. He was buried in Section 14, Lot 18. In 1960 the Lilly family plot was ennobled when sculptor David Krenz Rubins, a longtime professor at the Herron School of Art, installed his Lilly Monument. Rubins's statue was a stylized bronze angel with upright arms set on a pink granite base.

J. K. Lilly Jr., the Eli Lilly and Company scion and president from 1948 to 1953, died in 1966. A prodigious philanthropist, J. K. Jr. arranged for his former 3,500-acre estate, Eagle Crest, to be transformed into the city's Eagle Creek Park. Beyond his business and civic interests, J. K. Jr. was a renowned collector. He assembled an immense collection of 20,000 rare books and 17,000 manuscripts, which he donated to Indiana University as the beginnings of the Lilly Library's fabled holdings. The Smithsonian acquired J. K. Jr.'s collection of 6,000 antique gold coins. After his death, J. K. Jr.'s collection of 77,000 stamps was dispersed at three days of auction that netted more than $3 million. J. K. Jr. was interred in the family plot in Section 14, Lot 9, not far from his father's grave.

Eli grew up on Tennessee Street (later renamed Capitol Avenue), which was the customary route to Crown Hill Cemetery. As a boy he watched brass bands lead the funeral precessions with slow dirges on the way north and then return playing sprightly numbers such as "A Hot Time in the Old Town Tonight." In 1907 Eli married Evelyn Fortune. They stuck close to home, living in various locales in the old north side neighborhood near his boyhood haunts and the extended Lilly family. Tragedy struck the young couple in June 1908 when their first child, named Eli, died only a month after he was born. The second son, also named Eli, was born in March 1910, but only lived seven months. Two small markers in the Lilly plot at Crown Hill memorialize the young lives. To the parents' great delight, a healthy Evie Lilly was born in September 1918.

Eli went on to a rich and extraordinary career as an industrialist, philanthropist, preservationist, and free-ranging intellectual that extended into his nineties. He always maintained a strong tie to Crown Hill, most vigorously illustrated by his generous financial support of the cemetery's historic structures. When the HLFI held an open house to celebrate the completion of the Waiting Station renovation, the administrators naturally invited elderly "Mr. Eli," as they called him. J. Reid Williamson, then the HLFI president, remembered the longtime president of Eli Lilly and Company being rolled into the offices in his wheelchair. "All that walnut and cherry paneling was just glistening, and he just looked around. We thought, 'Maybe he doesn't like it.' But then he smiled and said,

> But Lilly's passing was not to go unnoted. As the long funeral cortege entered the great Gothic Gates and passed the restored Waiting Station, the tower bell mournfully tolled in homage.

'Well, fellas, it was never this good out at the plant.'" Speaking of Lilly's lifelong connection, Williamson said, "Mr. Eli had a great love of Crown Hill."

In January 1977 Eli was ninety-one. While he tired easily, his mind was still crisp. Each day he still dressed in his business suit and tie. Though he had been diagnosed with liver cancer the previous month, he insisted on making the traditional New Year's call to the Indianapolis pharmaceutical wholesalers, a custom his grandfather and namesake had began. Eli entered University Hospital in mid-January. On January 24, 1977, he passed away.

As with most things in his life, Lilly had prepared for his funeral. He left complete instructions for the casket, the people to be invited, the funeral service in the Gothic Chapel, and the burial afterward in the Lilly family plot. He specified the regular Episcopal service be used—from the 1928 edition of the standard *Prayer Book*. Ever self-effacing, Lilly further specified, "I do not want any eulogies or remarks made at the service." But Lilly's passing was not to go unnoted. As the long funeral cortege entered the great Gothic Gates and passed the restored Waiting Station, the tower bell mournfully tolled in homage.

War hero and Indianapolis civic leader Robert H. Tyndall was born in Indianapolis in 1877. Enlisting at age twenty in the Indiana National Guard, he served in Puerto Rico during the Spanish-American War. After stints as a merchandise broker and tailor, Tyndall returned to the military as war in Europe loomed in 1916. By August 1917 Tyndall was a colonel commanding the unit that became the 150th Field Artillery of the famous Forty-second (Rainbow) Division. The division fought in crucial battles, including the September 1918 attack against the strategic Saint Mihiel salient that was the American forces' first independent offensive. The division also fought in the Meuse-Argonne campaign. For his service, Tyndall was honored with numerous decorations and awards, including the Distinguished Service Medal, and France's Croix de Guerre and Legion d'Honneur. Following the war, Tyndall served in the Reserve Corps, and by 1924 was a major general.

Tyndall's postwar civilian career also went well, serving as a Fletcher American Bank vice president and national treasurer of the American Legion up to about 1925, when he began working with Carl G. Fisher on his Miami Beach and Montauk Beach developments. When World War II erupted in 1941, old warhorse Tyndall mobilized the 50,000 troops of the Thirty-eighth Division at Camp Shelby, Mississippi—mobilized, that is, until the statutory retirement age of sixty-four forced him to other

fields. Throwing himself into politics, Tyndall won the Indianapolis mayoral race in 1942, and ably administered the city's government until a sudden heart attack felled him on July 9, 1947. To honor his memory, the downtown headquarters for the Indiana Army National Guard's Seventy-sixth Infantry Brigade was named Tyndall Armory. At Crown Hill Tyndall was memorialized with the modest gray granite marker that was erected in Section 36, Lot 162.

George L. Denny took over as Indianapolis mayor after Tyndall's death, serving through 1948. Like so many Indianapolis mayors, Denny was buried in Crown Hill after his death in 1958. Walter C. Boetcher was mayor from 1937 to 1939. He died in 1951. Albert H. Losche died in 1966 after serving as mayor from 1962 to 1964. In 1971 Christian J. Emhardt died after serving as mayor in the early 1950s, and as a judge from 1959 to 1963.

Homer E. Capehart was a Hoosier politician out of central casting. Born on a farm in southern Indiana's Pike County in 1897, Capehart made his fortune in the jukebox industry, refining a record-changing mechanism that he eventually sold to Wurlitzer. In 1938 Capehart launched his GOP political career with a giant "Cornfield Conference" that he held in one of his farmfields. He went on to narrowly defeat Henry Schricker in 1944 for the U.S. Senate seat that he also won in two successive

The Cold War also brought new groups to Crown Hill. Displaced by the takeover of their Baltic country by the Soviet Union in 1940, Estonians found a new home in Indianapolis in the years after World War II.

elections. Considered a Latin American policy sage, Capehart presciently warned about a missile build-up in Cuba, and called for a "crack-down" on that county. Capehart held his seat until an upstart attorney named Birch Bayh upset him in the 1962 election. Following his defeat, Capehart relocated to a comfortable home on North Pennsylvania Street, where he focused on his Indiana business and farming interests, while occasionally advising Washington officials. After a slow decline, Capehart died of complications from hip surgery at Saint Vincent Hospital

on September 3, 1979, at the age of eighty-two. He was interred in the family plot in Section 46, Lot 241, where the dignified pale gray Capehart memorial stood near his grave.

The Cold War cast a long shadow in Crown Hill. In 1951 nuclear war's chilling reality impacted Crown Hill. At the request of the Civil Defense officials, the corporators set aside twenty-one acres in the undeveloped northwest corner of the cemetery for "temporary mass burials" of people killed in an unexpected "air or bombing attack by an enemy of the United States" that would kill "thousands of persons within a short period of time." There would be, the corporator minutes read, no time for "the observance of customary burial practices."

The Cold War also brought new groups to Crown Hill. Displaced by the takeover of their Baltic country by the Soviet Union in 1940, Estonians found a new home in Indianapolis in the years after World War II. Many of the transplanted Estonians were urban dwellers, primarily from the capital city of Tallinn. Most had been in refugee camps in Europe for a number of years awaiting permission to relocate. While many of the educated urban families had to initially take menial jobs, they soon found work in their fields, especially teaching and engineering. Once situated, they sought a final home for their departed. In 1962 the Estonian-Americans purchased a large plot in Section 235 of the north grounds, where they erected an imposing monument that read, "Final Resting Place of Estonian Americans and their Families," and the Estonian phrase, "*Su Üle Jumal Valvaku*," which translates to the request, "That God would watch over you." As part of their drive to maintain their culture during their hegira, the Estonian community had put down roots in Crown Hill.

With more than 400,000 American soldiers and sailors killed in World War II and the nation girding for confrontation with the Communist bloc, Memorial Day was meaningful in the late 1940s. Even though the revived Indianapolis 500 was again drawing enormous crowds back to the Speedway, tens of thou-

sands of people still crowded Crown Hill each Memorial Day. A postwar Indianapolis editorial writer stated the importance of honoring the fallen and voiced concerns about the Communist menace: "The nation pauses today in grateful remembrance of those who rendered loyal service to the flag." In the midst of the Red Scares, the editorialist connected Memorial Day to vigilance against enemies, both foreign and domestic: "Responsibility of the present generation has increased because of new threats to our liberty," the unnamed editor wrote, going on to lash out at the "disloyal citizens who take advantage of national defense for selfish gain and the subversive alien who seeks to overthrow our institutions with the poison of dangerous philosphies," urging citizens to crush "every trace of disloyalty." Memorial Day in the 1950s was a big event at Crown Hill. An Indianapolis paper warned motorists to be alert when inching west on Thirty-eighth Street: "Traffic officials today issued a gentle warning to out-of-town race fans that all roads do not lead to the Speed-way. Every year for fifteen years before the war, half a dozen or so cars, Speedway bound, become entangled in the bumper-to-bumper line of autos headed for Memorial Day services at Crown Hill Cemetery. Barring a miracle, it probably will be no different this time, officials said."

By 1950 the Cold War was heating up. America had scarcely noticed the "police action" in Korea when fallen soldiers began arriving at Crown Hill. Some of the first were members of the Twenty-fourth Infantry Regiment, which General Douglas MacArthur had hurriedly deployed in the summer of 1950, along with other woefully unprepared U.S. troops posted in Japan. Comprised of African American soldiers, the Twenty-fourth's predecessors led back to the U.S. Colored Troops of the Civil War. Stationed in peacetime duty in Japan, the Twenty-fourth

*Andrew S. Bowman portrays his grandfather, Sergeant Andrew Smith of the Fifty-fifth Massachusetts Volunteer Colored Infantry, at the Spirit of Freedom; an annual collaboration with Crown Hill and the Indianapolis Public Schools Office of Multicultural Education. Smith was awarded the Medal of Honor on January 16, 2001, by President Bill Clinton.*

had scant time for proper combat training before being thrust into fierce fighting with hardened North Korean troops. The Twenty-fourth also suffered the inequities of an African American unit in a segregated army. The officers were not held in high regard by their soldiers, and morale was low. The regiment initially got high marks for its actions in the breakout by U.S. forces from the Korean seaport of Pusan, where the North Korean troops had besieged the Americans. The Twenty-fourth also received accolades at battles at the Han and Hant'an River

*The* Recorder *blarred "Tan Yanks Hit Korean Reds," reporting that African American GIs had won the "first big U.S. 'tilt' in Korea."*

crossings, and elsewhere in the theater. The *Recorder* blarred "Tan Yanks Hit Korean Reds," reporting that African American GIs had won the "first big U.S. 'tilt' in Korea." The national news media declared the African American unit had pushed forward under heavy fire and repulsed a fearsome North Korean charge. Later, things did not go well for the regiment. The unit suffered high losses and a reputation for being "unreliable," but the Twenty-fourth's experience was little different from elements of other equally unseasoned American troops in the first days of the Korean War. As decades of Memorial Days rolled along in Crown Hill, a new tradition began to emerge: each year before the ceremony, a small group of aging African American men met behind the Gothic Chapel on a slope near the National Cemetery. Gathered together, the men paid a personal tribute to their fallen comrades, some of the 54,246 American soldiers and sailors who made the ultimate sacrifice in Korea before the indecisive truce was declared in July 1953.

Robert Groves Jr. was among them. Nineteen years old, Groves had been a Crispus Attucks High School student. The private first class died on August 29, 1950, during a day of ferocious fighting with the North Koreans that climaxed in hand-to-hand combat. Groves was posthumously awarded the Purple Heart, the Combat Infantryman's Badge, the Korean Service Medal, the United Nations Service Medal, the National Defense

Service Medal, and the Korean War Service Medal. After his death, the *Recorder* published a letter Groves had written home to his fiancée, Doris Watkins. In his last letter, he wrote, "I have aged ten years since July 1. . . . The only thing that keeps me going is thinking how happy we'll be together again someday." The remains of Groves, the first Indianapolis African American to die in Korea, were interred in Section 9, Lot 2033.

Another member of the Twenty-fourth, William Watkins, died on December 8, 1950, during the bitter cold that left several hundred of his comrades horribly frostbitten. Despite the cold, the fighting continued. Watkins died during battle and was posthumously awarded the Purple Heart, the Combat Infantryman's Badge, the Korean Service Medal, the United Nations Service Medal, the National Defense Service Medal, the Korean Presidential Unit Citation, and the Republic of Korea War Service Medal. He was buried in Section 9, Lot 2080.

The dramatic entry of a half million Chinese troops into the war in late 1950 forced the American troops to retreat, leading to the legendary Chosin Reservoir battles. By the summer of 1951, the war was a fixed-position slugfest, akin to World War I's trench warfare. As the meat-grinder war continued into 1952, other Indianapolis soldiers came home to Crown Hill. A high school football star, Golden Gloves boxer, and New York Central employee, Corporal Wilson J. Beene, was a member of Company F, Second Battalion, Fifth Infantry Regimental Combat Team. He had entered the army in March 1951 and arrived in Korea six months later as the war solidified into a static, casualty-mounting conflict. On July 27, 1952, his unit came under heavy fire. Grievously wounded, Beene died the same day. Posthumously decorated, Beene was interred in Section 9, Lot 2048.

An Indianapolis native, Private First Class Herman Russell was a marine, a member of the First Battalion, Seventh Marines, First Marine Division—the "first of the seventh," part of the fabled "Magnificent Seventh" that had achieved so much glory in Pacific battles during World War II. When Korea erupted, the Seventh was reactivated and took part in MacArthur's brilliant

IN
MEMORY
OF ALL
VETERANS

CALL OUT OUR NAMES
AS THE YEARS GO BY
REMEMBER
AND WE SHALL NEVER DIE.

A NATION THAT HONORS IT'S VETERANS.
IS A NATION DEDICATED TO THE
PRESERVATION OF A FREEDOM WON BY
THE SACRIFICE OF LIFE ITSELF. THESE
EMBLEMS ARE APPROPRIATELY DEDICATED
TO THE VALIANT DEAD. OF THE
ARMED FORCES WHO VENTURED FAR.
FOUGHT BRAVELY. AND GAVE THEIR LIVES
TO PRESERVE FREEDOM AND LIBERTY
IN OUR LAND. TOGETHER THEY LIE
HERE IN MUTE TESTIMONY TO THE
MANNER IN WHICH THEY LIVED. WORKED.
AND FOUGHT TO ACHIEVE THE VICTORIES
IN ORDER THAT AMERICA MAY LIVE

Inchon gambit that forced the North Korean forces to withdraw north toward the Yalu River and the Thirty-eighth Parallel. The Seventh fought all the way to the Thirty-eighth Parallel. After the American retreat following the Chinese army's incursion, the Seventh fought in the frigid "Frozen Chosin" Reservoir action, which many call out as the U.S. Marine Corps' finest hour. Born on March 8, 1928, twenty-four-year-old Russell was killed in action in Korea on October 26, 1952, and was buried in Crown Hill's Section 9, Lot 2050 on January 12, 1953. He was awarded the Purple Heart, the Combat Infantryman's Badge, the Korean Service Medal, the United Nations Service Medal, the National Defense Service Medal, the Korean Presidential Unit Citation, and the Republic of Korea War Service Medal.

Even as the stalemate between the democratic and communist forces continued in Korea in the early 1960s, another Cold War front opened up: Vietnam. More than two dozen American soldiers killed in Vietnam eventually came to rest in Crown Hill, including the last burial in the National Cemetery. On October 6, 1969, Major Robert W. Hayes of the 774th Tactical Airlift was navigating his C-130 plane over Chu Lai, South Vietnam, toward the Da Nang airbase when the reportedly sabotaged plane exploded. Thirty-one-year-old Hayes lost his life, as did four other crewmen. The Crown Hill

National Cemetery was officially full, and there had not been any burials there for decades. But the administrators found space for Hayes. On October 27, 1969, he was interred in Section 10 Lot 730A, the National Cemetery's final burial.

In March 1965 President Lyndon Johnson ordered a major escalation of American forces, which reached 536,000 troops by 1968. The fallen from Vietnam began arriving at Crown Hill not long after the first U.S. combat troops arrived. More than 58,000 American soldiers and sailors died during the Vietnam War. There were more than 350,000 casualties. Staff Sergeant Kenneth Leroy Reed, a Hamilton County native, died in a helicopter crash on June 12, 1965, and was buried in Section 232, Lot 271. Marine corporal Alvin Carver Forney died when he stepped on a mine in Quang Nam Province on September 1, 1965. The twenty-two-year-old Indianapolis native was buried in Section 99B, Lot 122. Twenty-four-year-old Private First Class David Jesse from Indianapolis died in a firefight with entrenched Viet Cong in Ap Nha Mat, a jungle area near Saigon on December 5, 1965. He was buried in Section 224, Lot 1353.

As the war expanded through 1968, so did the American casualties. Private First Class Eurey Lee Hatchett was a natty, likable Crispus Attucks graduate who attended Indiana University–Purdue University at Indianapolis. On July 3, 1966, he was

*Opposite and above:* Flowers placed by the public during the 2008 Memorial Day ceremonies to honor the fallen hoosier heroes of the wars in Iraq and Afghanistan.

serving with the Thirty-fifth Infantry Regiment as a rifleman in Pleiku Province's Ia Drang Valley, where the previous November American and North Vietnamese forces first engaged in a set battle. The engagement ended inconclusively, with both sides claiming victory. But the region remained disputed territory, resulting in Hatchett's presence in the valley, where he was cut down by small-arms fire. He was posthumously awarded the Combat Infantryman Badge, the Bronze Star with V, the Purple Heart, the National Defense Service Medal, the Vietnam Service Medal, the Vietnam Campaign Medal and the Vietnam Cross of Gallantry with Palm Unit Citation. After a funeral attended

> Back on the home front, some members of old Indianapolis families were also coming to ther final resting place.

by an overflow crowd, Hatchett was buried in Section 99B Lot 325. On April 22, 1968, Staff Sergeant William Lewis Chifos was killed in Long An Province. Chifos was awarded two Silver Stars and one Bronze Star before being interred in Section 46, Lot 156. Lance Corporal Virgil Lee Larkins was a nineteen-year-old marine rifleman, who died when his helicopter was shot down in Quang Tri Province on May 10, 1969. He was buried in Section 99, Lot 4127, where his family memorialized him with bronze marker embellished with a cross.

Like so many soldiers of the era, John Thomas Pettitt was drafted. A graduate of Ben Davis High School, Pettitt had worked as a draftsman at Detroit Diesel-Allison Division before being sworn in as a member of the Indianapolis Police Department on June 23, 1969, just three days before the Indiana Selective Service inducted him into the army. He arrived in Vietnam in January 1970, as American opposition to the war was rising and President Richard Nixon was implementing his Vietnamization and withdrawal strategies. By November Sergeant Pettitt was serving as a reconnaissance tank commander with the

Twenty-fifth Armored Tank Division in Hua Nghia Province. On November 6, Pettitt was killed by indirect fire—an artillery or mortar round. He was interred in Crown Hill's Section 46, Lot 60. Twenty-seven-year-old Pettitt left a son, John Pettitt Jr., and a daughter, Kelly.

Back on the home front, some members of old Indianapolis families were also coming to ther final resting place. Skiles Test was from a prestigious Indianapolis family, descended from a Diamond Chain Company founder. A millionaire in his own right, Test owned a large estate at 6700 Fall Creek Road, what came to be known as the House of Blue Lights. A true eccentric, Test harbored hundreds of cats and dogs, burying them in tiny, carpet-lined coffins with a Lord's Prayer recitation and little headboards. Underground tunnels of unknown use and destination laced the grounds. A small-scale train and a gondola hauled Test around his land and up one of the hills. Teams of his Saint Bernards towed him in a small jitney. He hoarded enormous stashes of various commodities and components, and lit his house, pool, and grounds in his favorite color, blue. And—according to the vivid tales told by Indianapolis teenagers—Test also kept his dead wife's glass coffin in his big rambling house, where he bathed the casket in a lurid blue light. The fact that the last macabre eccentricity was wholly and totally untrue did not keep generations of thrill seekers from sneaking into the Test estate for heart-thumping attempts to view the coffin. For decades, a late-night foray to the House of Blue Lights was an Indianapolis rite of passage.

Rather than the bizarre, frightening image painted by thrill seekers, friends, family, and employees of Test speak of him as a kind and generous man who supported several Indianapolis charities. He bequeathed his estate to Lawrence Township School District, which honored his name with the Skiles Test Elementary School and Skiles Test Nature Park. When he died

*Opposite: Indiana National Guard Bravo Battery, 2-150 Field Artillery, employs a howitzer in a twenty-one-gun salute on Memorial Day 2011.*

in March 1964, the estate sale was a major event, as curious throngs elbowed for views of the late hoarder's possessions. On March 21, 1964, Test was laid to rest in the family plot in Section 23, Lot 34, where seven other Tests also lay. A beautiful stone sundial decorates the plot.

At some point in Crown Hill's early history, the prominent Fletcher family arranged for a remarkable boulder to be place at the verge of the sprawling family plot, which encompassed an expanse of Section 7. A massive, dark-gray orb of metamorphic rock striated with thick bands of pink crystal, the boulder was formed deep in the earth by enormous pressure and heat. After its creation in the far north, glaciers tumbled the multihued boulder to the terrain now called Crown Hill. Geologists called the complicated rock a glacial erratic.

The lodestone of the Fletcher clan was stern Calvin Fletcher, the flinty Vermont Yankee who pioneered Indianapolis and helped start Crown Hill. Calvin's brother, Stoughton A., loaned the corporators the initial capital to buy the Crown Hill property. Generations of the perennially wealthy and important Fletchers owned wide swaths of Indianapolis property, cannily invested in the city's most profitable enterprises, and served on the Crown Hill Board of Corporators. The Fletchers gave their name to American Fletcher National Bank, a rock-solid Indiana financial institution for many decades.

When Stoughton A. Fletcher II was born in 1879 he was given the name of his honored grandfather. The Fletcher heir apparent initially appeared to be a chip off the old block, joining the S. A. Fletcher and Company Bank after graduation from Princeton University. When his bank president father, Stoughton J.'s health failed, Stoughton A. stepped forward to run the institution. By 1920 he had steered the bank through a merger, making the American Fletcher National Bank Indiana's larg-

est national bank. With some of his banking booty, Fletcher built Laurel Hall, a forty thousand square-foot mansion with thirty-two bedrooms, twenty-seven fireplaces, and twenty-two bathrooms. Built on wooded hills above Fall Creek, the house cost about $2.1 million when it was completed in 1916. Fletcher and his wife, May, lived large at Laurel Hall, hosting enormous parties, where the martinis were stirred, not shaken, in a cement mixer. The lawn parties reportedly featured his celebrated trotting horse, Peter the Great. The horse sometimes had the run of the house, as Fletcher rode Peter the Great into the mansion for canters across the parquet floors.

But even as the parties continued through the 1910s, Fletcher's luck was changing. An attempt to corner the American sugar market failed, costing him $17 million. More disastrously, his untimely merger of two companies to manufacture diesel engines for a U.S. military contract resulted in the firm's collapse after the government canceled the contracts at the end of World War I. The collapse cost Fletcher additional millions and his financial situation devolved.

After resigning from his position as bank president and selling Peter the Great and his horse farm to politico Thomas Taggart, Fletcher declared bankruptcy in 1924, listing $481.39 in assets and $1,763,602.54 in liabilities. The next year the American Fletcher National Bank sold Laurel Hall to the Sisters of Providence, who opened Ladywood, a Catholic girls boarding school, a dramatic departure for the infamous party place.

On October 8, 1957, Fletcher died in New York. After his cremation, his ashes were buried in the family plot in Crown Hill Cemetery, not far from the Fletchers' complicated and well-traveled boulder.

Sports heroes also made Crown Hill their final home. Robert "Tiny" Baldwin played shortstop in the Negro National League

*Opposite: Visitors on a guided tour of the cemetery pass the glacial erratic rock on the Fletcher lot.*

in 1921. Born in 1904, he died on May 14, 1959, and was buried in Section 41, Lot 11, where the Baldwin headstone lists ten family members. Specializing in "shine balls," Horace Owen "Hod" Eller was a pitcher for the Cincinnati Reds from 1917 to 1921. Eller had perfected the pitch, polishing the ball with talcum powder to a slick finish, and then throwing it in a special way that caused the ball to wobble erratically on the way to the batter. It was a fastball and knuckleball combined. Using his pitch, Eller helped the Reds win the 1919 pennant with a 20–9 win-loss record, and 2.39 earned run average. But when baseball officials outlawed the shiner after the season, Eller lost his edge, dropping to 13–12 in 1920. Traded to a minor league team, he played in the minor leagues until 1925, when he returned to Indianapolis. Eller joined the police force and served for twenty-two years. Born in 1894, Eller died on July 18, 1961. He was interred in Section 223, Lot 1017.

Born in 1955, John Ed Washington won a basketball scholarship to the University of Evansville, where he was the leading scorer for the last of celebrated coach Arad McCutchan's thirty-one basketball teams. He returned as a senior All-American candidate to play for the Purple Aces at the NCAA Division I-A level under the new coach Bobby Watson. Washington appeared headed to the National Basketball Association ranks. But on December 13, 1977, the team took off from the Evansville airport for a game in Tennessee. Due to pilot and ground crew error, the plane crashed ninety seconds later, killing all twenty-nine on board, including fourteen team members. Washington was buried in Section 98, Lot 1418, where his marker read, "Asleep in Jesus." He was memorialized with the John Ed Park on Roosevelt Avenue.

William L. "Bill" Garrett was a basketball pioneer. After leading Shelbyville to the state championship in 1947, he was named Indiana's "Mr. Basketball." It was the same year Jackie Robinson broke the color line in major league baseball. It took convoluted negotiations involving Indiana University president Herman B Wells, coach Branch McCracken, an influential IU trustee named Nate Kaufman, and Faburn DeFrantz, the

progressive Senate Avenue Young Men's Christian Association executive director, but Garrett played basketball for IU, becoming the first African American to play in the Big Ten Conference. He went on to win All-Conference honors and in 1951 was named an All-American. The Boston Celtics drafted Garrett in the second round, but a draft call prevented him from playing in the NBA. After serving in the army in Japan, and playing with the Harlem Globetrotters for two years, he coached Indianapolis Crispus Attucks High School to its third state basketball championship in 1959. Garrett later served as the Crispus Attucks athletic director, as an Ivy Tech instructor, and was serving as an IUPUI assistant dean when he died of a heart attack on Aug. 7, 1974, at the age of forty-five. His death was front-page news around the state. Before the memorial service at Witherspoon Presbyterian Church on Michigan Avenue, police had to direct the lines of traffic. When Garrett's hearse reached Crown Hill two miles away, the cortege of mourners still stretched all the way back to the church. Garrett's marker in Section 224, Lot 745, was inscribed with his basketball legend and an image of him as an IU player. In September 2000 Shelbyville High School named the new gymnasium in his honor. DeFrantz served for thirty-five years as the director of the Senate Avenue YMCA and as an outspoken advocate of African American rights. When he died in 1964, he was buried in Section 26, Lot 64.

Record-setting mothers were also interred at Crown Hill. Sareptha Jane Evans was eighty-seven years old when she died in March 1947. She was reportedly the mother of thirty children, including two sets of quadruplets, three sets of triplets, and three sets of twins, along with a number of babies the family called "singles." Evans's teamster husband, Ephraim, had relocated the family from Ohio around the turn of the twentieth century. He died seventeen years before his wife at the age of seventy-seven. Though most of the twenty-five girls and five boys lived through infancy, only three survived their mother. Sareptha was buried on March 11, 1947 in Section 99, Lot 2063.

The Roma people—Gypsies in the American argot—have

been coming to Indianapolis for a long time. A 1917 *News* article described an annual convention held along the banks of Eagle Creek east of Kentucky Avenue, where three hundred Roma were camping. The paper noted the "gaudily-dressed women" with numerous children standing next to the Romani automobiles—"fifteen six-cylinder up-to-date automobiles. Not a flivver in the lot." The "gipsy king," Ephraim John, was dressed in a Panama hat and Palm Beach suit, directing the camp affairs and preparing for a wedding that was going to unite two clans.

The Roma have long used Crown Hill for their burials. In 1946 *Star* columnist Lowell Nussbaum quoted Crown Hill's superintendent Raymond Siebert talking about a "Gypsy King" being buried in the cemetery some months prior. He described the dead king arriving for his interment sitting bolt upright in the back seat of an automobile between two "tribesmen." When the gravediggers were down in the grave tamping the dirt down over the king's coffin, the mourners began tossing in coins—and then watched until the grave was filled to insure the diggers did not take any of the money. Once a year through the 1950s and 1960s, a cavalcade of Romani arrived at Crown Hill to celebrate at their ancestors' graves, leaving offerings, such as food, money, cigarettes, and jewelry. In 1963 another Gypsy king came to Crown Hill: Max Eli was buried in Section 223, Lot 121, and his wife, Ruby, joined him in 1970. When he died in 1965, Pete Ziko was the next Roma leader to come to Crown Hill, beginning a long line of Zikos to be interred along the road in Section 223, where the family erected a number of impressive granite Ziko monuments. Being wayfaring people, the Roma prefer roadside graves. Why Crown Hill? One Indianapolis funeral director who has organized Ziko funerals thought the Roma chose Crown Hill because the size and age were like the vintage cemeteries of Europe—"the maturity of Crown Hill, the old monuments, the diversity," he said. "The Old World feel probably appealed to them." By 2011, about two-dozen Elis and Zikos were buried in Crown Hill, their graves regularly attended to by family members. At Christmas 2011 the monuments were

gaily decorated with tinsel, silver reindeer, and tiny artificial Christmas trees. A fresh grave was outlined in a garland of red tinsel.

Through the decades, the Roma funerals in Indianapolis were well attended, as Romani show their solidarity by rushing from all parts of the country for the emotional multiday ceremonies. In the United States, the Roma typically practiced a syncretistic brand of Roman Catholicism that blended their traditional, ancient Hindu-tinged customs with standard Catholic liturgy. During traditional Roma funerals, the close relatives of the deceased did not shave, bathe, change clothes, comb their hair, or wear jewelry for three days after the death until the bodies were buried. In part to placate the *mule*—the spirits of the dead—Romana women expressed their grief with shrieks of despair, rending of clothes, and pulling hair. Beyond their own lamentations, the Romani men manifested their distress with marathon drinking. According to the Roma, the *mule* were vague wispy apparitions who wandered for up to a year after death, frequenting the houses where they lived to snatch bits of food and use the toilet, before finally reconciling themselves to their new situation. The mourners spent three days of grieving with the deceased, who in the Roma custom cannot be left alone. After the burial, the Roma assembled for a lavish *pomana* funeral dinner.

When Gypsy king Pete Ziko died in Indianapolis Methodist Hospital on September 28, 1965, after a heart attack the day prior, the lobby was already filled with gathered Roma holding vigil. The *Star* related that the forty Roma "broke into hysterics" when they heard the news of his death—"screaming and wailing," according to a hospital spokesman. Ziko had been the elected national Roma leader for more than twenty years, while working as a coppersmith in his East Washington Street home until his death. He led about 10,000 Roma around the United States, and his son, Larry, was expected to succeed him. Roma were en route from Chicago, New York, California, and other locales. At the Dorsey Funeral Home on East New York

Street a few days later, a *News* journalist reported incense from Jerusalem wafted through the air, along with the heady scent of "enough flowers to equip a florist shop," and the "almost incessant wailing of the women," who were wailing in Romanian. "It rises in a crescendo and ends in a sob," the journalist indicated. Eating and sleeping were "haphazard" until the burial, he wrote, and reported all of the city's palm-reading parlors were closed until the funeral was over.

On October 1 the Roma cortege moved Ziko from Saint John Catholic Church to his final resting place in Crown Hill to the sound of a brass quartet playing "Oh My Papa." At the gravesite, a hundred Roma men and women tossed in coins as the gleaming brown casket was lowered into the grave—so their leader would have money to pay his way into heaven, they told the reporter. When the grounds crew finished filling the hole, the mourners drenched the grave with beer, wine, and whiskey, along with their adjacent relatives' graves—"a tribute to the dead," they said. Afterward, the family milled around, drinking. "Occasionally, one or more looked back at the grave and cried," the journalist reported.

Through the decades, the Roma continued to have notable burials at Crown Hill. Tina Conner of Indiana Landmarks (formerly HLFI) worked in the Waiting Station at Crown Hill during some of the Roma funerals. "The Gypsy king funeral was the second-longest cortege I ever saw—Eli Lilly's was the longest," Conner said. "They just kept coming and coming. The Gypsies wanted to stay all night in the cemetery, but Crown Hill drew the line." In the winter of 2011 Crown Hill employee Clifford Jackson was digging yet another grave in Section 223. He talked about the festive air around the Roma burial sites: "It's a party," he said. "They're having fun. A little drinking, you know. They know how to send you off."

Herbert Wirth was a bird of a man, scarcely five feet tall, maybe a hundred or so pounds. Each day, six days a week, he would head out on his route, an elderly, stooped man with two shopping bags filled with his wares: kitchen towels, washcloths, potholders, bandannas, and an array of shoelaces in various hues. Everything was a quarter, except the fancy potholders a teenage neighbor girl crafted. They were fifty cents, but he did not take a commission. Door to door he would go with a smile,

from Sixteenth Street to Broad Ripple. It was his neighborhood, where he lived in a small house his mother left him when she died in 1957. "I'm your neighbor," he would say to his customers in his high-pitched voice. Winter and summer, three times a year, he visited each door in his neighborhood, hurrying along in his polished shoes with his odd kind of shuffle-jog. He did it for more than twenty-five years, since 1944 when he was laid off at age fifty-seven from his job in a dry goods store. Herbie, his customers called him.

Wirth was always polite, always smiling, happy to hear no, ready to hear yes, always ready to chat. For those who took the time, he would tell them he should have gotten married when he was young. It was a lonely life without a family. Not self pitying, just telling the truth. Sometimes a housewife would say he was not without friends, all his neighbors knew him. "Well, I do run into a lot of people in my work," he would say before heading to the next door.

Wirth knew Crown Hill well. Each Sunday in the warm months he visited his mother's grave in Section 78, Lot 89 to leave a bouquet of flowers. Her headstone was a double one, with his name and birth date already inscribed. Knowing he was alone, he had also taken care of his funeral, paying Flanner and Buchanan $749.26 for a gray casket and the burial expenses. Not too many years later, *Star* columnist Tom Keating wrote a profound article about Wirth, who explained his sales psychology and philosophy of life. He understood his place in the social hierarchy, yet recognized his capacity to make the world a better place. He told Keating, "There won't be much of a dent in the world when I die, but at least I can say I made an honest-to-God try to do what I did as a nice man."

On January 30, 1971, Wirth died of a heart attack in a north side supermarket, where he was waiting for the weekly shipment of his favorite bread. There was some initial concern about the funeral arrangements, but then folks learned that Herbie had taken care of things. He had specified he did not want a service in a funeral home or church. He just wanted a graveside service at the cemetery—"And that some people be there." Keating again wrote about Wirth in the *Star,* telling his readers that the Crown Hill service for him would be at 10:00 a.m. on Wednesday morning, and the minister would be at the Thirty-fourth Street gate to meet anyone wishing to attend. "It would be a shame if no one showed up," Keating wrote.

People showed up. Droves of people showed up. Hundreds of cars. A thousand mourners. Rich and poor, black and white, young and old, hippie, soldier, businessman, all gathered together in Crown Hill to remember a nice man. As it turned out, one of Crown Hill's largest memorial services was not for a statesman, a celebrity, or a plutocrat. It was for Wirth. Inspired by the outpouring of care, Robert C. Braun, HLFI director, rushed to the Waiting Station tower, where the freshly reroped cemetery bell had hung unrung for forty years. Braun began pulling the bell rope, tolling, tolling, for a half hour until his hands were blistered, and then he tolled the slow, mournful death knell for one small man who succeeded in making the world a little better place.

According to Keating, "Someone brought a large guest book to the grave and most of the people present signed it before leaving. Because Herbie had no relatives, the book was placed in the casket with him. It was a very full book."

GLORY OF GOD WITH THANKSGIVING FOR THE WONDERFUL

DISCIPLINE
COMPASSION

GREAT
EXPECTATIONS

TO THE
MEMORY OF
THE FAMILY
OF ELI LILLY

# 7

## THE GREAT CITY, 1980–2000

Urban revitalization saved Indianapolis just in the nick of time. During the 1970s and 1980s, urban decay ate at Indianapolis. Unigov, the 1970 consolidation of city and county governments, had pushed the city's energy far out into the suburbs. Though the city's population had dramatically risen to 744,624 with the Unigov expansion, the Indianapolis downtown slumbered—Naptown was the city's discomforting, but appropriate, moniker.

Intense urban planning and ambitious public-private initiatives led by the Richard Lugar and William Hudnut III mayoral administrations, however, began to turn things around. Indianapolis wanted to be "the Great American City." And a great American city needed a professional football team. In 1982 construction began on the $77.5 million Hoosier Dome. Then in the morning hours of March 29, 1984, the city got its team when fifteen Mayflower trucks rolled into town with the former Baltimore Colts organization. With Maryland's eminent domain seizure of the Colts imminent, owner Robert Irsay chose to take Indianapolis up on its generous offer. Nothing signaled Indianapolis's arrival in the big leagues like the Colts.

Other civic initiatives were coming together as well. By the 1980s the enormous capital and social investment in the Indiana University–Purdue University at Indianapolis campus was paying dividends. Gargantuan sports facilities arose in the central city. In 1987 the Pan-American Games and the Indianapolis Museum of Art's blockbuster Latin American show, *Art of the Fantastic*, built further confidence. As the 1990s dawned, skyscrapers began to rise, and after a stutter-step beginning, the landmark Circle Centre started to take shape. Restorations of the Circle Theater and the City Market reinvigorated culture and cuisine. The Indianapolis Canal Walk, the Eiteljorg Museum of American Indians and Western Art, and the White River State Park added further tourist draws that were later bolstered by the Indiana State Museum, Victory Field, and the National Collegiate Athletic Association Hall of Champions. From the 1970s to the late 1990s, about $4 billion of public-private money was spent in downtown Indianapolis. Another $168 million was invested in professional and amateur sports facilities. By the mid-1990s, people had a good reason to come back downtown. Naptown had reawakened.

Crown Hill was part of the city's renaissance. Despite the challenges in the decades following World War II, Crown Hill was in good shape at the beginning of the 1980s. The cemetery was worth about $10 million. The Perpetual Care Fund, the endowment mandated by state law for ongoing cemetery maintenance, was worth almost $3 million. There were annual sales of about $250,000, with an operating budget of $895,000. The staff had fifteen salaried employees, twenty-one full-time maintenance workers, and twenty-five seasonal employees. There was solid leadership and a strong board. The place was decently maintained, but the corporators wanted to make it better.

In 1984 the Board of Corporators organized the Crown Hill Heritage Foundation, a 501(c)(3) not-for-profit corporation dedicated to preserving the cemetery's historic buildings and grounds. In 1985 the cemetery embarked on a much-needed rehabilitation of Crown Hill's three miles of brick and wrought-iron fencing. Time, weather, and repeated car crashes had wreaked havoc on the old fence that was completed in the 1920s. All 615 brick columns needed to be "restructured." The $600,000 restoration work was projected to take a few years to complete. Not long after, the Subway got a $150,000 restoration. In 1993 Stewart D. Tompkins, the foundation's president, announced that the foundation had spent $1 million in recent years and anticipated spending a like amount in the following six years.

The same year the fence project began, Crown Hill commissioned sculptor David L. Rodgers to construct a massive limestone sculpture, called *Equatorial Sundial*. Designed as a site-specific sculpture to be installed in front of the Community Mausoleum, the sundial was fabricated in five giant pieces at the Woolery Stone Company in Bloomington, Indiana, during 1986 and 1987, and then assembled and finished on site by Rodgers during 1987. Rodgers wanted his sundial to stimulate cemetery visitors to consider their place in time, space, and nature, as well as the relationship between human time and cosmic time. Through the passage of the day's light on his functional sundial, Rodgers artistically connected the day's cyclic birth, maturation, and conclusion to the beginning, development, and passing of each human life. "We wanted to build something that would catch the interest of the public," said Tompkins.

The construction of the popular garden crypts continued apace. In 1987 the corporators learned that preselling was going well on garden crypt IV, which was scheduled for completion in 1989. A subsidiary of the Gibraltar corporation, a diversified Indianapolis cemetery and mortuary organization, was bidding on the construction project. Within a few years, Gibraltar owned fifty-one cemeteries and nineteen funeral homes in fourteen states, besides the crypt construction company and a third-party sales organization. In 1993 the corporators announced plans for the Abbey, a new $1.2 million garden mausoleum complex. Designed by Patrick L. Fly, the Abbey was clad in Indiana limestone and Carnelian granite. In 1996 Gibraltar won the Crown Hill contract to build the 448-crypt, seven-level Pine Garden mausoleum in the southeast quadrant of the cemetery.

In 1996 Crown Hill established the cemetery's Scattering Garden in a wooded area of the south grounds. Located on a half-acre plot, the Scattering Garden's winding mulch pathways lead through a forest glade. The cemetery was responding to requests by family members who wanted a natural setting to scatter the ashes of their loved ones. In part, Crown Hill organized the garden to ease the concerns of family members about the need to obtain a legal permit to scatter remains outside of the cemetery.

The undeveloped land at the north edge of Crown Hill attracted interested parties in the 1990s. Woodstock Country Club wanted to lease it for a golf course. The International School wanted it for playing fields. Butler University inquired about buying it for a School of Religion. After consideration, the corporators concluded in early 1999: "Crown Hill is not interested in looking to utilization of the land, at this point." At the 1999 annual corporator meeting, President Keith Norwalk presented his assessment on Crown Hill as it approached the millennium. He listed the accomplishments: a growing Perpetual Care Fund, increasing cemetery and funeral home sales, and "facilities that are unparalleled in scope and quality." He summarized by saying, "The last few years have presented Crown Hill with some great challenges and some unique opportunities. The dynamics

*Opposite:* Equatorial Sundial, *a work of polished limestone by sculptor David L. Rodgers, purported to be Indiana's largest functioning equatorial sundial.*

of a changing market have challenged us. The interfacing of a new corporation with a 135-year-old corporation has challenged us. But, we are moving in the right direction."

As it has been since the beginning of Crown Hill, grieving families arranged for the cemetery's most heartfelt art. Jeffrey Bratton was a student at North Central High School who had an idea for a contemporary bronze sculpture of akimbo forms. He constructed a model of seven brooding upright rectangles, but before he could execute his plan, he died of cancer. After he was buried in June 1980 in Section 75, Lot 1, his parents commis-

sioned an Ohio artist to cast a bronze sculpture of Bratton's art in tribute to his memory.

In spite of the cost, many still yearned for the beauty and prestige of a private mauso-leum. William Ramier Amthor ran a successful import-export company in San Francisco. When he died in early 1983 he left money for an elegant Gothic-influenced mausoleum with a stained-glass mosaic window. But Amthor did not leave his family enough money for a whole tomb, so they just built the front wall and called it done. They erected the monu-ment in Section 9, Lot 18, where it stood as mute testimony to Amthor and his fine taste. The gravestone inscription read, "God is my strength and power and he maketh my way perfect."

In 1989 the Bane family, who owned an advertising agency and an international carpet-cleaning corporation, built the most recent of Crown Hill's fifty-seven mausoleums. Situated on the slope of Crown Hill, the restrained gray Bane tomb with its graceful staircase winding through landscaped hedges resonates solemnity. "It was my mom's original thought," William J. Bane told author W. C. Madden. "She thought a mausoleum

was the way to go. She didn't want to be buried in the ground." Mom must also have had a grand sense of whimsy. The Banes had a stained-glass window installed in their mausoleum that included a squirrel, a rabbit, and a red-bearded leprechaun wearing a large green hat.

After a long and fruitful sojourn at the Waiting Station, Historic Landmarks Foundation of Indiana moved into its own office building on Michigan Street near IUPUI in 1990. With HLFI gone, the Center for Attitudinal Healing of Indianapolis, later named The Life Center, subleased the Waiting Station. But in the mid-1990s the Crown Hill management decided to reoc-cupy the building after a twenty-five-year hiatus. The managers first considered using it for a flower shop, then as a Rock of Ages monument showroom. The Crown Hill Heritage Foundation soon also moved into the Waiting Station. The foundation had raised $1.8 million by 1997. A few years later, $500,000 was used to restore the Waiting Station. Shortly thereafter, the founda-tion raised $3.2 million for the restoration of the Gothic Chapel, the new vestibule, planting of the Fortune Family gardens, and installation of the street lamps leading from the Thirty-fourth Street Gate to the chapel.

The Waiting Station was also used as a gathering point for the cemetery's increasing number of tours. As part of the cemetery's ongoing strategy of public relations, the foundation's staff and volunteers expanded the cemetery's specialized tours program, including ones focused on the Civil War, women, African Americans, literary and art figures, trees, and Crown Hill found-ers, just to name a few. In the late 1980s the cemetery started presenting Victorian Days, with role players depicting India-napolis's yesteryear. Popular almost immediately, eight hundred people were attending the event by 1993; that figure jumped to 3,200 people in 1997. The "Run through Hoosier History" run/walk event was pulling another throng into the cemetery. More than five hundred attended the rededication of the Confederate Mound in 1993 when Representative Andrew Jacobs Jr. spoke. There were concerts, art fairs, poetry readings, Easter egg hunts, and photography contests. The Susurrus Dance Company per-

formed a sacred dance at the James Whitcomb Riley memorial, where a crowd of spectators circled around the monument as they followed the dancers, sometimes joining the dance themselves—an *Indianapolis Star* reviewer called it "a once-in-a-lifetime work." Through the promotion and participation in these events, a new generation rediscovered Crown Hill as something far more than a burial place.

Thieves and vandals also unfortunately discovered Crown Hill. Theft and vandalism was a perennial problem in most cemeteries, and Crown Hill was no different despite round-the-clock security. Missing statuary and pots were not uncommon. Gravestones were pushed over—and sometimes the tombstones retaliated: A 1986 *Star* article noted one hapless vandal who was trapped under a headstone he had toppled. Administrators talked of a monument with a mounting pin sticking up where a bronze sculpture used to stand; of General Abel Streight's bronze bust being found on the ground near the National Cemetery, where the thieves had abandoned it.

In 1995 a brazen (and strong) thief made off with the eight-hundred-pound stone hunting dog that had faithfully lay at Charles Frese's grave since the 1880s. The cemetery publicized the theft. Some months later, a former Crown Hill docent, Sheila Riley, spotted an article in an antiques publication about the arrest of a gang of graveyard thieves operating out of New Orleans and upstate New York. She immediately recognized Frese's pooch in the story's photograph. The dog was sitting outside a storage unit in Ray Brook, New York. After contacting the police and going through eight months of procedural complexity, Crown Hill paid seven hundred dollars in shipping to get the Frese dog back to his rightful home in Section 34.

A year after the Frese dog returned to Crown Hill, another gang of thieves stole six antique funerary urns, including an ornate cast-iron vessel from the grave site of President Benjamin Harrison. In late June 2000 an individual was charged with the theft of hundreds of pieces of funerary art from Indiana cemeteries, including the six urns from Crown Hill. The urns had been sold to southern Indiana antique dealers for two to three hundred dollars each. By June 28, 2000, the Crown Hill urns were back, with even better security measures.

Memorial Day services wound down in the decades after the Cold War. The grass was still clipped and the flags still snapped. The military bands still played and the leaders still gave their stirring speeches. But by 1993 only about a thousand people attended the Crown Hill service, a dramatic departure from the tens of thousands that thronged the cemetery earlier in the century. A small Memorial Day contretemps erupted in 1995 when the local media ballyhooed Crown Hill's decision to prohibit flower poles and standing baskets. "Crown Hill Cemetery to Ban Hanging Flower Stands," the headlines read. Returning to Crown Hill's historic landscape aesthetic and standards, the cemetery management had decided to eliminate the poles and urns, as they created an untenable maintenance problem. Though television crews flocked to cover the flap, the Crown Hill administrators soon had the story under control with well-organized spin control. Through the 1990s the Memorial Day crowds continued to dwindle. When only about two hundred people showed up for the Memorial Day observances in 1998, R. L. Judd wrote a letter to the *Star*, noting the Broad

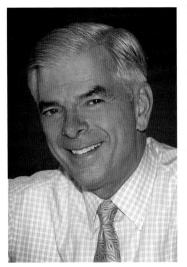

*Keith Norwalk*

Ripple bars were overflowing when he drove home from the sparsely attended Crown Hill ceremony.

The Crown Hill organizational chart had changed since 1945, when Howard T. Wood was hired as the replacement for Superintendent Raymond E. Siebert. In 1960 Wood's title was changed to executive vice president, and then in 1988 he was named as Crown Hill's

president. In 1991 Tompkins, Crown Hill's executive vice president, retired after more than fifteen years of service.

At its April 1991 annual meeting, the board of corporators welcomed Keith Norwalk as the new Crown Hill president. Cut from the same cloth as other important Crown Hill superintendents, Norwalk was destined to be another strong, long-lived leader.

At the 1991 annual meeting, the corporators again focused on the feasibility of adding a funeral home to Crown Hill. The board discussion about adding a mortuary to Crown Hill had been long and complicated. Feeling the industry pressure, the board of corporators increasingly saw funeral services as an outgrowth of the cemetery's mission and as a way to increase revenues to insure Crown Hill stayed on a strong financial footing. In 1987 the corporators began discussions with funeral home chains about opening an on-site mortuary. By 1988 the corporators were entertaining proposals from four funeral home

chains, though it voted the following year to put the funeral home project "in abeyance."

It was an idea that would not die, and in early 1992 the board approved a contract with J. Stuart Todd, Architect, to draw up plans for the mortuary, and the ground breaking was held in May 1992. The budget was $1.5 million. When the Crown Hill Funeral Home opened March 1, 1993, Norwalk stated the funeral home was "a culmination of many years of research and effort by the staff and Board of Managers." Norwalk told reporters that the fifteen thousand-square-foot funeral home would eliminate "logistical challenges" for grieving families who could now take care of everything in one place. "We have space for burials for over the next 200 years," he said.

By 1995 the increasing popularity of cremations was impacting Crown Hill's revenue stream, as they were less expensive than burials. As the numbers increased through the 1980s, the cemetery added a new crematorium in 1990 to handle the need.

*Opposite and above: Crown Hill Cemetery administrative offices, Crown Hill Funeral Home, Memorial Chapel, and Celebration Hall located on the north grounds of the cemetery at Thirty-Eighth Street and Clarendon Road.*

While cremations in Indiana were relatively low by national standards, the percentages were rising. With the funeral home, Crown Hill also faced the legal need to keep the not-for-profit cemetery financially separate from the for-profit mortuary, so combined sales forces needed rigorous accounting. Running the combined cemetery-mortuary operation proved to be a challenging balancing act.

As the decades progressed, the stewardship of Crown Hill was passed down to generation after generation of corporators: the Lillys, Fletchers, Ayres, Peacocks, Hollidays, Rhodehamels, Woollens, Liebers, Elders, Ruddells, Adams, Browns, Mothersheads, and Frenzels among them—each generation's sons following fathers or uncles in cadenced lineages. "It became very much a family affair," said Berkley W. Duck III, himself the fifth in his family line to sit on the board, going back to his great-great-grandfather, John S. Spann, who joined the corporators in 1880. While the corporators continued their multigenerational task of sustaining an enormous community institution out of an enduring sense of honor and loyalty, board membership was understood to be a lifetime commitment.

In the 1990s Norwalk began to talk about the need to "contemporize" the board of corporators with diversification, specifically with women and African Americans. The board agreed it was time to change. "We began to pull back from the family lineage concept. Some thought it was somewhat of a birthright," said Duck. In the spring of 1997, the Crown Hill Board announced the cemetery's first female and African American corporators. It was big enough news that the *Star* ran a large article, headlined, "Crown Hill Cemetery welcomes first female, black board members." Hilary Stout Salatich, a Conseco Capital Management executive and civic leader, was asked to join. "My uncle, Walt Kuhn, served on the Board, so I had a connection. But I think they were really trying to add a woman," Salatich said in 2011. "Since then they've added a number of other women, so I'm not the Lone Ranger."

Milton O. Thompson was part of a groundbreaking African American family. His father, O. C. Thompson, started the Thompson Brothers Unit Step concrete step company in 1958, when he relocated his family from Illinois to Indianapolis. Over time, O. C. and a brother built the company into one of the city's

# The Corporators
# A Roll of Honor

*From* The Story of Crown Hill *(1928) by Anna Nicholas*

One who delves even in a limited way into the early history of Indianapolis can hardly fail to be impressed by the number of really big men who figured in the development of the city—"big" in the sense of possessing public spirit, a broad outlook, foresight and an unselfish willingness to do their part in promoting the fortunes of their home community.

This one transaction alone is enough to put the names of the thirty citizens on a roll of honor, so important an institution has Crown Hill become, so greatly has it added to the city's prestige by the unusual character of the system by which it is financed and by its remarkable natural beauty, aided and abetted by art.

They were men of vision, these corporators, which is quite a different thing from being visionaries. They looked ahead with prophetic eyes and saw possibilities that to others were not visible. They saw the State capital as a future city in the line of traffic between the growing riches of the West and the markets of the East; they saw a good class of enterprising citizenship in their town and state; they foresaw growth—and they put their projected cemetery as far out from the existing town as they dared. They did not have the prescience to envisage a city that reached to Broad Ripple miles beyond Crown Hill, or they might have faced greater ridicule than any at first received—for their venture was regarded as impractical and ill-judged—and have chosen a site more than three and a half miles from the town's center. But they did insist on a large acreage. Six hundred acres seemed to some of their fellow townsmen a preposterous over-estimate of future needs. No cemetery in the country, even near the largest cities, had at that time so much ground.

These men were right. The thirty men who organized the Crown Hill Corporation were only typical of the settlers who had brought Indianapolis through its forty years of life to where it was in the early sixties.

These thirty men were unselfish because, when they might have made the cemetery a personal commercial undertaking and an investment for their own profit, as had been and still is a common procedure in many communities, they unanimously agreed that no money from the sale of lots should go to individual or corporate benefit, but as related elsewhere, that all profits beyond expenses of maintaining the cemetery in proper condition should go into a fund for future maintenance and care of the grounds when income should cease. This agreement, which is one of the articles of association, has been scrupulously observed. Its existence has given the place an element of permanence that seldom exists in a cemetery overtaken by the growth of a city, and that no doubt adds greatly to the sense of security and satisfaction with which lot owners and those who have friends sleeping their last sleep there regard the place.

The board of corporators is self-perpetuating. When a vacancy occurs through death or resignation the board elects another to fill his place, giving a preference to a son of the former member when possible. The consequence has been a harmony of feeling and unity of action quite unusual in so large an association. There has also existed among the corporators a sense of responsibility and a pride in the care and improvement of the cemetery that could not be greater if the undertaking were of personal benefit. Men have a distinct pride of membership.

# CROWN HILL CEMETERY BOARD OF CORPORATORS

This chart shows in chronological order the individuals who have held the various chairs of the Board of Corporators of the Cemetery. The original corporators are shown in the left column with their successors to the right. The current board member's names are in bold on the far right.

| | | | | | | | | | |
|---|---|---|---|---|---|---|---|---|---|
| ROACHE Addison L., 1863 | AYRES Frederic M., 1906 | AYRES Lyman S., 1940 | PEACOCK John E. D. Jr., 1997 | | | | | | |
| MARTINDALE Elijah B., 1863 | LILLY Josiah K. Sr., 1910 | LILLY Eli, 1948 | HANLEY William A. Jr., 1977 | | | | | | |
| HUBBARD William S., 1863 | HUBBARD William H., 1908 | DANIELS Joseph J., 1920 | HOLLIDAY John H., 1973 | ROGERS Randall D., 2001 | | | | | |
| KITCHEN John M., 1863 | LANDON Hugh McK., 1916 | CAIN Joseph E., 1947 | RAUCH John G., 1963 | SALATICH Hilary S., 1997 | | | | | |
| BROWNING Robert, 1863 | RUNNELS O. Solis, 1891 | McCULLOCH Carleton B., 1930 | HOKE Frank, 1957 | WISHARD Gordon D., 1990 | | | | | |
| WALLACE William, 1863 | ELDER John R., 1891 | ELDER William J., 1908 | ELDER Bowman, 1940 | ELDER William J., 1955 | ELDER William L. Jr., 1994 | | | | |
| VAJEN John H., 1863 | RUDDELL Almus G., 1917 | RUDDELL James H., 1949 | LILLY Eli II, 1984 | RUDDELL Richard A., 2004 | MacALLISTER Chris, 2012 | | | | |
| FLETCHER S. A. Jr., 1863 | WALLICK John F., 1895 | MARTINDALE Charles, 1922 | BOHLEN August, 1937 | FAILEY Robert B. Jr., 1971 | FAILEY John N., 2007 | | | | |
| NEW John C., 1863 | NEW Harry S., 1906 | MacDONALD John A., 1937 | BRADLEY C. Harvey, 1953 | BRADLEY C. Harvey Jr., 1973 | PEACOCK Sally Bradley, 2003 | | | | |
| McCARTY Nicholas, 1863 | NICHOLSON Meredith, 1916 | NICHOLSON Meredith Jr., 1948 | ALIG C. O. Jr., 1969 | BINFORD Thomas W., 1982 | ALIG Cornelius, M., 1990 | | | | |
| LORD John M., 1863 | HOLLIDAY John H., 1880 | HOLLIDAY Alex H., 1922 | HITZ Benjamin H., 1932 | RHODEHAMEL Harley W. Jr., 1950 | RHODEHAMEL William A., 1997 | | | | |
| ARMSTRONG John, 1863 | MALOTT Volney T., 1902 | WOOLLEN Evans, 1922 | WOOLLEN Evans Jr., 1942 | WOOLLEN Evans, 1959 | FORTUNE Russell III, 1990 | | | | |
| ROCKWOOD William Otis, 1863 | SPANN John S., 1880 | SPANN Thomas H., 1898 | DUCK Berkley W., 1922 | DUCK Berkley W. Jr., 1940 | DUCK Berkley W. III, 1989 | | | | |
| LIEBER Herman, 1863 | LIEBER Otto R., 1908 | LIEBER Herman P., 1934 | LIEBER Kurt, 1940 | LIEBER William L., 1977 | TOBIAS Marianne W., 2011 | | | | |
| MORRIS Thomas A., 1863 | FLETCHER Jesse, 1904 | DAY Thomas C., 1910 | DAY Frederick H., 1935 | DAY Frederick H. Jr., 1952 | DAY Frederick J., 1998 | | | | |
| LOVE John, 1863 | BATES Hervey Sr., 1881 | BATES Hervey Jr., 1929 | APPEL Fred G., 1936 | APPEL John C., 1962 | APPEL Daniel C., 1990 | APPEL Steve, 2011 | | | |
| MORRISON William H., 1863 | JAMESON Patrick H., 1881 | FLETCHER S. A., 1911 | FRENZEL John P. Jr., 1935 | FRENZEL Otto N. Jr., 1950 | FRENZEL Otto N. III, 1988 | FRENZEL Otto N. IV, 1994 | | | |
| HAUGHEY Theodore P., 1863 | DUNCAN John S., 1893 | CHISLETT John, 1915 | BROWN Arthur V., 1917 | BROWN Volney M., 1950 | MOTHERSHEAD Wilson, 1967 | KRUSE Katharine Mothershead, 2001 | | | |
| TOUSEY George, 1863 | MANSUR William, 1874 | CLAYPOOL Edward F., 1893 | MARMON Walter C., 1911 | GRIFFITH William C., 1941 | GRIFFITH William C. Jr., 1970 | GRIFFITH C. Perry Jr., 1986 | | | |
| SHARPE Thomas H., 1863 | HARRISON Benjamin, 1893 | BARNES Albert A., 1901 | STALNAKER Frank D., 1928 | CANNON Fermor S., 1933 | KUHN Walter W. Jr., 1974 | WOOD Richard D., 1978 | | | |
| RAY James M., 1863 | BROWN James W., 1881 | BALS Henry G. C., 1892 | DANIELS Edward, 1907 | BENNETT Henry W., 1919 | BENNETT Edward J., 1936 | BENNETT Edward J. Jr., 1976 | | | |
| BUTLER Ovid, 1863 | BLAKE John G., 1882 | HOLLIDAY William J., 1893 | HORNBROOK Henry H., 1918 | SULLIVAN Reginald H., 1936 | HOLLETT Byron P., 1970 | TOBIAS Randall L., 2000 | THORNTON Lindsay Elder, 2013 | | |
| SHEETS William, 1863 | CHURCHMAN Frank M., 1871 | VINTON Merrick E., 1892 | MANSUR Charles W., 1896 | HUME George E., 1914 | BROWN Garvin M., 1935 | SUTPHIN Dudley V., 1967 | SUTPHIN Charles P., 2006 | | |
| CARMICHAEL Jesse D., 1863 | EKIN James A., 1867 | JACKSON William N., 1871 | HENDRICKS Victor K., 1901 | ENGLISH William E., 1908 | MORRIS Donald S., 1926 | FAIRBANKS Richard M., 1965 | BIRGE Jonathan L., 2000 | | |
| VINTON Almus E., 1863 | FERGUSON James C., 1871 | HENDRICKS Allen W., 1885 | HANNA Hugh H., 1888 | HOWE Thomas C., 1921 | LESH Perry W., 1934 | LESH Charles Perry, 1984 | THOMPSON Milton O., 1997 | | |
| BLAKE James, 1863 | FLETCHER Elijah T., 1871 | FLETCHER Ingram, 1880 | FLETCHER Allen M., 1885 | FLETCHER S. J., 1900 | REVEAL William O., 1910 | ROCKWOOD William M., 1928 | COLLETT John P., 1946 | BELL Tanya, 2012 | |
| FLETCHER Calvin, 1863 | KING Edward, 1866 | AYRES Lyman S., 1888 | MILLER Wm. H. H., 1896 | FESLER James W., 1917 | MARTINDALE Elijah B., 1950 | CRAFT Edwin M. Jr., 1968 | DUNN Edward G., 1979 | DUNN Edward G. Jr., 2000 | |
| TODD Charles N., 1863 | YANDES George B., 1889 | FAIRBANKS Charles W., 1913 | MILLER Samuel D., 1920 | MILLER Sidney S., 1940 | MILLER Samuel D. II, 1948 | WILLIAMS John G., 1954 | CHAMBERS David L. Jr., 1973 | TUCKER Fred C. III, 1985 | |
| CROSSLAND Jacob A., 1863 | NEWCOMER Freeman S., 1882 | RAND Frederick, 1890 | MAYER Ferdinand L., 1897 | DICKSON Fred C., 1915 | OGLE Kenneth, 1937 | GALLAHUE Dudley R., 1943 | JOHNSON Nelson G., 1971 | JOHNSON Jefferson N., 1998 | LAWSON Catherine W., 2008 |
| YANDES Daniel, 1863 | MORTON Oliver P., 1867 | HORD Oscar B., 1878 | COBURN John, 1888 | JORDAN Arthur, 1908 | ADAMS William Ray, 1935 | ADAMS Roy Elder, 1940 | ADAMS Reily G., 1950 | ADAMS R. Morris, 1983 | WOODARD-VAN RIPER Edna, 2004 |

most respected contractors, wholesaling steps regionally and constructing stairs for high-profile projects, such as the Hoosier Dome. In November 1963 the Thompson brothers' success garnered a front-page article in *Ebony* magazine.

After playing quarterback for the North Central High School football team in the early 1970s, Thompson went on to Wittenberg University, where he was an All-American baseball player. With his family emphasizing education, Thompson graduated from the Indiana University School of Law. He served as deputy Marion County prosecutor before founding the Grand Slam sports and entertainment management companies, and continuing his work as an attorney. Beyond serving on numerous boards, Thompson was also the voice of the television game show, *Hoosier Know It Alls*. Thompson talked about his connections to board members that began in high school and were strengthened through his university years and extensive civic work. Thompson said, "Keith Norwalk approached me about Crown Hill's need for a 'more contemporary governance structure.' I saw myself serving a bridging responsibility." As his parents were both buried in Crown Hill's Section 100, Lot 278, Thompson also was a "property owner," a critical requirement to be a corporator. "I was a safe choice," he said about his

appointment as the first African American corporator. Speaking of his parents' economic and civic success in a country of racial discrimination, and of the long respectful funeral cortege for his mother, Mary Lee, which stretched in a seemingly endless stream back up Route 421 from the cemetery, Thompson said, "I've got a responsibility."

In 2001 Katharine Mothershead Kruse was the second woman appointed to the board. Kruse's great-grandfather, Volney T. Malott, began serving as a corporator in 1902, then the line switched to the Browns, her grandfather, Arthur V., and uncle, Volney M., passing on to her father, Wilson Mothershead. When he died, his position passed on to Gordon Wishard, as there were no males in the family to take the seat. "It always went to gentlemen, not ladies," Kruse said. It was painful to her, someone who had absorbed the sense of duty toward Crown Hill from her forebears. "So many memories," she said, "so many ancestors, so much feeling. It's that sense of history, of belonging. People take that seriously. There was a real sense of duty. It sunk in." So

> In 2001 Katharine Mothershead Kruse was the second woman appointed to the board.

# HARRISON ULLMAN

Harrison Ullman was a crusading journalist who used provocation and wit to uncover the truth. Born in Mishawaka and educated at Indiana University, Ullman was a forty-five-year veteran of Indianapolis journalism, including a ten-year stint at the *Indianapolis Star* and a decade as Indiana University–Purdue University at Indianapolis's director of public relations. His most visible posi-

tion was as the editor of the alternative newsweekly *Nuvo* from 1992 until just before his death in 2000. During his long career, Ullman exposed controversial issues, from animal rights and arts support to court-mandated busing, drunk cops, unconstitutional drug busts, environmental disaster cover-ups, and criticisms of Mayor Stephen Goldsmith's privatization initiatives. During his editorship, *Nuvo*'s

circulation grew from 20,000 to 55,000. He was a hard-nosed editor. *Nuvo*'s publisher/editor Kevin McKinney told a reporter after Ullman's death, "He understood that power corrupts. He knew that he was a force because of his memory, and because of his craft, he was able to protect people."

In February 2000 Ullman learned he had cancer. Within two months, he was when Kruse was named to the board she and Salatich agreed, "OK, 'bout time." Kruse said the corporators have continued to reach out to diverse groups since then. "They saw the light," she said. "They continue to see the light."

Beyond the tens of thousands of African Americans buried in Crown Hill, the cemetery is the final destination for an extraordinary spectrum of humanity, including the Muslim departed in Section 114. Syed Anwar Shah, the head of the Indianapolis Muslim Community Association's burial committee, talked about the importance of cemeteries in the Islamic tradition: "At our holiday of Eid—a prayer festival—after we go to the mosque, before we go to the parties, we stop at the cemetery and pay our respects. When Muslims come from out of town, they go to the local cemetery to pay respects. It is part of our tradition." The Muslim community was drawn to Crown Hill because, in Shah's words, the cemetery was "multi-cultural, multi-religious. It is a very historical place in Indiana. And it is very close to our mosque."

Shah's uncle was the first interment in Section 114 in 1994. His uncle, Syed Esmail Shah, had come from Pakistan to visit Indianapolis in 1993. To give his uncle a sense of America, Syed and his sons took him on a monthlong, nearly nine-thousand-

mile tour of the western United States. "He was very happy I showed him the United States," Shah said. "At the Grand Canyon, he started praying about the beauty of God; the beauty of heaven. He saw it in the mountains."

While still in Indianapolis in February 1994, Shah's uncle died of sudden heart failure. He contacted his family in Pakistan about making arrangements to fly his uncle's remains back. But within a few hours, the family called back, saying that he should be buried in Crown Hill. As part of his tour of Indianapolis, Shah had taken his uncle to visit Crown Hill. "My uncle, he said, 'What a beautiful place to be buried.' He quoted the prophet, who said, 'If there is greenery on your grave, God will have mercy on your body.' My uncle had written his daughter in Pakistan and told her, 'If I die in America, I want to be buried in America.' He had a premonition." Syed was interred in Section 114, Lot 78A on February 21, 1994. There are now more than a hundred Muslims buried facing Kaaba in Crown Hill's Muslim Section 114, with room for more than 3,500 interments.

Lawrence P. "Larry" Godfroy was an Indianapolis resident for many years. He was also the chief of the Miami Indians, one of the state's most powerful tribes in the early days of European settlement. Under the charismatic Little Turtle, the

gone, as the aggressive cancer quickly spread to his lungs and spine. "Man, Harrison Ullman died fast," *Indianapolis Business Journal*'s Chris Katterjohn wrote in a begrudging salute column. There were many other salutes to Ullman from across the full political spectrum: the Indiana State Teacher's Association, the Indiana State Medical Association, and the American Civil Liberties Union all honored him.

Conservative congressman Mike Pence praised his integrity and journalistic professionalism. The day before Ullman died, Governor Frank O'Bannon named him as a Sagamore of the Wabash. In 2003 Ullman was inducted into the Indiana Journalism Hall of Fame, the only editor of an alternative weekly to be so honored. "He had the journalistic courage to take on the power structure, tell the king he

had no clothes, unmask deceitfulness and self-righteousness, and raise important questions about conflicts of interest and unintended consequences of public policies," former Indianapolis mayor William Hudnut III said about Ullman. "Every community needs at least one Harrison Ullmann, preferably more." Ullman was entombed in the Court of Remembrance in the Community Mausoleum.

Miami successfully fought the incursions of the white settlers into the Miami homeland in the late eighteenth century. Godfroy's great-grandfather was Francois Godfroy, the last war chief of the Miami. Primarily centered along the upper Wabash River, the Miami had stubbornly maintained their tribal identity. "The persistent people," they sometimes called themselves, as they repeatedly petitioned for tribal recognition by the federal government. In 1961 the Indiana Miami council elected Godfroy as their council chairman. Lumkekumwah the Miami called him, meaning Stamp Hard. When Godfroy was eighty-eight, he joined the Council of the Miami Nation that represented the far-flung Miami tribe. After his death, Godfroy was buried May 6, 1986, in Section 60, Lot 509.

By 1993 there were more than 173,000 people buried in Crown Hill. Among them were many notable sports, entertainment, and arts figures who were interred in the 1980s and 1990s. Born in 1935 Bailey Robertson was a basketball star at Crispus Attucks High School. Known as "Flap" because of his flamboyant wrist-flipping shots, Bailey served as a role model for his younger brother, Oscar. Bailey took the Crispus Attucks team to the Final Four in 1951. After graduation, Robertson helped Indiana Central College (later known as the University of Indianapolis) get into the top ten small college rankings. At the school, he ranked in the top five in the country in scoring, was an All-American twice, and also achieved renown for his world-class trash talking. He was not called Flap for nothing. After college, he played for both the Harlem Ambassadors and with Harlem Globetrotters in Europe and Latin America, as well as with the U.S. Army Special Services unit in Europe while he was in the service. Like so many African American athletes of his day, Robertson's career was circumscribed by racism at the high school, collegiate, and professional levels. After returning from the army, Robertson worked for the City of Cincinnati. He was inducted into the Indiana Basketball Hall of Fame in 1990. Robertson died on January 6, 1994. Following his funeral, he was buried in Section 73, Lot 77 in Crown Hill, just a few miles from the high school where he first achieved glory.

Jim Hurtubise was an old-school race driver. Besides driving sprint and stock cars, he drove in the Indianapolis 500 ten times, including his first 500 run in 1960, when he was the fastest qualifier and rookie of the year. Born on December 5, 1932, in upstate New York, he raced in various circuits for decades, finishing in the top ten of the United States Auto Club Championship Car series thirty-eight times. After suffering serious burns in a crash during the 1964 Rex Mays Classic in Milwaukee, doctors asked Hurtubise how he wanted them to shape his mangled hands. "Just make 'em so I can hold a steering wheel," he replied. After his death of a heart attack on January 6, 1989, near his home in Port Arthur, Texas, he was returned to Indianapolis to be entombed in the Community Mausoleum, D-8, 2DD.

Most people knew Thomas W. Binford as the Indianapolis 500's chief steward. He served twenty-two years in that position, longer than anyone else. But that was just his most public face. For decades, as CEO of Indiana National Bank, Binford was among Indianapolis's liveliest movers and shakers, instrumental in bringing the Indiana Pacers and Colts to town. He was the founder and leader of numerous businesses and civic institutions, including the Urban League of Indianapolis. Beginning in 1982 he served as a Crown Hill corporator. A Phi Beta Kappa Princeton graduate, Binford served as DePauw University's president, and as the Pacers president. He had some range. He was seventy-four when he died on January 14, 1999, of a cerebral hemorrhage. He was buried in Section 61, Lot 26, where a sleek, contemporary Binford family monument memorialized him, as did renaming a northwest Indianapolis street as Binford Boulevard.

Born in 1883 in the Illinois border hamlet of Hymera, Indiana, Lottie Lyons Grow was a lifelong Hoosier, who had a very long art career as a painter, etcher, writer, and lecturer. She studied at the Saint Louis Art Institute, the John Herron Institute of Arts, and Marian College (now Marian University). As a member of the Brown County Art Association and the Indiana Art Club, Grow was an active artist, producing her oeuvre of

well-received flower and landscape art. She wrote for numerous publications, including *Newsweek* and *Art Digest* and wrote two books. She presented the first art programs on Indiana television and radio. Prominent in the community, Grow took part in many social organizations, including the American Pen Women, Phi Beta, and the International Platform Association. At the age of eighty-seven she was still submitting her paintings to the Indiana Artists Club exhibitions. When she died in late 1981, Grow was buried in Section 60, Lot 184, next to her husband, Doctor Walter S. Grow, who died in 1945.

Artist and iconoclast Elmer "Taf" Taflinger proclaimed himself to be "a revolting Hoosier." An Indianapolis native, Taflinger studied art under Otto Stark at Manual Training High School while working as a stagehand at the Murat Theatre and at the English Opera House. After high school, he studied art at the New York Art Students League before stage producer David Belasco hired him. Under Belasco, he worked from 1914 to 1922 as an art director, stage manager, and general dogsbody, with duties that included costume, set, and lighting design. After his theater career ended, Taflinger divided his time between New York and Florence. In 1928 he returned to Indianapolis, where he worked with printmakers George Jo and Gordon B. Mess and taught at the Circle Art Academy. In 1934 he established his own art and teaching studio on East Fourteenth Street, and also taught at the Indianapolis Art League (now the Indianapolis Art Center). Taflinger was a volcano of artistic opinion. In 1933 he petitioned the court to change his birthplace to protest the decision by Indiana's Chicago World's Fair committee to award Missourian Thomas Hart Benton a commission to create a set of murals for the state exhibition.

Taflinger remained a controversial figure for the balance of his long and productive life. His best-known art works included the *Apotheosis of Science* mural done in 1938, the fresco *The Triumph of the Ideal* completed in 1940, and the hotly debated Holliday Park installation *The Ruins*. It took twenty years of divisiveness and contention for Taflinger's *Ruins* to finally be dedicated in 1978. Taflinger eventually called his complicated

piece, *Constitution Mall*, which included limestone tablets representing the three races of mankind and three branches of government, a fountain and reflecting pool, twenty-five Grecian statutes, and four classical female figures from the demolished Marion County Courthouse. (Three sister statues from the courthouse went to Crown Hill.)

Taflinger spent his last thirty years working on his autobiography, "Revolting Hoosier, A Modest Autobiography." Unlike *The Ruins*, Taflinger's autobiography never reached full fruition, though a documentary based on his book did come out in the 1990s. After Taflinger's death on August 13, 1981, he was buried in Section 73, Lot 439, where an exceptionally restrained granite gravestone marked the final resting place of a remarkably outspoken artist and activist.

Born in 1915, Jerry F. Daniels was an Indianapolis native, who joined with three other Indianapolis men in the early 1930s to form a singing and comedy act called Jack, King, and Jester. When they arrived at Harlem's famous Apollo Theater in 1934 to play a gig, the bandleader Paul Whiteman asked them to change their name to avoid confusion with another group. The Ink Spots were born. Playing three guitars and a cello, and singing in a style that prefigured rhythm and blues and doo-wop, the Ink Spots garnered international acclaim later that year when they toured the United Kingdom. A *Melody Maker* review praised their "natural hot rhythm," "terrific single-string solo work," and their "beautifully balanced and exquisitely phrased vocalisms." A busy recording career followed, on labels that included Victor, MCA, Jasmine, Waldorf Music Hall, King, Vocalion, Mayfair, and Decca. Their first big hit, "If I Didn't Care," reached number two on the R&B charts in 1939. But by that time Daniels had already left the group. When a music journalist told him that the other band members said he quit because of illness, Daniels retorted, "the only thing he was 'sick' of was making so little money." Though the Ink Spots went on to a long, influential career with numerous band members, musicologists always considered Daniels, with his distinctive tenor and guitar and ukulele playing to be an "original" Ink Spot. The Ink Spots were inducted into the Rock and Roll Hall of Fame in 1989. After Daniels died on November 7, 1995, he came to rest in the Abbey Mausoleum A-7-F.

Etheridge Knight did "poeting," his personal phrase for writing poetry. Over a thirty-year career, Knight transmuted African American argot and oral form into a powerful, inclusive literary expression. Through his poetry, Knight transcended racism, poverty, prison, and heroin addiction. Knight said his art allowed him to find a community—"it was because of poetry—that's what brought me into communion with other people."

Born in Corinth, Mississippi, in 1931, Knight excelled at the African American oral tradition of "toasting"—the rhyming, often obscene, couplets about the drugs, sex, crime, and violence of street life. After quitting school in the eighth grade, he drifted into the rough world of pool halls and bars, where his narcotics habit began. While living in Indianapolis, Knight joined the army in 1947. Posted to Korea at the height of the fighting, Knight was seriously wounded by shrapnel. The morphine treatment reignited his addiction, and he returned to Indianapolis with a serious monkey on his back. His descent into heroin addiction led to a conviction for robbery. While serving a ten- to twenty-five-year sentence at the Indiana State Prison, Knight rediscovered his talent for "toasting," and then written poetry. His first book, *Poems from Prison,* came out in 1968 when he was still an inmate. The slender volume was well received, opening a new world for Knight. He later told an interviewer, "I died in 1960 from a prison sentence and poetry brought me back to life."

Released from prison in 1968, Knight published his second book, *Black Voices from Prison*, in 1970. Both books focused on the angry realities of race, prison, and political engagement. He quickly became a prominent member of the Black Arts Movement that flourished into the mid-1970s. Over the next years he served as a writer in residence at several universities, including Harvard, Butler, and Howard, with his work expressing maturing views of love and race. Honors began to come his way. His *Belly Song* was nominated both for the National Book Award

and Pulitzer Prize. He won a Guggenheim Fellowship in 1974 and grants from the National Endowment for the Arts in 1972 and 1980, which permitted him to investigate the role of African American oral traditions in black poetry. He received the Shelly Memorial Award from the Poetry Society of America for his distinguished achievement. While Knight's literary career was soaring, his personal life was rife with addiction and marital discord.

Divorced three times, with continuing problems with drugs and alcohol, he returned in the 1980s to Indianapolis, where his family still lived. In 1987 his collected works, *The Essential Etheridge Knight,* received the American Book Award. When not giving readings around the country, Knight was methodically studying toward a bachelor's degree from Martin University, where he was Poet Laureate. By the late 1980s, Knight was a poet for all people, adapting his readings to the audience, reaching out for the revivifying universal community of art.

Not long after he graduated with his bachelor's degree, Knight died on March 10, 1991, of lung cancer. But his community of poetry lived on. Martin University named a building the Etheridge Knight House. The annual Etheridge Knight Festival of the Arts in Indianapolis continued to celebrate his dream of

uniting all people with poetry. Knight's small discrete gravestone in Section 62, Lot 173 reads "Poet son father brother," and includes an epitaph that was the title of one of his most moving poems, "We Free Singers Be." The first stanza of the poem reads:

> We free singers be
> Sometimes swimming in the music,
> like porpoises playing in the sea.
> We free singers be
> come agitators at times, be
> come eagles circling the sun,
> hurling stones at hunters, be
> come scavengers cracking eggs
> in the palm of our hands.

Continuing a tradition that began with Indianapolis's pioneers, Hoosier political, military, and civic leaders chose Crown Hill for their last home. Larry A. Conrad was a young Indiana University at Indianapolis law school graduate when he managed Birch Bayh's U.S. Senate campaign against Homer Capehart in 1962. After his unexpected victory, Bayh named Conrad

as his legislative assistant and later appointed him to be chief counsel to the Senate Subcommittee on Constitutional Amendments. While serving as counsel to the subcommittee, Conrad crafted what became the Twenty-fifth Amendment, which clarified the provisions for presidential disability and succession. After his successful foray to Washington, Conrad returned to Indiana in 1969, where he became an influential political and civic leader. In 1970 Conrad won the election for secretary of state, often considered the stepping-stone to the governorship. The next year, Conrad accordingly tossed his hat in the ring for the Democratic nomination for governor. He lost the Democratic primary to former governor Matthew Welsh in 1972. Conrad was reelected secretary of state in 1974. In 1976 he won the Democratic nomination for governor, but lost to Republican incumbent Otis R. Bowen.

When his term as secretary of state ended, Conrad went private, practicing law and then joining Melvin Simon and Associates as vice president of corporate affairs. As part of his

# WILLIAM SHIRLEY

William Shirley was born in Indianapolis on July 6, 1921, and attended Shortridge High School. At the age of nineteen, he moved to the Enchanted Kingdom. Well, there was a stop in Hollywood, before his cinema career transformed Bill Shirley into Sleeping Beauty's Prince Phillip, Walt Disney's first fully realized (and named) prince.

Shirley moved to Hollywood to study voice and try to break into the movies. Republic Studios soon signed him to do bit parts in seven pictures, including *Flying Tigers*, *Doctors Don't Tell*, *Rookies on Parade*, *Hi Neighbor*, *Ice-Capades Review*, and *Sailors on Leave*. Before his Republic contract ended, the army drafted Shirley in 1942. After the war, he appeared as Captain Kidd in *Abbot and Costello Meet Captain Kidd*, and in late 1952 had the leading part as Stephen Foster in *I Dream of Jeanie*. Through the 1950s, Shirley had a yeoman entertainment career, with regular radio, stage, nightclub, and television appearances. In 1959 Shirley got his defining role—but it was only his

voice that endured in film history. Walt Disney's organization cast him as Prince Phillip, the mythically charming aristocrat who awakened Sleeping Beauty from her slumber. Dubbing for actor Jeremy Brett, who had the part of Freddy, Shirley's final cinematic warble was in the 1964 film, *My Fair Lady*. Shirley, who gave voice to the eternal prince charming, died of lung cancer in Los Angeles on August 27, 1989. He was entombed in the Community Mausoleum, C-18, B.

community work, Conrad was involved with the planning for the Circle Centre Mall and the White River State Park. A major promoter of Indianapolis's renaissance, Conrad was a central planner for the opening ceremonies for the 1982 National Sports Festival, as well as for the 1987 Pan-American Games. In 1989 Conrad formed his political consulting firm, The Conrad Group. The following year he was attending a conference sponsored by Partners of Livable Places in Lyon, France, when he suffered a ruptured aorta. Following open-heart surgery in a Lyon cardiology hospital, Conrad died on July 7, 1990. He was fifty-five years old. He was interred on the slope of Crown Hill in Section 88, Lot 5. His gravestone illustrated his pride and joys: his family, Indiana birthplace, his secretary of state office, his authorship of the constitutional amendment, and an outline of the Indianapolis skyline he helped build.

"General" Cleo Brown, Indianapolis's last Spanish-American War veteran, died on September 11, 1982. Born on May 21, 1880, he served in the Third Armored Cavalry Regiment, "the Brave Rifles." Brown was the commander in chief of the Spanish-American War Veterans encampments held in Indianapolis in 1975–76 and in Anaheim, California, in 1980–81. His role as commander in chief gave Brown his unofficial rank of "general," which he delighted in using. His official encampment photograph showed a small, wizened man in a vintage campaign hat holding a tiny American flag. Long a stalwart at Crown Hill's Memorial Day ceremonies, Brown was 102 years old when he went to his final rest. He was buried next to his wife, Eva May, in Section 60, Lot 57. The marker included a small heart inscribed with the words, "Married 70 years."

John Morton-Finney was born on June 25, 1889, in Uniontown, Kentucky, the son of a slave whose ancestors had migrated from Ethiopia to Nigeria before being swept up in the trans-Atlantic slave trade. One of seven children, Morton-Finney grew up in a family who read poetry and debated politics as the evening's entertainment. His mother died when he was fourteen, and his father sent the children to live on their grandfather's farm in Missouri.

By the time Morton-Finney died on January 28, 1998, he had earned twelve degrees, including a law degree from Indiana University and a degree from Butler University when he was seventy-five years old. Fluent in six languages, Morton-Finney was a dedicated teacher in the Indianapolis public schools for forty-six years. After serving as a young trooper in World War I with the Buffalo Soldiers of the Twenty-fourth U.S. Infantry, Morton-Finney was still practicing law at the age of 106. In 1991 Martin University bestowed an honorary doctorate degree on him. After his death, Morton-Finney was buried with full military honors in Section 46B, Lot 445, with other honors quickly following. In February 1998 Congresswoman Julia Carson gave a tribute to Morton-Finney on the floor of the U.S. House of Representatives. The Indianapolis Public Schools Board unanimously voted in 2000 to rename the Center for Educational Services to the Dr. John Morton-Finney Center for Educational Services. At the dedication, Commander Carlton Philpot, the chairman of the Buffalo Soldiers Monument committee at Fort Leavenworth was the keynote speaker. In 2003 the IU Board of Trustees named an IUPUI residential house in his honor.

Reverend Mozel Sanders began serving as the pastor of Mount Vernon Missionary Baptist Church in 1959. Born on May 25, 1924, in East Saint Louis, Illinois, Sanders took part in Martin Luther King Jr.'s momentous march on Washington, D.C.; was a stalwart of the Indianapolis Opportunities Industrialization Center and the Fare Share Organization that pushed for greater opportunities for African Americans, especially as managers; and spread the word through his gospel radio show on WTLC. Sanders, however, was best known for his work feeding the hungry, especially his Thanksgiving Day dinners that fed thousands. The Thanksgiving meals started in 1970, and by 1976 they were a community-wide event. City hospitals donated the use of their kitchens to cook hundreds of turkeys and all the trimmings. In 1987, the year before Sanders died, two hundred volunteers fed 16,000 people at the Thanksgiving Day feast at Arsenal Tech High School.

Sanders died in 1988. A large crowd that included numerous civic leaders gathered at a memorial service at the Indiana Convention Center. He was entombed on September 10, 1988 in Crown Hill's 2A, D-13.

Sanders's memory was honored with the renaming of an Indianapolis street, a housing project, and a twenty-nine-acre park. In 1996 Crown Hill named him as one of the Pillars of Society, whom are recognized in the cemetery with a photograph and plaque. The Thanksgiving tradition also lived on. In 2011, the fortieth anniversary of the first event, an estimated 43,000 people broke bread at Sander's great dinner.

After Walter S. Blackburn graduated from Howard University, he returned to Indianapolis and founded Blackburn Architects, where he was soon joined by his wife, Alpha, as a partner. Blackburn's award-winning buildings and projects permeate the fabric of the city. The firm's designs include the RCA Dome, the Indianapolis Artsgarden, expansions of the Convention Center, Conseco Fieldhouse (now Bankers Life), the United Airlines Indianapolis Maintenance Center, the Indianapolis International Airport and airport public art projects, and numerous school, church, and corporate developments.

Blackburn served as a visiting professor at Ball State University, a member of the board of managers for Rose-Hulman Institute of Technology, a commissioner of the Indiana Arts Commission, and a member of the dean's advisory board for IUPUI. He was named a Fellow of the American Institute of Architects, an honor bestowed by their peers on less than 1 percent of the country's architects. He received U.S. presidential appointments to the General Services Administration Review Board and the National Institute of Building Services.

In 1998 Blackburn received a commission to design the National Underground Railroad Freedom Center in Cincinnati, Ohio. Unfortunately, he died in August 2000 before the project's completion, but Alpha oversaw the remaining work. Today, the center is "a symbol of the commitment to freedom throughout the world" and "an international beacon for racial reconciliation."

Blackburn, the son of Cleo Blackburn, who developed Flanner House in Indianapolis into one of the Midwest's greatest social service institutions in the 1940s and 1950s, is buried on the Crown in Section 88, Lot 3.

A broad spectrum of humanity has come to be buried in Crown Hill. Some lived modest lives, remembered mainly by friends and family. Others have had international impacts, but never received the acclaim that came to others. Howard S. Garns was one of those. Garns was a nicely turned-out architect in Indianapolis's Daggett architectural firm. The Daggett group had designed James Whitcomb Riley's house a generation or so before Garns arrived just after World War II. Born in Connersville in 1905, Garns graduated from Indianapolis Tech High School and then studied architecture at the University of Illinois. While at Daggett, he supervised a staff of draftsmen cranking out the bread-and-butter work of a mid-century architectural firm: shopping centers, public schools, Roselyn bakeries, and the like. He was known for his sharp custom suits, pencil-thin moustache, and a penchant for whistling. But Garns had another passion: puzzles. As depicted in David Zivan's *Indianapolis Monthly* article, "A Puzzling Life," Garns was often bent over a spare drawing board, working on his "game," which looked like a crossword puzzle but used numbers instead of words. After he retired, Garns began publishing his games in a puzzle magazine in 1979. He called the puzzles "the Number Place."

In 1984 an editor of the Japanese puzzle company, Nikoli, saw one of Garn's puzzles and began publishing the games under the transliterated name of "*suuji wa dokushin ni kagiru*," which meant "the numbers must be single." With some refinements, the publisher shortened the name to "Su Doku," then "sudoku." It was the name that went into puzzle history. A New Zealand professor became addicted to the puzzle when he encountered them while traveling in Japan, and developed a computer

program to generate more. When the *Times of London* began publishing the professor's games, Garns's puzzle went viral, first picked up by other British newspapers and then the *New York Post* in America. Sudoku became a twenty-first-century phenomenon, with thousands of published puzzles, hundreds of books, game shows, championships, and a plethora of branded products. But Garns did not benefit financially from his little game. In the 1970s Garns and his wife, Evelyn, sold their modernist ranch in Devon Court and moved into a condominium. There were money problems at the end. In the late 1980s, Garns was diagnosed with cancer and died on October 6, 1989. Garns, the inventor of Sudoku, was interred in Crown Hill's mausoleum behind one of the elegant marble markers that lined the tomb's wall like crossword graphs—a perfect end for a natty architect with a bent for puzzled-out order.

> Crown Hill honored people who have made quiet, but vital contributions with a memorial to those who donated their bodies to medical science.

Crown Hill honored people who have made quiet, but vital contributions with a memorial to those who donated their bodies to medical science. In 1978 the Anatomical Education Board of the Indiana University School of Medicine arranged to purchase Section 41-A in the cemetery to inter the cremains after the bodies have been studied. The Medical Science Donor Memorial was initially installed in 1991, and renovated about a decade later. Each October, a Protestant chaplain, a priest, and a rabbi hold a memorial service at the Garden. In 2011 the monument recognized more than a thousand medical donors. The marker read, "Dedicated to those persons of good will who have bequeathed their bodies for the advancement of medical science."

Some graves are so poignant and puzzling, they require investigation. Pieter Grootendorst was born in the Netherlands and was buried in Crown Hill. Grootendorst's grave marker was carved to resemble a traditional Dutch house or barn of the early twentieth century. On the roof of the tiny structure, the stone carvers inscribed Grootendorst's final statement to the world: "Here lies the body of Pieter Grootendorst, born in Holland, September 29, 1918. I came to America in 1949 and wanted to love this beautiful country and I found out it was corrupt and that there is no opportunity for people who want to do right. So I am gone and may the Lord take my soul."

Grootendorst had good reason to be disillusioned with America. About 9:00 in the evening on Saturday March 23, 1974, thirteen-year-old Lankie Lee Whisenant Jr. and his uncle,

Troy Statz, came into Grootendorst's little Humpty Dumpty Carry Out Restaurant with its funny peaked roof at 1316 East Michigan Street. Lankie's dad, Lankie Sr., waited in the car. Grootendorst was working on the American dream. He owned a small wholesale poultry business, Farm Fresh Eggs and Florida Juice, on East Market Street and his house at 2041 New Jersey Street. Grootendorst had started the restaurant to bring in a few more dollars. He was buying six investment properties on the old north side and could always use the cash. The people in the neighborhood knew him well, a gruff but fair guy.

Lankie Jr. and his uncle stamped the snow off their feet and ordered three coffees and four egg sandwiches. When the cook brought the food, Statz walked over to the register and pulled out a massive .357 handgun. He pointed it at Grootendorst, and said, "This is a holdup." Grootendorst was prepared. He pulled out his .32 revolver he carried in a holster under his apron when he was working late at the restaurant. He started firing. Statz fired back. Within minutes the Humpty Dumpty would never be put back together again. The windows were blown out; the walls wrecked by gunfire. Grootendorst was hit four times—in the stomach, chest, and legs. Lankie Jr. took a couple of bullets in the stomach and staggered out the door.

Lankie Sr. was waiting in a red 1971 Chevrolet when the shooting started. He saw his son fall in the snow and got out and tried to get the boy inside the car. But when people began to run up, Lankie Sr. got in his car and drove off. His son was pronounced dead a half-hour later at the Marion County General Hospital, despite surgeons' efforts to save him. Twenty-four hours later, no one had yet claimed the body.

Grootendorst was in critical condition. He was not expected to live. Grootendorst spent a long time in the intensive care unit in Marion County General Hospital, and was then transferred to University Hospital for treatment of the kidney wound. A year after the shooting, he was still hospitalized and bitter. His attorneys were forced to dispose of most of his hard-earned properties, which declined rapidly without his attention. His

> After a brief flare of success in the mid-1970s, the Colts languished in the lower rungs of the league. By 1984, there was little love lost between Irsay and the Baltimore fans.

health was, quite literally, shot. He told a *Star* reporter, "I lived in America for twenty-five years, but I never thought this would happen to me." And then he said, "It is funny that our government spends so much money on foreign aid, but they won't spend enough money to keep our own streets safe."

Though the doctors said Grootendorst was going to die, one of the detectives who knew him said, "Old Pete will fool you—he really is a tough old guy."

And he was. Grootendorst lived until November 13, 1990. The *Star* obituary for Grootendorst noted the funeral at Stuart Mortuary Chapel, and the graveside service at Crown Hill, where he was laid to an uneasy rest in Section 41, Lot 250. The obituary suggested that memorial contributions could be made to the Kidney Foundation of Indiana.

Robert Irsay was a former marine, and a very successful businessman, who had relentlessly built his heating and air-conditioning company into a substantial corporation. When he sold his company, he grabbed a good deal on the Los Angeles Rams NFL franchise for $19 million, and then swapped it in 1972 to Carroll Rosenbloom for the Baltimore Colts. After a brief flare of success in the mid-1970s, the Colts languished in the lower rungs of the league. By 1984, there was little love lost between Irsay and the Baltimore fans. He contended he needed a new stadium and major financial concessions. Accustomed to successful pre-Irsay seasons, the fans claimed they needed a winner. Soon Baltimore and Irsay were at loggerheads. And Irsay was not backing down, entertaining offers from a number of cities eager for a pro football team, including Indianapolis, Phoenix, Memphis, and Jacksonville; Indianapolis won out. When the team left Baltimore in the early morning hours of March 28, 1984, one of the city's sports columnists famously wrote that the Colts left "with all the grace of a snake-oil salesman backing out of a prairie tank town."

Indianapolis fans embraced the Colts. In April 1984, 20,000 Hoosiers crowded the Hoosier Dome to welcome Irsay and the Colts; 143,000 applied for season tickets. The fans endured through some tough seasons, especially as rumors swirled that Irsay was shopping the team around. Irsay tried to calm the concerns in an interview, where he pointed out the Colts' lease on the stadium was for twenty years. "And with that," he said, "I signed my life away."

In November 1995 Irsay suffered a stroke that confined him for many months to Saint Vincent Hospital. After his release in the summer of 1996, he contracted pneumonia, and had to be transferred to the Mayo Clinic in Minnesota to recover. After being discharged from the Mayo Clinic, Irsay returned to Indianapolis. In early 1997, he was hospitalized with heart and kidney problems. Shortly after 10:00 a.m. on January 14, 1997, Irsay died with his son, Jim, and wife, Nancy, in the room. Irsay rests on the slope of Crown Hill in Section 88, Lot 5, with a view of Lucas Oil Stadium and the Indianapolis skyline. His gravestone is emblazoned with the Colts' trademark horseshoe, a symbol of Indianapolis's rebirth as a great All-American city.

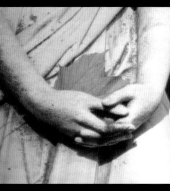

ALBERT REINKEN Jr.

# 8

## CROWN HILL IN THE TWENTY-FIRST CENTURY

The trauma of 9/11 changed everything. Even as the nation was reeling from the attacks on the World Trade Center and the Pentagon, legislators were hurrying bills through Congress to tighten security, the military was readying for wars in Afghanistan and Iraq, and across the homeland communities prepared to deal with terrorism. In the midst of the turmoil, the American public rediscovered Memorial Day.

"Resurging Patriotism Revitalizes Indiana Ceremony," read an *Indianapolis Star* headline about Memorial Day in 2002. A large crowd gathered at Crown Hill to honor the nine Hoosiers killed on 9/11 at the World Trade Center and the Pentagon, and Sergeant Jeannette Winters, who was killed in Afghanistan. They belted out "God Bless America," and Lee Greenwood's "God Bless the U.S.A.," a song written to honor veterans returning from Vietnam, which got a second life during the Persian Gulf War. They listened intently to Indiana Republican Party chairman Rex Early tell them, "Freedom is not free."

The Crown Hill Corporators were dealing with their own turmoil. They were increasingly concerned about the Perpetual Care Fund, the long-term endowment needed to maintain the cemetery's day-to-day operations when all the burial sites were sold. Despite vigorous oversight by the board of managers, investments had continued to yield insufficient returns to build the fund. Increased sales, which had stagnated for years, were

not going to fix the problem. The corporators realized that they needed to dramatically increase the fund's capital base.

To solve the problem, the Crown Hill Corporators began to explore several options, one of which was the potential sale of the underperforming funeral home, and another the possible sale of the unused land at the northern edge of the cemetery. Purchased in 1889 and 1911, the acreage along Forty-second Street was still a tangle of forest and brush. Based upon the rates of interments and the growing popularity of cremations and crypt entombments, the Crown Hill management projected in 2003 that the cemetery had enough land for 268 years of burials. Soon thereafter, Crown Hill announced it was planning to sell sixty-six acres along Forty-second Street. Negotiations began with several interested parties, which culminated in a proposal from a developer from Carmel, Indiana, the following month.

There were, however, wetlands on the property that, according to *Nuvo*, were under the protection of the federal Clean Water Act and would force any developer to work with the U.S. Army Corps of Engineers to avoid impacting the wetland. In March 2006 the initial developer pulled out of the deal, citing the problems caused by the wetlands, but the corporators felt they needed to pursue a sale of the property to infuse the Care Fund with cash. An *Indianapolis Star* editorial supported an upscale housing development on the cemetery site, saying the city needed to balance "smart development and natural preservation." An ad-hoc group named the Crown Hill Advocates called for "grassroots participation" in decisions about the cemetery land.

By May 2006 Crown Hill was considering three different proposals, one of which included a seven-acre light retail development and 320 custom homes, townhouses, and "urban-style homes" on seventy acres of Crown Hill land. A growing consortium of environmental and neighborhood groups continued to oppose the project. In January 2007 the Metropolitan Development Commission heard the necessary zoning request. After a very contentious hearing, filled with remonstrators arguing against the zoning request, the commission voted against the petition.

As Crown Hill was in the midst of the final stages of the issue of securing a rezoning variance, another impending development created a different opportunity to take the pressure off of the Perpetual Care Fund. An offer extended by Gibraltar Remembrance Services, LLC, was accepted for the purchase of the funeral home assets and a management agreement for the operations of the cemetery. The purchase doubled the Care Fund and would bring new resources to Crown Hill. Co-owned

by brothers Tim and Jay Brammer, Indianapolis-based Gibraltar was founded in 1963 and rather than relying on the cemetery-chain model of drastic cost cutting, they focused on building community relationships. Unlike the contentious land sale, Crown Hill's deal with Gibraltar went quickly and smoothly. "From the first discussion until we started managing, it was about six months," Jay said.

Crown Hill's board members initially wanted to be assured that the Brammers shared the same vision as the corporators. "The board wanted to be sure we were interested in long-term development of the cemetery, and that we shared the same belief in the heritage of the cemetery," said Jay. "The size, prestige, the history of the cemetery, in our hometown—it was just a natural for us," said Tim.

Beyond the contribution to the Care Fund (according to Jay, now the state's "best-funded"), a 9,500-square-foot expansion of the funeral home, accompanied by substantially increased sales, allowed Crown Hill to be on firm financial footing for the future.

Even during the years the cemetery officials were grappling with some very complicated challenges, they, and the Crown Hill Heritage Foundation, worked to make Crown Hill an ever more meaningful place. On Sunday, October 29, 2000, a crowd gathered to dedicate the Indiana AIDS Memorial with the event, "A Day of Remembrance, Celebration, and Recognition." A twelve-foot high bronze sculpture by Indianapolis artist Guy R. Grey represented intertwined hands forming an AIDS support ribbon. Behind the bronze, limestone tablets listed many of the names of the 4,000 Hoosier AIDS victims who died between 1982 and 1999, including teenage AIDS activist Ryan White. To celebrate the dedication, dancers, musicians, and a poet presented original works. Funded by the Indiana AIDS Fund, the Joseph F. Miller Foundation, and Crown Hill Cemetery, the monument was the first permanent AIDS memorial in a cemetery, and the third in the country. "Throughout its history," said Keith Norwalk, Crown Hill president, "Crown Hill has represented the lives of Indianapolis-area families,

and the events that have been significant to the community. Memorializing victims of AIDS does both."

Greg Powers was one of the AIDS victims memorialized on the monument. A former principal of Bob Powers Toyota, he was best known as the owner and guiding light of Our Place, one of Indianapolis's oldest gay bars that was established near Sixteenth and Alabama Streets. The bar served as a second home and political locus for many in the Indianapolis gay community. Powers was a quiet force in the community, belonging to fifty-three groups, twelve of them national. "He was a very generous person," said Betty Wilson, president and CEO of the Health Foundation of Greater Indianapolis Inc. Powers helped fund a thrift store that was part of the Indiana AIDS Foundation outreach. When he died on February 1, 2002, Powers was forty-nine years old. The Greg R. Powers Direct Emergency Financial Assistance fund, which was organized to provide aid to HIV/AIDS sufferers, was founded in his honor. "As a result of his generosity and high profile," Wilson said, "there is now a fund to assist the disadvantaged who are dealing with the disease." The staff and customers of Our Place, which was renamed Greg's following his death, embraced the Indiana AIDS Walk, and by 2011 had raised $400,000 for a plethora of groups serving the needs of the Indianapolis gay, lesbian, bisexual, and transgendered community.

On *El Día de los Muertos,* the Day of the Dead, November 2, 2001, Crown Hill dedicated the Latino Section in the north grounds. A mariachi band played as Hispanic families ate bowls of chicken mole and rice, and distributed flowers, candles, and traditional candy in the shape of skulls. Located in Section 231, the one-and-a-half-acre Latino Section represents the cemetery's outreach to central Indiana's burgeoning Latino population. By 2002 there were already more than 34,000 persons of Hispanic descent living in the city—up 294 percent since 1990. The thousands of Latin Americans who relocated to Indianapolis brought the greatest cultural shift to the city in several decades. There was a Mexican consulate in downtown

# "A Place for Me at Crown Hill"

Alice Timmons Gochenour (1918–2010) learned to fish and shoot from her father at Wild Cat Creek near Frankfort, Indiana. At a young age she also learned the value of a strong work ethic when her father made her the candy purchaser for his variety stores.

The Timmons family lost everything in the Great Depression. Her father cried as he told Alice her university money was gone. He assured her, however, that they would make it somehow because Hoosiers were the salt of the earth.

Alice went on to find work with Pitman Moore Laboratories in Zionsville, Indiana, where she met Raymond Gochenour. They married and took up residence in a quaint log house in the woods. It was a time that held Alice's fondest memories.

Alice and Raymond moved to Washington, D.C., where Raymond worked at Walter Reed Army Institute of Research and Alice worked at the National Institute of Health. They became world travelers and eventually settled in California to live on the ocean.

was interred in the Crown Hill Community Mausoleum. Alice was heartbroken, lonely, and alone in their home by the sea.

Raymond always loved trees. Alice made a gift in his memory to fund the Gochenour Tree Nursery at Crown Hill. Alice never forgot her father's words and throughout her life thought of herself as a Hoosier. She made a gift through her will to the Crown Hill Heritage Foundation to support Crown Hill's preservation programs.

Alice came home to Indiana. She lies at rest with Raymond in the Crown

**Alice came home to Indiana. She lies at rest with Raymond in the Crown Hill Community Mausoleum, C-11-2D.**

Before leaving Zionsville, Raymond insisted that they make arrangements to come home to Indiana for burial at Crown Hill when the time came. Raymond became terminally ill on one of their world trips and

Hill Community Mausoleum, C-11-2D. Visitors to the cemetery are welcome to enjoy a lovely view of the grounds from the Alice Timmons Gochenour Memorial Garden adjacent to the Celebration Hall patio at the Crown Hill Funeral Home.

*Alice Gochenour and Marianne Randjelovic, vice president of development, visiting at Crown Hill.*

Indianapolis. Dozens of Latino restaurants blossomed along the byways of northwestern Indianapolis, not far from the cemetery. In 2010, when the census indicated that 9.4 percent of the Indianapolis population was Hispanic, it was clear that the Latino Section was a prescient addition to Crown Hill. *El Día de los Muertos* quickly became one of Crown Hill's most popular and colorful annual events.

While he was not buried in the Latino Section, Hilario "Larry" Rangel was a prominent Hispanic citizen in Indianapolis who came to rest in Crown Hill. His restaurant, La Margarita, located on Thirtieth Street at the north edge of the Indianapolis Motor Speedway, catered to the racing crowd, which led to his untimely death. On February 14, 2000, he was flying back from an auto-racing event in Florida with veteran 500-mile race driver and Champion Auto Racing Teams franchise holder Tony Bettenhausen. When the small plane hit a storm near Lexington, Kentucky, the wings began to ice. Bettenhausen, an instrument-rated pilot, tried to climb higher, but the plane went into a spin. It hit a hillside and killed all aboard, which included Rangel;

Bettenhausen and his wife, Shirley; and a CART partner, Russ Roberts. The Rangel family was a mainstay of the Indianapolis restaurant scene for decades. Beyond La Margarita, Larry and his brother, Raul, ran El Matador in Broad Ripple, and relative Joe Rangel was the raffish, but famously patriotic proprietor of Acapulco Joe's downtown until his death in 1989. Larry was buried in Section 58, Lot 140, near the Bettenhausens, who are interred in Section 58, Lot 110.

In the months after the 9/11 tragedies, the Crown Hill staff and community leaders organized a monument to the brave men and women who serve in public safety jobs, especially those who fall in the line of duty. The inception of the Heroes of Public Safety was the meeting of a national and local tragedy occurring within one week of each other. Dedicated on September 11, 2002, the twelve-foot-high granite monument was inscribed with the names of the fallen. It was sited in the heart of Crown Hill in Section 97. The one-and-a-half-acre plot included granite walks and room for fifteen hundred graves. The memorial has become a meeting place for officers to gather for events and

to honor and remember their comrades. In September 2002, Crown Hill began hosting the annual "Beyond the Badge Run & Walk" to honor and thank public safety professionals and raise funds for the Jason M. Baker Public Safety Scholarships.

Marion County Sheriff's Deputy Jason M. Baker tragically provided the local inspiration for the Crown Hill memorial. On the evening of September 17, 2001, Baker was responding to a domestic disturbance when he spotted a suspicious car near Fifty-second Street and Keystone Avenue. When the driver would not pull over, Baker gave chase. As they raced south, two  men in the car opened fire with AK-47 assault rifles. Though his car was hit and he was injured, Baker continued the chase, calmly calling back radio updates to his comrades.

Baker was born into a police family and as a young boy often accompanied his police-chief dad to the station. He dreamed of being a police officer. As part of North Central High School's community service Learning Unlimited program, he interned at Washington Township Fire Department's Station 223. During his internship, Baker logged a record number of community-service hours—a record that remained unbroken as of 2011. After joining the Sheriff's Department in 1995, Baker continued his community outreach. Only a few days before the chase, twenty-four-year-old Baker was speaking to a class of Indiana University–Purdue University at Indianapolis, students about 9/11. He told them to be vigilant, have faith, support government leaders, be reflective on national outcomes, and "say thanks to public safety, fire and police personnel."

With Baker still in pursuit of the renegade vehicle, the fleeing men careened around the corner of Thirty-second Street and Brouse Avenue, slammed on the brakes, and waited to ambush the deputy. When Baker turned the corner, the men, wearing body armor, raked his police car with automatic weapons fire. Baker was grievously wounded, and died en route to the hospital. "There was not an ounce of fear in him, and he still chased and fought to the end," a sheriff department chaplain later said.

The funeral cortege was seven and a half miles long. After a moving ceremony attended by many hundreds of people, Baker was laid to rest in Section 97, Lot 1709. The polished black granite marker included the inscription, "A family dedicated to service above self." Baker was posthumously awarded the Medal of Honor and his badge was retired.

Firefighter Paul Jolliff was named for his grandfather, Paul K. Jolliff, who was an Indianapolis firefighter from 1940 to 1966. Prior to following in his grandfather's footsteps, Paul served his country as an Airborne Ranger in the U.S. Army. At the age of thirty he joined the Indianapolis Fire Department in 1995, working out of Fire Station Number 10. As a firefighter/paramedic, Jolliff, already the recipient of a Community Service Medal, began training to become a department dive team member. On June 14, 2002, he began his twenty-second and final practice dive on the way to his certification. The practice mission simulated the rescue of a drowning child from a ten-acre pond, where the murky waters reached as deep as seventy feet. Jolliff was one of several divers from various area departments taking place in the training dive.

As the simulated rescue proceeded, the trainers realized that they had lost contact with Jolliff. The training exercise turned into a real rescue mission and certified divers were soon in the water trying to locate one of their own. It took them two hours to find Joliff in the dark waters. A later investigation determined that he had probably gotten entangled in the lines used to guide the training search and drowned in a confused struggle to free himself.

A service was held on June 18, 2002, at Trinity Episcopal Church, not far from Crown Hill's gates. The procession, which

*Opposite: The general public is invited to participate in the Beyond the Badge 5K Run & Walk at Crown Hill Cemetery every September. Proceeds go to the Jason M. Baker Public Safety Scholarships.*

made its way through Crown Hill's Thirty-fourth Street Gothic-gate entrance, included a horse-drawn caisson, bagpipers, and hundreds of fellow firefighters. Jolliff was survived by his wife, Wendy, and three-year old son, Timothy. The couple's second child, Katie, was born two months later on August 23, 2002. Jolliff was buried with full honors in the first grave west of the Heroes of Public Safety Memorial on Lot 1583.

On August 18, 2004, Indianapolis Police Department Patrolman Timothy "Jake" Laird responded to an early morning call about gunfire on the south side of the city. There was a report of a wounded officer. When the shooting stopped sixteen minutes later, Officer Laird was dead, four officers were wounded, and the shooter and his mother were dead. Laird's funeral was long, crowded, and emotional. Approximately 2,200 mourners, including hundreds of police officers, Governor Joe Kernan, U.S.

Representative Julia Carson, and other dignitaries attended the funeral. The long line of officers filing past the casket snapping salutes and wiping away tears delayed services for forty minutes. Honoring Laird's bravery, Police Chief Jerry Barker retired the patrolman's badge, Number 2479, and posthumously awarded Laird the IPD's Medal of Honor—only the fourth time in a century and a half that the medal had been presented.

The funeral cortege took a significant route to Crown Hill. Escorted by a procession of police vehicles, the hearse passed IPD headquarters, then turned south to the department's South District offices, where the cortege paused as officers stood at attention in front of their patrol cars. Over the radio came the formal message reporting Laird was no longer on duty: "There is no greater love than a man that would lay down his life for another. Timothy Jacob Laird, Charles 421, is 10-42. He has

gone home for the final time." The procession slowly moved on to Crown Hill. The cortege sometimes stretched seven miles along the city streets. The silent police cars' flashing roof lights made "a flickering river of blue and red," the *Star*'s Tim Evans wrote.

Reaching Crown Hill, the squad cars and motorcycles passed under a huge American flag hanging from the Gothic Arch. After the hearse arrived, an IPD honor guard carried Laird's flag-draped casket to a horse-drawn caisson. Four mounted police officers and a riderless horse with empty boots backwards in the stirrups, symbolizing a fallen warrior, followed. Twenty-five

bagpipers and drummers played the baleful tune, "Balmoral," as they led the procession to the gravesite, where hundreds waited in the hot sun. The service was succinct. Philip Bacon, IPD chaplain intoned the biblical words, "Earth to earth, ashes to ashes." There was a rifle salute, a trumpeted "Taps," and hundreds of uniformed officers placed white carnations tinged with red on the wooden casket till it was piled high. Laird was buried in Section 97, Lot 1582.

Officer James L. Davis worked in the neighborhood. He was a Butler University police officer, who responded on the morning of September 24, 2004, to a call about a suspicious person near the Hinkle Fieldhouse, where the suspect was intently watching a women's basketball practice. When confronted by Davis, the man attacked and shot him with his own service weapon. A thirty-one-year-old Indiana University graduate with a wife and three children, Davis had been with the Butler police since January 2003. A few hours later, police exchanged fire with the suspect, a mentally ill man, in the 4400

block of North Illinois Street, where he was fatally wounded. Officer Davis's funeral procession to Crown Hill included driving through the Butler campus, where students lined the streets throughout. In a reprise of Laird's services, 1,200 people came to Davis's funeral. Eight hundred police officers wearing black bands on their badges attended the burial ceremonies. A blanket of white carnations tipped with red lay on the casket. Davis was interred in Section 97, Lot 1581.

Indiana State Police lieutenant Gary E. Dudley was a veteran trainer at the State Police Academy, where as commander he mentored hundreds of troopers. Dudley also cared about the widows and families of officers killed in the line of duty. To help them out, he transformed a struggling survivors' fund into a thriving charity through an annual trans-Indiana bike ride to raise funds and awareness for the survivors of the fallen. In five years, the rides raised more than $100,000. Dudley ironically lost his life while bicycling in western Indiana on one of his charity rides. On August 22, 2006, a freight truck plowed into the group's support van that was following ten riders, killing fifty-one-year-old Dudley and Lake County Police Chief Gary Martin.

More than a thousand people gathered in Brownsburg for Dudley's funeral, more than half of them troopers he had trained. Hundreds of squad cars from many states joined the sixteen-mile funeral procession to Crown Hill, where Dudley was honored with the soulful sound of trumpet fanfares, wailing bagpipes, and volleys of rifle fire. His widow commissioned a monument to her husband that is located amidst the pine trees of the Heroes of Public Safety memorial.

Officer David Spencer Moore came from a family committed to community service. His parents, Spencer and Jo, both worked for the IPD, and sister Carol is an Indianapolis schoolteacher.

David's dream was to become an Indianapolis police officer. He attended Purdue University in the

Reserve Officers' Training Corps program. After three years an old knee injury kept him from reaching his goal of joining the marines, but it allowed him the opportunity to pursue his dream and he joined the IPD in July 2004 with the department's 102nd recruit class. He quickly found being a police officer was his calling and was given the department's "Rookie Officer of the Year" award for making the most radio runs in one year and in developing a working rapport with citizens in his North District. The community knew Moore as respectful and fair, and with his engaging smile he often garnered information that led to arrests. Early in his career he worked specialty street crime fighting units, receiving the department's Medal of Valor for interrupting a gunfight where four people had already been shot. He earned the department's Medal of Merit for formulating a crime-fighting plan that was implemented in the Broad Ripple area, culminating in several arrests.

On January 23, 2011, six and half years into his career, Moore conducted a routine traffic stop that quickly became a deadly encounter. The driver exited his vehicle with a gun in hand and fired, hitting Moore six times. As Moore lay dying by his police vehicle, the suspect fled in a stolen car. Indianapolis Fire Department Station 10 and Medic 10 quickly transported Moore to Wishard Hospital, where officers and citizens held vigil and prayed. Moore did not recover from his injuries, dying three days later in his mother's arms.

Because of the efforts of the officers and the emergency medical services on the scene, Moore's family was able to donate five of his organs and both corneas. Out of something so tragic to his department and to the City of Indianapolis, seven people were able to receive his gift, allowing them to live a full and active life.

Moore died on January 26, 2011, and is buried in the southwest side of the Heroes of Public Safety memorial on Section 97. His polished black-granite monument bears his likeness and four medals, including the Medal of Honor and Purple Heart, both awarded posthumously. The legacy on his monument includes perhaps his biggest medal, the Indianapolis Organ Procurement medal.

Even with the nation in turbulence, heritage and art remained an important part of Crown Hill's mission. In 2001 the Crown Hill Heritage Foundation commenced a restoration of the Waiting Station. When the construction was complete, the foundation began a major renovation and expansion of the Gothic Chapel. Designed by CSO Architects, the chapel renovation cost $3.2 million, which was funded through the Foundation's first capital campaign. The American Institute of Architects Indiana chapter awarded the project a 2007 Excellence in Architecture award. As part of the project, the chapel's organ was replaced with a new custom-designed Roger's pipe organ. Crown Hill Corporator and musicologist Marianne Tobias gifted the organ in memory of her parents, Russel and Mary Williams.

The American way of death continued to evolve in the twenty-first-century. The trend toward cremation grew, forcing casket makers to adjust and cemeteries to change their business models. As competition increased for the declining numbers of burials, cemeteries across the country opened their gates to a wide array of activities, including bird-watching, poetry readings, and jazz concerts. The *New York Times* caught the zeitgeist with its 2007 article, "In need of income, cemeteries seek breathing clientele."

To celebrate its 140th anniversary in 2003, Crown Hill inaugurated the Hoosier Artists Contemporary Sculpture Walk that included works by ten artists. Michael B. Wilken's *Social Attachments,* an abstract metal sculpture, was permanently installed. Eric Nordgulen's spindly *Antenna Man* was installed

*Opposite: Eagle Plaza in the Field of Valor military section on the north grounds of Crown Hill.*

HONOR AND RE[...]
LCpl Deryk L. Hallal ~ 06 [...]

OPERATION IRAQI FREEDOM
DERYK LYELL
HALLAL
AUG 23 1979
APR 6 2004

soon after. Looking like some extraterrestrial construct designed for ethereal communication, the sculpture was installed in a copse of pines in the south grounds.

The post-9/11 wars in Afghanistan and Iraq highlighted the need to expand the military sections of the cemetery. The Crown Hill administrators established the four-acre Field of Valor, which has space for 5,000 graves and 500 crypts, which doubles the cemetery's space for veterans. On Veterans Day, November 11, 2004, a large gathering of veterans, families, and supporters dedicated the Field of Valor Memorial on a prominence of the north grounds. Emblazoned with the golden seals of the army, navy, marines, air force, and coast guard, the black-granite monument surmounted the pale gray mausoleum. The keynote speakers were Jeffrey and Pamela Hallal, the parents of U.S. Marine Deryk Hallal, who had been

killed in action in Iraq not many months before. Their speech was "The Honor and Truth of American Veterans." A year later on Veterans Day, Congressman Mike Pence spoke to another large group assembled to dedicate the Field of Valor's Eternal Flame and Eagle Plaza that stood in front of the memorial. Conceived and donated by philanthropist Rachel H. Newman, the Eternal Flame and the accompanying preservation endowment was given in memory of World War II veteran Maurice W. Scearce.

On Memorial Day, 2004, Governor Joe Kernan—himself a navy veteran and Vietnam War prisoner of war—reminded the crowd at the Crown Hill ceremony, "This is a time to step back and reflect and remember—a time to say thank you." Hallal was one of those honored. He was an All-American kid when he graduated from North Central High School. A six-foot, five-inch wide receiver in school, Hallal had yearned to serve his country

after 9/11. In May 2003 he enlisted in the marines, and within a year he was fighting in Al Anbar Province during the height of the Iraqi uprising. During a major insurgent offensive on April 6, Hallal was serving as the point man for his squad as it moved through a dense urban area. When the insurgents attacked, he was caught in the open, the target of grenade, machine-gun, and rifle fire. Returning fire, Hallal eliminated three insurgents, which allowed his squad to ready themselves for the assault against the enemy stronghold. Hallal courageously led the attack against intense enemy fire. While shot in both legs, he continued to engage as his squad mates carried him into an alley. But another bullet struck Hallal. There was little his fellow marines could do but administer morphine and say a prayer as he died in the street. He was posthumously awarded the Bronze Star with Valor citation. Hallal's memorial service was held two weeks later, when he was interred in the Field of Valor, Section 213, Lot 292A. His parents had his three-foot-high granite tombstone inscribed with the U.S. Marine Corps insignia and the phrase: "Christ died for your sins. Our son died for your freedom."

Army corporal Antoine J. McKinzie was another tall Indianapolis man who fell in Iraq. His family called the six-foot, three-inch Pike High School and ITT graduate a gentle giant. McKinzie was manning his Humvee's machine gun in western Baghdad on March 21, 2006, when a sniper shot him. He was twenty-five-years old, on his second tour of duty in Iraq. An honor guard of Patriot Riders with snapping American flags on their motorcycles led the cortege into Crown Hill, where McKinzie's casket with his dogtags and flowers was interred in Section 213, Lot 498C. At the Memorial Day remembrance a few months later, McKinzie and the other twenty-one Hoosier soldiers killed in Iraq during the previous year were honored as the Indiana National Guard's Thirty-eighth Division band played and 105-mm howitzers gave off their thunderous salutes.

*Above: Pamela Hallal preparing to release a dove for her son, U.S. Marine lance corporal Deryk Hallal, who died in Iraq.*

Sergeant John Rankel of the U.S. Marine Corps had already served two tours of duty in Iraq when he reenlisted in 2009. As part of the military surge, Rankel was deployed to Afghanistan. A graduate of Speedway High School, where he lettered in football, baseball, and basketball, the twenty-three-year-old was on a foot patrol in volatile Helmand Province on June 7, 2010, when he was shot to death. Indiana governor Mitch Daniels authorized flags in the state to be flown at half-mast. Rankel was the thirtieth Hoosier to be killed in Afghanistan. After services on Saturday, June 19, 2010, at Speedway High School, the long cortege slowly rolled to Crown Hill, where Rankel was laid to rest in the Field of Valor.

Crown Hill also addressed the needs of children. Shepherd's Way, the cemetery's section for infants, was dedicated in May 2005. With its resting benches, the watchful shepherd statue, and bronzes of gamboling children in a beautiful landscape, the area offers grieving parents a place for meditation and acceptance. Some time before, a mourning mother initiated Shepherd's Way. She had told Norwalk she felt alone and isolated when she visited her baby's grave. Norwalk challenged the Crown Hill staff to transform Section 237 into a special place where families could find comfort amidst beautiful surroundings. The Shepherd's Way project was funded by Rachel Newman, whose own mother had been devastated by the loss of four of her children. At the foot of the shepherd statue, a bronze plaque was inscribed with the story of Newman's too soon departed siblings, Frances, Hazel, Carl, and May.

On Sunday, June 4, 2006, the 699 orphaned and abandoned children who lay in Section 37 at last got their monument. The nine-foot-high Hearts Remembered Memorial was commissioned in their honor. Most of the forgotten children had died while under the care of the Board of Children's Guardians, the Children's Bureau, the Indianapolis Children's Asylum, and the Home for Friendless Colored Children, and were buried in unmarked graves. Most died of neglect and maltreatment. Starvation, malaria, syphilis, whooping cough, diphtheria, and tuberculosis were some of the listed causes of death. All were

buried in Section 37 in unmarked graves. "We found a hill full of children with no stones," said Anna Sturgeon, a former intern at the Marion County Children's Guardian Home, who researched the forgotten children.

Harry Lockwood was one. Born to a prostitute in 1898, he was raised in what social workers often called "abodes of poverty and wretchedness." Soon after entering the city orphanage at age twelve, Lockwood was farmed out to a country family, who appeared to have been looking for another pair of hands. Lockwood was returned to the orphanage when he refused to work, asking the farmers if they thought he was a horse. It was going better for Lockwood with a Rush County family when three years later he was struck with appendicitis. After an operation to drain the fluid from his side, the doctors told the foster family that Harry needed an operation to remove the appendix. The family refused to pay. Some months later, the doctor insisted the boy had to have the operation, so Lockwood went back to Indianapolis to get indigent care at the City Hospital. But it was too late for him—the affliction had been allowed to fester too long. Lockwood died on August 10, 1913, just a few weeks before he turned fifteen. Two days later, he was buried in an unmarked grave in Section 37.

But that Sunday in 2006 was the children's day, as a host of dignitaries and celebrities, including Congressman Dan Burton and Rupert Boneham of *Survivor* fame, remembered them. Funded with donations from a broad range of corporations, foundations, and individuals, the memorial project was led by the Care for Kids Foundation, a not-for-profit group focused on the needs of vulnerable children. Joseph Miller designed the black-granite monolith to have an incised circle, where a bronze sculpture of two children holding hands stood. Two smaller monoliths inscribed with the children's names flanked the central monument. At the dedication, the Indianapolis Children's Choir sang hymns, and people held hands and prayed. The ceremony concluded with celebrators laying flowers on the new monument while children read the names of the no longer forgotten.

Indianapolis pioneers were still arriving at Crown Hill into the twenty-first century. In 1912 Crown Hill had established the Pioneer Cemetery in the north grounds for the reinterred remains of 1,160 people buried in Greenlawn Cemetery. Industrial expansion had necessitated the removal of the bodies, only thirty-five of whom were identified. Then, in the summer of 1999, the undertakers reinterred the remains of another thirty-three people, twelve adults, and thirty-four children, from the Rhoads Cemetery on the west side, where the country graveyard had stood since 1844. Construction on the new Indianapolis airport unearthed the Rhoads graveyard. An expansion of I-69 near Castleton in 2008 and 2009 threatened the tiny Wright-Whitesell-Gentry Cemetery, already marooned in an asphalt-surrounded islet of green. A team of forensic anthropologists led by University of Indianapolis professor Stephen Nowrocki exhumed the bodies, and at Crown Hill staff reinterred the remains in the exact configuration of the old graveyard. The

twenty-first-century interments brought the total buried in the Pioneer Cemetery to 1,239.

As the decades slipped by, monuments got more modern. Changing technology allowed more personalization. A muskie leaps on the Diehr monument. A navy jet roars on another. A score of musical notes dance across the Arvin marker. "Love never dies," it reads. An inscription on a memorial bench in the south grounds insisted, "I am still the boss." Computer-generated images of the departed began to gaze back from the inscribed surfaces of the gravestones. Technology now permitted talking tombstones, actualized by small stone tablets embedded with microchips and radio tags that can beam a thousand words and a picture to a cell phone for more than three thousand years. The dead speak.

Some new monuments celebrate the old. In 2009 a monument to commemorate the centennial of the Holy Trinity Greek Orthodox Church of Indianapolis was installed in the Greek

Orthodox section of the cemetery. Crown Hill's Greek area began in the 1930s with Section 236 and expanded to Section 224 after the first section sold out. The church began on South Meridian in 1910, serving as a center of Hellenism and Greek Orthodoxy for Indianapolis's small Greek community. For decades, the church was at 213 North West Street, near the current location of the Indiana Historical Society.

Pantelis Cafouros arrived in Indianapolis in 1893, a handsome, dark-eyed devil with brilliantine hair and a thick mustache. He was active in the Holy Trinity Church. When he and his wife's baby, James, was born, it was the first Greek son born in Indianapolis, an event Cafouros celebrated by buying a hundred dollars in fireworks. Fluent in many languages, Cafouros began a night school for Greeks to learn English in 1906. He and his wife owned the Devil's Café at 108 West Maryland Street. Mrs. Cafouros did not speak English, so thought the name

related to the French word, *de ville,* the city. When she discovered the real meaning, she strenuously objected to the name. To keep the peace, Pantelis divided the restaurant into two side-by-side eateries. He ran "The Devil" and his wife worked in "The Paradise." On March 15, 1924, Pantelis was buried in Crown Hill, Section 69, Lot 134.

Some new monuments resonate eternal yearnings. Crown Hill's most recent angel was designed as a caretaking angel. During a time of crisis in her life, Marianne Tobias purchased a cemetery plot in a glen in Section 87. "I decided I needed an angel," she said "I wanted my angel there to help. Her wings are folded—she is of the earth. She's holding a bird. There's a cat at her foot." Tobias worked with the Rock of Ages monument staff at Crown Hill to craft the angel, along with a sitting bench so people can sit for contemplation. "I wanted a very human angel," she said. As Tobias

weathered the storms in her life, she would come to Crown Hill, where her angel provided succor. "She has seen me through so much heartbreak," Tobias says. "I have a strong relationship with that angel."

Crown Hill offered meaning to people in myriad ways. Each spring, thousands upon thousands of daffodils bloom at Goethe and Helen Link's place in the hills south of Mooresville. Doctor Goethe Link was an Indiana University School of Medicine founder and practicing surgeon until his eighty-eighth year. He was also a pioneering aeronaut, with a national balloon race victory in 1909, as well as being a serious amateur astronomer with his own thirty-six-inch telescope. After his death in 1980 at age 101, he was interred in Crown Hill's Section 67, Lot 82. The daffodils were Helen's passion. She had carefully cultivated her 'Edward Buxtons,' 'Cloud Nines,' 'Lucy Janes,' 'Towhees,' 'Tutus,' and all the other 1,100 varieties that prospered at the seventeen-acre Link Daffodil Gardens. She said her love of daffodils began at eight: "My mom promised if we planted daffodils, we would have a pretty spring." Helen died in December 2002 and was

ROBERT D. BECKMANN JR.

A granite copy of Georgia Strange's *Do Not Go Gentle* rests atop the monument of Robert D. Beckmann Jr.: actor, photographer, arts patron, civic leader. Beckmann served as press secretary for Mayor Richard G. Lugar and commercial real estate broker for F. C. Tucker Company He was a founding board member of the Arts Council of Indianapolis and a driving force in the development of Massachusetts Avenue as a home for galleries and theaters. An inscription on his monument reads, "I worked for a city where the arts are central not peripheral, essential not optional, where the arts are not merely the icing on the cake, but truly the critical leavening in the cake itself! Carry on the battle!"

buried beside her husband. In Helen's honor, the Indiana Daffodil Society planted her daffodil cultivars around the Links' rusticated granite tombstone, as well as around Crown Hill's statue of Persephone. As Helen promised, it made for a pretty spring.

James Louis "J. J." Johnson was Indianapolis born and bred, one of the remarkable group of musicians who emerged from the Crispus Attucks High School and Indiana Avenue jazz crucible in the years between the two world wars. During his six decades of performing, recording, and composing, Johnson became an acclaimed international star. Music critics declared him to be the finest jazz trombonist of all time. In his performing career, Johnson played with the greats, among them Benny Carter, Duke Ellington, Dizzy Gillespie, Count Basie, Charlie Parker, Ella Fitzgerald, Billie Holiday, Miles Davis, Quincy Jones, "Cannonball" Adderley, Illinois Jacquet, Herbie Hancock, and Wynton Marsalis. Playing his sinuous style of slide trombone, he recorded on hundreds of albums, becoming so popular he won *Down Beat* polls even when he was not performing at all. "I've always known that a trombone could be played different, that somebody'd catch on one of these days," Gillespie said to Johnson. "Man, you're elected."

At the height of his popularity in Manhattan's booming post-World War II bebop scene, Johnson returned to Indianapolis to marry a local woman, Vivian Elora Freeman, the daughter of the Crispus Attucks founder. They were to be together until her death many decades later. He launched a successful composing career, including the music for his critically received *Naptown, U.S.A.* album that came out in 1956. In the 1970s, Johnson moved to Los Angeles to write scores for television shows, including the *Mod Squad*, *Starskey and Hutch*, and the *Six Million Dollar Man*, and for films that included *Shaft*. After decades living in New York, Europe, and Los Angeles, Vivian insisted they move back to Indianapolis in 1987 to be closer to family. Soon after, he wrote one of his best-known later works, "Why Indianapolis? Why Not Indianapolis?"

While on tour in Japan in late 1988, Vivian suffered a massive stroke. Though J. J. stopped playing to nurse her, she died three years later and was interred in Crown Hill. Johnson remarried, and continued to play and achieve accolades, including an honorary doctorate from IU, a National Endowment for the Arts American Jazz Fellowship, an Artist in Residence award at Harvard University, and acceptance into the *Down Beat* Hall of Fame. But he was struggling with depression. When he learned he had prostate cancer, he shot himself on February 4, 2001.

Johnson's place in musical history had long been secured. Celebrated contemporary trombonist Steve Turre said, "J. J. did for the trombone what Charlie Parker did for the saxophone. And all of us that are playing today wouldn't be playing the way we're playing if it wasn't for what he did. And not only, of course, is he the master of the trombone—the definitive master of this century—but, as a composer and arranger, he is in the top shelf as well." After a jazz-laced funeral at the Witherspoon United Presbyterian Church, Johnson was laid to rest beside his wife in Crown Hill's Garden Mausoleum, GMI C-14, not so far from the neighborhood that nurtured his genius.

A sixth-generation Hoosier, Governor Robert D. Orr was an Evansville industrialist who parlayed his civic involvement and

Republican Party activism into two terms as lieutenant governor under Otis R. Bowen. He then stepped into the governor's office, serving from 1981 to 1989. After leaving office, Orr was appointed by President George Bush to be the U.S. ambassador to Singapore.

Born on November 17, 1917, into a wealthy industrialist family, Orr attended Yale University and the Harvard Business School before joining the army in 1942. Serving in the Pacific, he left with a major's rank. It was in the Pacific that he met his future wife, Joanne "Josie" Wallace, who was a transport pilot. They married in 1944 and had three children.

Orr's governorship was marked by budget, public utility, and education controversies, but he generally prevailed with his initiatives, such as the "A-Plus" education package, which extended the school year, required student achievement exams, and established a performance-based school accreditation system. While the "A-Plus" program was eliminated in the years following his terms, Orr's PrimeTime program that reduced class sizes in kindergarten through third grade remained a lasting educational reform. His leadership in economic development led to the Japanese investment in the $500 million Subaru-Isuzu plant near Lafayette. Though the $86 million in incentives that were part of the economic development package received criticism, subsequent governors followed his model.

When Orr returned to Indianapolis from his Singapore ambassadorship in 1992, he formed a consulting firm, Alliance for Global Commerce, which focused on international trade and export consultation. In 2000 Robert and Josie divorced. In January 2001, at the age of eighty-three, Orr married Mary K. Davis. Orr entered University Hospital in 2004, where he died of heart arrhythmia on

# RUTH LILLY

Crown Hill Cemetery benefits greatly from the civic leadership and great philanthropic tradition of the Lilly family. Josiah Kirby Lilly Sr. joined the Crown Hill Cemetery Board of Corporators in 1910. Eli Lilly became a Corporator in 1948 and was followed by his grand-nephew, Eli Lilly II in 1984.

In 1970 Eli Lilly saved the Waiting Station at Thirty-fourth Street and Boulevard Place from destruction and financed its restoration. Ruth Lilly continued the family commitment to the historic preservation of Crown Hill. Personally and through the Ruth Lilly Philanthropic Foundation, she supported the restoration of the Gothic Chapel, the Waiting Station, the barn and workshops, the cemetery's winding roads, the brick and wrought-iron fence, and numerous historic monuments in the original sections of the cemetery developed in the 1800s.

Ruth lies at rest adjacent to family members in Section 13 and 14. Their latest philanthropic gift to the Crown Hill Heritage Foundation is the sponsorship of *Crown Hill: History, Spirit, and Sanctuary*, a gift for the ages.

*The Lilly House at Oldfields on the grounds of the Indianapolis Museum of Art. Ruth Lilly was seventeen years old when her parents, Josiah K. Lilly Jr. and Ruth Brinkmeyer Lilly, moved the family to Oldfields. In 1966 Ruth and her brother Joe (J. K. Lilly III) donated the forty-four-acre family estate to the Art Association of Indianapolis for a new museum.*

From *A Little Book: The Poems and Selected Writings of Ruth Lilly*

## Memories

> Wealth may go, gold decay
> Friendships and hearts may sever,
> Youth and beauty – will pass away,
> But memories last forever.

## Ideal

> I want a home in the southland
> Away from the city's eyes,
> Where I can walk alone at night
> Beneath the purple skies.
> There will be light and airy rooms
> Broad firesides and soft, old chairs
> And round-eyed children, whose footsteps
> Sound on the wooden stairs.
> Tall pines will rise to guard the house,
> Mysterious, spicy, still,
> And at their feet warm violets
> Dance with the wind at will.
> I know that someday I shall find
> Free from mortal bonds and bars,
> This dream castle. And I shall walk
> Alone beneath the stars.

March 10, 2004. After services in the Crown Hill Funeral Home, Orr was interred in Section 24, Lot 63, where the curving stone Orr monument was designed to serve as an exedra, an outdoor seat, for visitors. Orr was the eleventh Indiana governor to be buried in Crown Hill.

John Y. Woodruff was an Olympian, an African American who won a gold medal in Hitler's 1936 Berlin games with an extraordinary tactic that lives on in track-and-field lore. Woodruff was born on July 5, 1915, in Connellsville, Pennsylvania, and went to the University of Pittsburgh with the support of local businessmen impressed with his running. On August 4, 1936, twenty-year-old Woodruff was running in the Olympic finals of the 800 meters, when he suddenly found himself boxed in by veteran runners. He realized if he tried to break through the pack, he could be disqualified for fouling another runner. "I knew I had to do something drastic if I was to have any chance of winning the race," he told a journalist years later. So he did do something drastic: he stopped. Letting the other runners pass him, and then he started the race again. Making up ground with his long legs, Woodruff overtook one runner after the other to win the race in 1:52.9, becoming the first of five African Americans, including the legendary Jesse Owens, to win gold medals in Berlin. The *New York Herald Tribune* called Woodruff's restart "the most daring move ever seen on a track."

When Woodruff died on October 30, 2007, in Fountain Hills, Arizona, he was ninety-two. He asked for a service in the Connellesville stadium, where he long before began his storied athletic career. It was near the massive oak tree that had grown from the sapling he brought home from Berlin. On November 14, 2007, Woodruff was buried in his wife's family plot in Crown Hill's Section 46, Lot 86, where an inscribed granite memorial bench reads, "1936 Berlin Olympics—John Y. Woodruff—800 Meter Gold Medalist."

For a few generations, Ruth Lilly was an Indianapolis enigma, famously generous and famously reclusive. Born in 1915, Lilly was the daughter of Josiah K. Lilly Jr. and was the heiress to the Eli Lilly and Company fortune. She made major donations in central Indiana, supporting youth support programs, historic preservation, health care, and medical education. Butler University, Wabash College, DePauw University, Franklin College, IU, and Anderson University received her gifts, as did Methodist Hospital, Riley Hospital for Children, Saint Vincent Hospital, the Brain Injury Association of Indiana, Indianapolis Art Center, the Indianapolis Symphony Orchestra, the Ballet Theater of Indianapolis, the Indianapolis Opera, and the Indiana Repertory Theater. In Indianapolis, the Ruth Lilly Hospice, Ruth Lilly Special Collections and Archives, Ruth Lilly Medical Library, Ruth Lilly Health Education Center, Ruth Lilly Law Library, and Ruth Lilly Young Men's Christian Association Outdoor Center spoke to her philanthropic impact. She was also a very generous donor to the Crown Hill Heritage Foundation.

In November 2002 Lilly stunned the country with news that she had pledged Lilly stock worth $100 million to the Poetry Foundation, a small, Chicago-based organization that published *Poetry* magazine with a staff of four and annual revenues of $700,000. Lilly had a great love of poetry, and reportedly had a soft spot for *Poetry* because they had sent a kind rejection letter when she submitted a poem decades before. She was also connected to another poetry enigma. For many years, she was posited as the "Poe Toaster," the shadowy figure who left three roses and a partially filled bottle of cognac at Edgar Allen Poe's Baltimore grave on January 19, his birthday.

On December 30, 2009, Lilly died of heart failure at the age of ninety-four. After funeral services, she was laid to rest in the Lilly family plot, in Section 13, Lot 21. But Lilly's vision lived on. In April 2011 IU received two generous gifts from her estate worth an estimated $10.7 million, directed to the Center on Philanthropy and the Herron School of Art and Design. The Center on Philanthropy announced it was establishing the Ruth Lilly Professorship Program to create endowed faculty chairs. Herron officials indicated the school was naming its administrative offices the Ruth Lilly Dean's Suite. But some things changed. After her death, the "Poe Toaster" abruptly stopped appearing.

Doctor Charles and Sarah Test were pillars of Indianapolis society. Charles Test was born in Indianapolis on January 10, 1916, as part of the Newby family, whose oligarch, Arthur Newby, bicycle and automobile pioneer, was known as the "quiet philanthropist." After education at Park Tudor, Princeton University, and the University of Chicago, where he earned his medical degree, Test returned to Indianapolis, where he served as a physician, IU School of Medicine faculty member, and civic stalwart. In 1954 Sarah Davol, an adventurous woman from Maine, who had served as a World War II Red Cross volunteer in the Pacific Theater and then worked in east Asia after the war, visited Indianapolis. There she met Test, a widower with two small children; they were married two months later, and had two children of their own. They were destined to be married for fifty-six years. Charles was an enthusiastic polymath. He was an avid stamp and rare book collector, and gloried in fishing, boating, and steam-powered locomotives. And like his family forebears, he was a quiet philanthropist. Sarah was likewise engaged in a dizzying array of organizations, including the Nature Conservancy and the IU School of Medicine's Kenya Partnership in El Doret, Kenya. The Tests were part of all the best clubs in Indianapolis and kept connected to Sarah's native Maine with a second home in Westport Harbor. Charles died on November 15, 2011. Sarah Test died four days later. They were interred in Section 23, Lot 34.

On December 22, 2007, 2,000 people attended Representative Julia Carson's funeral, including U.S. senators Richard Lugar and Evan Bayh, Governor Mitch Daniels, former senator Birch Bayh, Mayor Bart Peterson, and Nation of Islam leader Louis Farrakhan, all of whom spoke. But the memorial service was a long way from somber. When the pallbearers carried Carson's casket into the Eastern Star Church sanctuary, the mourners broke into sustained applause. Rousing music and prayer punc-

tuated the remembrances. Lugar remembered Carson's passion: "It didn't matter where she was, she talked about justice." Evan Bayh talked about her humanity, and willingness to help others. "I don't think she ever said no to anybody who needed her," he said. Former congressman Andy Jacobs Jr., who gave Carson her start in politics, said, "the public hasn't scratched the surface of her accomplishments. Over time, her accomplishments will grow." Farrakhan said, "She lives in the spiritual sense. She lives in those whom she touched."

While still in her twenties, voters elected Carson to the Indiana House of Representatives in 1972. After two terms, they voted her to the Indiana Senate, where she served until 1990. She then served as Center Township trustee for six years, a meaningful post for her, because when she was a twelve-year-old girl she asked for help for her sick mother, Velma, a cleaning woman. The trustee staff disrespected her, told her to get out. Carson vowed that no one who needed help would ever be disrespected in her office. In 1996 voters elected her to Congress, a post she held until she succumbed to lung cancer at the age of sixty-nine.

Carson was the first woman to lay in state at the Indiana Statehouse. After her four-hour funeral at the Eastern Star Church, the cortege, more than a hundred cars, slowly traveled to Crown Hill, where a large American flag hung from the Thirty-fourth Street gate. American flags lined the lane to Carson's gravesite near where her mother, Velma, was buried. There was a rifle salute, the American flag covering her casket was crisply folded, a song was sung, and a brief prayer was said. Then hundreds and hundreds of mourners lined up to place flowers on her coffin.

**Carson was the first woman to lay in state at the Indiana Statehouse.**

# RACHEL NEWMAN

Rachel Newman was a kind woman who wanted to bring beauty to the visitors of Crown Hill. In the spring of 2003 she donated *Spring*, the stained-glass window in the Community Mausoleum, and the following January donated *Summer*. The windows depict an exuberance of life, an elegant spreading tree with twittering birds in its branches. Flowers bloom, butterflies flit. A rabbit sits alert at the base of the tree. She donated the windows in honor of her husband, Chester, who

was interred in the mausoleum. Newman told the cemetery staff she wanted her husband and all the visitors to have something beautiful to see. She also donated trees around the mausoleum, along with a sound system, because Chester had been an organist.

Newman had worked at the Real Silk Hosiery Company, Eli Lilly and Company, and Sam's Club. She recalled meeting Eli Lilly on an elevator and thanking him for the company's insurance, which allowed

her to take care of Chester's blindness. Lilly said he appreciated her thanks.

In May of 2005 Newman gave the *Shepherd's Way* sculpture to Crown Hill. It was in honor of her mother and four siblings who died young. And the following November, Newman embellished the Field of Valor with the Eternal Flame and the Eagle Plaza. She also helped build the Pioneer Cemetery to honor the early Indianapolis settlers.

Newman died on June 17, 2008, at ninety-eight years of age. Two days later, she was entombed next to her husband in the Community Mausoleum, D2, D-2. In a newsletter commemorative article, the Crown Hill Heritage Foundation staff wrote of Newman's remarkable generosity and her vision of Crown Hill as a beautiful final resting place. "Rachel talked of Crown Hill as her home," they wrote.

GROW
OLD
ALONG
WITH
ME THE BEST
IS YET TO BE

KAUTSKY

JAMES · IRVING · HOLCOMB ·

# EPILOGUE

## CROWN HILL: A "MONOPOLY ON PERPETUITY"

Memorial Day 2011 was perfect, an azure sky, flowering trees in full resplendent glory, birds twittering, and the green grass precisely cropped. It was the 143rd consecutive observance of Memorial Day at Crown Hill. In the broad meadow of the south Grounds, pale smoke curled up from a Civil War encampment, where reenactors marched in their campaign hats and woolen uniforms, loosing musket volleys to remember the fallen brave hearts of both sides interred nearby.

At the Field of Valor, a group gathered to honor and remember fifteen Hoosier soldiers who died in Afghanistan and Iraq the previous year. Amidst the memorial stones and fluttering American flags, a black pirate flag snapped, the "Jolly Roger" of the Second Battalion, Fifth Marines' Golf Company, whose soldiers fought and died in Iraq. The most highly decorated Marine Battalion, the 2/5 has fought since World War I under the motto, "Retreat, Hell!" Jeff Hallal, the father of marine Deryk Hallal, who died in action in Iraq, gave the address, invoking Abraham Lincoln at the Gettysburg battlefield, where he charged America to never forget those who gave "their last full measure of devotion." As a tall marine sergeant in full dress uniform solemnly nodded his assent, Hallel said, "There is no greater honor than to give your life for your country." Zack Phillips, one of Deryk Hallal's Golf Company comrades, stood nearby. He said about the Memorial

Day remembrance, "It's kind of like laying to rest the ordeal we all experienced. It's a way to say goodbye."

As the sun reached its zenith, crowds began to congregate near the National Cemetery, with the Gothic Chapel soaring above it like some magnificent stone sentinel. In a tradition that began with the first observance in 1868, Crown Hill honored the soldiers who gave their lives. The Indiana National Guard Thirty-eighth Infantry Division Band played patriotic songs. Crown Hill president Keith Norwalk welcomed the visitors. The Color Guard posted the colors as small American flags waved in front of each gray marker in the National Cemetery. The crowd stood for the national anthem, then the pledge of allegiance.

Stretching back to Governor Oliver P. Morton's stirring speech just after the Civil War, a long line of Indiana leaders, including General Lew Wallace, U.S. senator Albert J. Beveridge, Congressman Andy Jacobs Jr., and Indianapolis mayor Alex Clark have given the Memorial Day address. At the 2011 observance, Congressman Mike Pence said, "In May, we remember those who put on the uniform and did not come home." He talked about the sacrifices of those who went, and the pain felt by loved ones who waited at home; the lifelong burdens carried by those who came back, when many of their compatriots did not. Pence concluded, "We gather today because of what Lincoln in his first inaugural called, 'The mystic chords of memory stretching from every patriot grave.' They bind us to the great and the humble, the known and the unknown. Who did great things, who suffered more than we suffer. Who gave more than we give, and pledged their lives, their fortunes, and their sacred honor for us whom they did not know. For we drink from wells we did not dig, and we're warmed by fires we did not build, in this, the freest and most prosperous nation in the history of the world. They were faithful in their time. And so we must be in ours."

A century and a half has transpired since a group of forward-thinking civic leaders gathered in an old bank building to discuss a new cemetery for Indianapolis. Crown Hill is no longer in the far hinterlands, and generations have laboriously transformed the hardscrabble farms the early corporators acquired into this sylvan expression of idealized nature. The provincial capital of 20,000 souls is now a pulsing international metropolis pushing two million in population. With its

relentless campaign for sustainability, Crown Hill is now a twenty-first-century institution, well positioned to prosper into its third century. Within the leafy environs of the cemetery, the importance of heritage constantly jostles with the imperative for change—it's the unending spiritual quest for dynamic equilibrium played out amidst the gravestones and ancient trees.

Some things endure: the vast rolling green space, the thousands of trees, the seasons' eternal cycle: spring's explosion of life, and the exuberance of summer giving way to autumn's melancholy grandeur and the quietude of winter. The many tens of thousands who repose here continue to ennoble and hallow the ground with their presence. More than 200,000 heroes and villains are here. Among the villains, John Dillinger's grave continues to be Crown Hill's most popular stop, where visitors still chip away at his battered gravestone and leave coins, bullets, and a baseball glove in return. But there are far more heroes in Crown Hill. There are military heroes and civic heroes, a U.S.

# ORIGIN OF MEMORIAL DAY AND THE FLOWER LEGEND

In March 1868 John A. Logan, a congressman and former major general in the Union army who had helped establish the Grand Army of the Republic, an organization for Union veterans of the Civil War, was invited to tour the battlefields of Virginia.

Prevented by congressional commitments from going, he sent his wife. When she returned to Washington, she gave her husband a full account of what she had seen. Her most vivid impressions, however, were not of the battlefields themselves, but of the

care being given to the graves of the Confederate dead.

Her impassioned report so moved Logan, who was then serving as GAR commander in chief, that within two months he had issued a general order to the organization that led directly to the establishment of what we now know as Memorial Day.

Although the order directs only the decoration of the graves of Union veterans, legend has it that at an early observance, after flowers had been strewn on the Union graves, a sudden wind came

up that blew the flowers across the graves of the Confederate dead as well. Those in attendance took it as a sign that the Almighty wanted all soldiers honored equally, whether they had worn the Blue or the Grey.

Thus it is that we take this day to honor all of the soldiers who have answered their last bugle call, those buried in the National Cemetery at Crown Hill as well as the 1,600 Confederates buried a short distance away, and, indeed, all those who have worn the uniform of their nation, in war and in peace, throughout its history.

*U.S. Congressman Mike Pence and Command Sergeant Major Doug Gibbens, U.S. Army (ret.), place a wreath at a cross to honor fallen hoosier heroes on Memorial Day, 2011.*

crickets to accompany the long view down Martin Luther King Jr. Boulevard, past the modest neighborhoods to the spires and monumental buildings of the Indianapolis skyline, a vista that mirrors the cemetery's obelisks and tombs and no-less-beloved markers of common humanity. The view gives rise to the realization that a cemetery is a mirror, however imperfect, of its society—reflecting a people's grandiosity, pettiness, pain, and inequity, along with their soaring hopes, unshakable courage, and enduring love.

A hundred and fifty years after its founding, Crown Hill Cemetery continues to serve the deep physical, psychological, and spiritual needs of an ever-evolving city. Like their predecessors, the corporators take a long view. Jay Peacock, board chairman, whose linage on the board reaches back generations to the Ayres family, said about his fellow Indianapolis citizens: "They want an institution to put their family in perpetuity. If we didn't keep it together, we'd be letting down a whole community, not just our families. That's damned serious." Gordon Wishard, another corporator with a long family linage, talked about the cemetery's extraordinary assets, its history, beauty, and strong corporate structure, all focused on maintaining the institution for eternity. "Crown Hill," he said, "has a monopoly on perpetuity." It's a big job, but as they have since 1863, the stewards of Crown Hill will continue to shoulder the burdens of preserving and developing this great cemetery. As Peacock said, "It is a grave responsibility."

president, three U.S. vice presidents, fourteen U.S. senators, a full caucus of congressmen, eleven Indiana governors, fourteen Civil War generals, a couple of dozen Indianapolis mayors, giants of industry and finance, groundbreaking artists and writers, and the moms and dads and sisters and brothers who are family heroes. A lot of heroes.

Then there's the eternal poet's view from Crown Hill: the quietude and scent of juniper, the chirp of birds and rasp of

DOUGLAS A. WISSING

# SPIRIT

In the 1830s a new memorialization of human life in beautiful American cemeteries grew within context of the American Rural Cemetery Movement. Previously, in the seventeenth and eighteenth centuries, death was abhorred. People were quickly placed, perhaps abandoned, in utilitarian urban grave sites, their bodies possibly uprooted by growing factories as capitalism advanced. Human death was feared and marginalized. As the nineteenth century philosophy of romanticism grew, so did the notion of the significance of death in the human experience. In particular, death became exalted as a bridge to the ecstasy of transcendent, eternal life.

Cemeteries matched this positive ideological change. They grew and developed into parklike settings; they became a place for social gatherings before city parks existed. This change of spirit was reflected in the profound change of cemetery settings.

Response to death and response to the dying process became inextricably linked to spirituality. Religious or not, spirituality has continued to be the strongest component that has bequeathed hope and comfort, both to the dying and to those left behind. In this regard spirituality has consistently given meaning, interpretation, and a means or method for coming to terms with the death experience. Is dying the beginning stage of eternal life, or is it simply, and no more, the cessation of life? One thing is certain: spirituality provides a personal connection to the mystery and the meaning of life. In *Tractatus Logico-Philosophicus*, Austrian philosopher Ludwig Wittgenstein wrote, "If we take eternity to mean not infinite temporal duration but timelessness, then eternal life belongs to those who live in the present."

In addition to the stories of those interred, Crown Hill Cemetery offers the continuing tales from the amazing diversity of animals and plants that have found a hospitable matrix for generations. The spirit of life's momentum is visible in many aspects. Crown Hill offers a vibrant urban forest, home to 4,156 inventoried trees containing 130 separate species. A tree map is offered to those interested in discovering this amazing collection. Provisions are made for those wishing to plant a memorial tree in memory of a loved one. In addition to the trees, approximately 120 species of shrubs adorn the grounds. Additionally, Crown Hill provides sanctuary for white-tailed deer, small mammals (such as coyotes, foxes, and hundreds of red squirrels) whose needs are tended to by groundskeepers. Red-tailed hawks and fabulous birds live and soar above the grounds, providing a birders' delight. Crown Hill stands by its dictum: "We like to think of ourselves as an outdoor classroom." A free classroom that is open 365 days a year!

One of the most pristine classrooms is the seventy-acre woods on the north side of the property. Rebecca W. Dolan,

director of the Friesner Herbarium at Butler University, noted that this remarkable place features burr oak trees approximately 350 to 400 years old, ash trees with long vines "catching a ride" on their beautiful trunks, a carpet of wildflowers in the spring, and various shrubs and plants such as the pawpaw that offer sustenance to the deer population and other fauna.

There are abundant small ponds that are called "ephemeral ponds" because they come and go according to rainfall. These offer drinking water and spawning areas for peepers and salamanders. Butler often uses the woods as a teaching laboratory for its students, who study this area in all seasons. One of the interesting features of "the woods" is that there are no trails. Nature is left alone, and a walk through this area is both challenging and unforgettable.

The living spirit of Crown Hill also emerges through its guided tours, private tours, and self-guided tours for visitors. Among these tours are those that feature Women of Crown Hill, Famous and Infamous Grave Sites, Skeletons in the Closet tours offering tantalizing facts and incidents at Crown Hill, Civil War Tours, and Art and Architecture tours. Hundreds of runners participate in the annual "Beyond the Badge Run & Walk" event in September. In nice weather, bikers ride through the twenty-five miles of paved roads and picnickers regularly take advantage of the grounds' beauty. Concerts are held in the Gothic Chapel. A photo contest invites professional and amateur photographers to memorialize special visions and moments in the life of Crown Hill. Many of these pictures are displayed in the administrative offices. The calendar of events is striking: for example, eleven distinct events were scheduled for October 2011. Online registration and invitations make it easy to participate.

The Spirit of Crown Hill is multidimensional. For the 200,000 bodies at rest therein, a living spirit embraces their final earthly destination with tenderness and caring. The past is very much a part of the present. For the living, Crown Hill teaches many lessons about life and the living of it. It is a magical place.

MARIANNE TOBIAS

# OAK TREE COMMUNICATION AND FAIRY SPUDS
## THE NORTH WOODS AT CROWN HILL CEMETERY

A wonderful remnant of an Eastern Deciduous forest has been secured on the grounds of Crown Hill Cemetery for 150 years. The woods on the northern edge of the cemetery, between Michigan and Clarendon Roads, are a sanctuary for plants and wildlife that sustained our pioneers and were characteristic of early Marion County. Just as the inscriptions on the grave markers are a reminder of, and tribute to, our forebears, the woods are a legacy of the past, linking generations. Woods of this size and quality are not found in many places in central Indiana.

These woods are special. Most of the parks with natural areas in Marion County are along rivers, creeks, and streams—places such as Holliday Park, Marott Park, and parts of Eagle Creek Park. The relatively steep topography of these sites prevented their being cleared for agriculture. The Crown Hill woods are close to White River, but far enough away to be out of the floodplain and flat.

Rebecca W. Dolan, director of the Friesner Herbarium, Butler University.

This terrain hosts flatwoods with shallow depressions called spring ponds that hold several inches of water in the spring. Because of the spring ponding, flatwoods were the last areas to be developed or farmed by settlers. Now these special places are some of the last truly natural areas in the city. The presence of spring ponds adds habitat diversity to the Crown Hill woods. At least forty-seven species of trees grow here. Impressively, the interior of the woods is largely free of invasive, nonnative pest plants that are a scourge in many urban natural areas.

Forests such as the woods at Crown Hill can be divided into three layers based on height above the ground. The upper layer, closest to the heavens, is the canopy. Just like with a canopy bed, this is the layer over your head. Very large and old trees hold their leaves up to the sun. Among the largest and oldest are burr oaks. Some in the woods measure more than fifteen

feet around and are likely several hundred years old. Although the woods at Crown Hill are isolated from other woods with burr oaks, the trees are able to communicate across the landscape via their pollen. The pollen of oaks travels on the wind and is able to cross fairly large spaces. Trees at Crown Hill preserve the gene pool of early Indiana and so connect the past with the present. Ashes, tulip poplars, sycamores, hickories, cottonwoods, silver and sugar maple also thrive at Crown Hill. At least two dozen trees are more than three feet in diameter.

The canopy is home to tree-nesting fox and gray squirrels. Raccoons and opossums hang out in its branches. Pileated woodpeckers, large birds up to two feet in length with calls sounding like Woody Woodpecker, fly through the treetops like parrots through the rainforest. Both woodpeckers and squirrels nest in hollow parts of mature, often dead, trees in forest habitat. Squirrels also build leaf nests to protect their young and to keep warm in winter. Squirrels usually have two litters of three or four young, one in late winter or early spring and the other in early summer. Young squirrels nurse for around five weeks before venturing to find their own food. They remain close their mother for five or so months before breaking from the family group. Pileated woodpeckers need large tracks of mixed hardwoods. Parents work together to excavate new nest holes each year, at an average height of forty-five feet off the ground. They lay one brood of three or four eggs. No special nest material is brought in. Eggs

are laid in the hole and incubated by both sexes.

The middle layer of the forest is a shrub layer. Indiana does not have a large diversity of shrubs in its flatwood forests, but the plants that are here are important food for wildlife. Pawpaw and spicebush are plentiful. Both are host plants for large elaborate butterflies (zebra and spicebush swallowtails) that lay their eggs only on these bushes. Spicebush berries are high in fats and nutrients needed for migration of neotropical birds stopping over to rest on their semiannual flights from North America to Central and South America. Redstarts, ovenbirds, wood thrushes, red-eyed vireos, and scarlet tanagers are just a few of the globally rare birds that stop in the Crown Hill woods. The woods are large enough to support a population of deer that can often be seen feeding at dawn and dusk in the field outside the woods at Forty-second Street and Clarendon Road. Only a small population can be sustained by the resources available here.

The layer of forest closest to the earth is the herb layer: nonwoody plants. The woods are alive in the spring with wildflowers and their pollinators. These spring ephemerals leaf out and bloom at the same time as garden crocuses and tulips. They grow from underground bulbs that store energy between growing seasons. Flowering is done quickly, before the trees leaf out and while sunlight can still get to the forest floor. Familiar plants such as trout lilies, mayapple, and jack-in-the-pulpit abound. Almost forty species have been seen. One of the most striking in terms of numbers is spring-beauty, a diminutive early bloomer with light pink flowers lined with dark pink veins. The plant is also known as fairy spuds. Folklore has it the underground storage organs of these plants are edible and were eaten by Native Americans. The tubers are only the size of a little fingernail, hence the name. It would take quite a few of these plants to make a meal.

Many of these woodland spring wildflowers are pollinated by specialist insects that only visit a single species of plant. Decline, or worse yet, loss of these plants, results in a cascading loss of biodiversity. Many have also coevolved with animal dispersers that carry seeds away and help the species spread. Tiny fat bodies, a high-quality food source for ants, are often produced by spring wildflowers, attached to seeds. The ants are attracted to the fat bodies like ant candy and carry the attached seeds back to their nests. Once there, the ants eat the fat bodies, but not the seeds. The seeds are left in a nice, fertile place to germinate and grow.

The forest floor is also home to land-dwelling animals. When winter snowmelt and spring rains are caught in the clay soils of ephemeral ponds, salamanders and other amphibians lay their eggs. Salamanders lay clutches of three hundred to eight hundred eggs attached to the undersides of leaves and sticks by gelatinous film. If the pond dries up too

soon, the eggs will die. If all goes well, many hundred tadpoles from a clutch will complete metamorphosis to develop into land-dwelling adults.

Beneath the forest floor, roots of trees absorb rain and help keep soils porous. Forest blocks help retain rainwater on site, reducing flow into overburdened combined sewer systems. Mature trees filter harmful chemicals and particles from the air, remove carbon dioxide from the atmosphere as photosynthesis converts this

gas into living plant material, and cool surrounding areas. All of the asphalt and concrete in built-up urban environments tends to trap the sun's heat. Trees provide respite from this heat-island effect. These are just some of the ecological services provided by the Crown Hill Woods that benefit all citizens of Indianapolis. This impressive wooded remnant of the past is serving our present and improving our future.

REBECCA W. DOLAN

# SANCTUARY

Death inevitably leaves a void. Reaction to the loss and the need for comfort can be evidenced from prescriptive customs that vary from culture to culture. The personal mourning experience, contrasted to state and national mourning and its dictates, are part of the solace humans require.

In the United States, many of our mourning customs stem from or are adapted from the elaborate customs of the Victorian era. Victorian mourning had specific social expectations involving clothes, behaviors, and periods of time set aside to show proper respect for the deceased.

Victorians expected that curtains in the home be drawn and clocks stopped at the time of death. Three or four days were allowed for a "wake," when visitors and relatives came to visit the bereaved family. At that time, flowers and candles were necessary to provide fragrance to cover the smell of decomposition. A widow was expected to wear black for a full year, and if she was wealthy, to clothe her servants in black as well. A weeping veil to cover the face and a cap or special hat were expected accoutrements. Jewelry, if worn at all, was to be black. Sometimes a lock of hair of the deceased was snipped off and combined with the jewelry. If mourning customs were not observed, ostracism and heavy criticism followed. In 1900 *The Wonderful Wizard of Oz* was first published. At the end of the book, Dorothy explains to Glinda (the Good Witch of the South), "My greatest wish now is to get back to Kansas, for Aunt Em will surely think something dreadful has happened to me, and that will make her put on mourning; and unless the crops are better this year than they were last, I am sure Uncle Henry cannot afford it."

Some of these customs persist today. Most can remember the beautiful veil covering Jacqueline Kennedy's face at the funeral of President John F. Kennedy. Black is still customarily worn for funerals. Flowers adorn caskets and gravesites. Wakes, or receptions in the home, are also common.

Aside from the social and cultural response to mourning, personal mourning is an individual response of indeterminate dress and times. Sometimes humans become overwhelmed in the mourning process and struggle to overcome a perpetual state of sadness that influences every aspect of their life. The goal of personal mourning is no less and no more than coming to peace and acceptance of the death at hand. One of the most eloquent poets, Joseph von Eichendorff, wrote in his poem "Im Abendrot" (At Sunset):

> We have gone through sorrow and joy hand in hand; Now we
> can rest from our wandering above the quiet land.
> Around us, the valleys bow; the air is growing darker. Just
> two skylarks soar upwards dreamily into the fragrant air.
> Come close to me, and let them flutter. Soon it will be time
> for sleep. Let us not lose our way in this solitude.
> O vast, tranquil peace, so deep at sunset! How weary we are
> of wandering—Is this perhaps death?

Modern psychology has determined that mourning is inevitable, healthy, and necessary to regaining one's emotional equilibrium. In fact, this science posits that there are "stages of the process" that are generally true for humans within their specific cultural matrix. In the 1960s Doctor Elisabeth Kubler-Ross determined a specific mourning pattern for those who knew of their own impending death. More usual, however, is grieving for a loved one.

Behavioralists have examined this human experience. Mourning can be defined as behavioral patterns, usually derived from the nature of the death at hand. For example, an unexpected departure based on natural causes or a gruesome sudden accident (the shock death) can trigger different, but nonetheless predictable, sets of behaviors. Anticipated death also creates its own special mourning syntax. Anticipated death and predeath mourning can also occur if the death was "expected." The ending of a natural long life, illness, or a more or less predictable lifespan determined by medical science during an illness or at birth. These scientific "findings" are filled with "exceptions." The mourning cycle for each human is individual and often painful. It is also inevitable.

Crown Hill Cemetery is prepared for this process. The Gothic Chapel stands ready to provide shelter, privacy, and quiet. The tranquil grounds offer spacious areas for walks and contemplation. Grave sites are beautifully and consistently tended. The administration provides connection to stone carvers for statues or special markers. Marking of a grave can be therapeutic for those left behind, and in this cemetery there are amazing tributes to the lives of those who died.

Sometimes the marking involves written remembrances and commentary on the deceased etched into tombstones and individual benches for rest. The emotional demands of mourning can easily deplete human energy. On a modern note, Crown Hill offers online memorials, a Grief Library, flower placement and delivery, the possibility to create a "virtual candle," and an online map to find a specific grave. For those wishing to have a reception, Crown Hill offers catering menus for service in several venues and Sympathy Dinners to send to a stressed family.

There is a singular drama to the final moment of burial. The land has been prepared, the tents placed, final prayers are said, and then the departure of family and friends. Preparation and continuing care of the grave site and the environs is a responsibility shared by a fascinating team: the groundskeepers. Their stories are amazing, their commitment to their work is intense, and their commitment to each other is bonding and beautiful. These are the men who keep the cemetery's grounds and animals safe and tended. Long after families have gone, these are the men who respect the memories, the final resting places, and also lovingly comfort the needy.

Sometimes there are twenty to thirty burials a week, Saturday being "the big day." Interviews with these men have been extraordinary. They have witnessed hundreds of mourners and private moments in the human experience with death. Their memories, their feelings, and their philosophies are shared below. Each person stated their love of their work, their loyalty to one another, and their feelings of being in a special place every day they come to Crown Hill.

At Crown Hill for more than twenty years, Larry Johnson has found the cemetery to be a peaceful place. He noted that there is a spirit of sanctity. He also explained that the team "treats each grave like it was a family member" and that there is, in spite of all the big machinery and heavy lifting, a tenderness about their work.

Johnson gently laughs when telling that the deer sometimes come after a funeral to munch on flowers—a treat and a buffet for them—and he feels like a "part time deer keeper." There are some mourners or family members who come on a daily basis, with a lawn chair or two, to be close to the deceased. He noted a growing fashion has been the placement of solar-powered lights on grave sites, lending a glowing candlelight in the night that is very beautiful.

Chris Hensley, assistant superintendent, explained that the barn and service yard areas lie at the physical heart of Crown Hill. For him, the parklike nature of the cemetery has been very

## THE GRAVEYARD BEES

Thousands of busy workers live atop Crown Hill's art deco Community Mausoleum. Come morning, they buzz off to pollinate the cemetery and make some memorable honey. For some years, England's Apiary of Indianapolis has kept hives on the mausoleum's roof. Subject to weather and the blossoms, the beekeepers come to gather the honey a couple of times each year. "We get twenty to thirty pounds of honey per hive, depending on what's pollinating, what's flowering," said Kim England, garage and maintenance assistant supervisor. Once gathered and processed, members of the cemetery's interment crew sell the dark, flavorful honey, along with a gravely delicious spread made of honey mixed with blackberry preserves.

compelling, making his work "very special" and providing him with a daily sense of peace and tranquility as he goes about his tasks. "I find myself every day in a little piece of the country," said Hensley. One of his most interesting comments was that he often calls the families back after the funerals to see how they are doing, to see if everything is all right, and to solve problems or complaints—from small concerns such as a missing vase to larger concerns having to do with headstones and perpetual care. "I always try never to say no," he said. Flexibility is the key to his success. "Every day is different" said Hensley, adding "there is always an answer to new problems." He has been at Crown Hill for more than twenty years, and has "worked doing everything" and would not ask his team to "do anything I would not do or have not done." He is a man of optimism, sincerity, and dedication. He especially loves the animals, and the red foxes are his favorite residents.

Jim Troy has worked at Crown Hill more than ten years and described himself as a jack-of-all trades. He is full of colorful stories, and he has strong institutional memories. The camaraderie of the team is especially important to him. Clearly he has a passion for his work, which primarily focuses on special operations, particularly in plumbing and the fountains.

When speaking of the families, Troy noted, "I have such respect for what they are going through; I treat everyone as if they were my own family." Burials of soldiers and babies have been particularly moving for him. He enjoys the tree recycling project: pruning the trees, cutting them, selling the logs and lumber, developing mulch from the chipper, and growing the small saplings that will be planted on the grounds. From time to time he has served as a pallbearer if the family did not have enough to fill the job. His heart and his talent are clearly in everything he does.

Attracted by its people, its atmosphere, and its beauty, Bob Buergler has been at Crown Hill for fourteen years. Part of his work involves the actual interment of the deceased, and he spoke movingly of the interactions he has had with families. "We are not in a hurry," he tells the families. "Just take your time at the site: I will wait." People "open up to him" and he listens: part psychologist, part friend, and most of all a comforting presence. "Everybody is different," he said. Buergler has a broad and embracing personality and presence. He also has been a regular contributor to the Crown Hill Heritage Foundation, and in particular feels close to his work at the Gothic Chapel.

Greg Ratcliffe is a gentle, caring presence on the team as well. He has worked at Crown Hill for eleven years and "loves every minute," noting that "being outdoors certainly beats being in an office." Among his many missions is offering comfort to the grieving. "I want them to know we are there for them," said Ratcliffe. While working he will often take time out to "talk to the families or visitors" or act as an impromptu tour guide. He noted that every time he comes to work he feels that he is "entering a unique place in the world," a place that is "different from the hustle and bustle of traffic, noise, and telephones. One of his particular interests lies in the different nationalities of persons buried and Crown Hill and the cultural differences in burial customs and memorializations within the fabric of our citizenry. He spoke too of a certain numbness to the pain of death—he can distance himself from the turmoil; and can be strong, offering solace and concern for people in their weakest and most fragile moments.

Kim England has worked for nineteen years at Crown Hill. With a gentle laugh, he recalls that he answered an advertisement in the paper wherein a "100 year old" unnamed institution was looking for a mechanic. He was most surprised upon arrival for his interview that it was a cemetery that needed his services. What has also surprised England has been how comfortable the job has been emotionally, and how beautiful it is to go to Crown Hill every day: "I love the out of doors. I love the parklike atmosphere. I love all of the animals. I love my professional family here, we all work together."

John Meredith is in his fifteenth year at Crown Hill. "I grew up as a child working for a funeral home," he remembered. "I had a friend who worked at Crown Hill and was going to leave . . . and then next thing was, I landed at Crown Hill. I would never work anywhere else. I am back to my roots." He added, "We always say we are tucking in people for the last time. Actually, we do not use the word bury."

Meredith noted that he always wants people to feel when they leave that their loved ones are going to be tended to. "You know what these people are going through and what it feels like and how important it is to make that day in their lives just right," he said. "We are going to take care of your loved one, even if you are not here." He considers himself almost like a therapist or counselor, and from time to time has given his card to people who might want to call him later. "When I see someone alone, I always take note: I want to be sure they are all right," Meredith said. Sometimes he has prayed with people, listened to their stories, or shared their pain. "And I have learned a lot: for example, I have a great relationship with the Muslim community now, and we have educated each other," he noted.

"This is what life is all about—helping people," said Meredith. He is generous of both his spirit and his time. "I am proud to be where I am," he said, viewing Crown Hill's employment not only as work but also as a mission of humanitarian depth and empathy.

Solace lies at the heart of Crown Hill. In the middle of a large, noisy, bustling city, this unique institution stands proudly in its mission. The institution speaks quietly, respectfully, and powerfully of life's final transition. With its natural beauty and its caring people, Crown Hill is a magical place with an elegant culture, the highest standards, and an enduring strength that seems to cleanse death of morbidity, offering hope, acceptance, and peace to all.

MARIANNE TOBIAS

# OCTOBER SKY

Sitting beside me on a blanket at Crown Hill Cemetery, placing flowers on a grave, my daughter, then age four, asked me what it meant to die. I thought of the October sky. Nature seems to me most beautiful during its yearly cycle of dying.

I can still remember an October sky from the autumn of 1975, the year engraved on the cemetery marker. My mother passed away the previous June. I lay on a worn blanket staring at the contrast of the leaves against the vibrant blue backdrop of the sky. Brilliant in death, the leaves were various hues of deep orange, bright gold, and scarlet. The sight comforted me, but at the time I did not know why. I believe I now do.

Death, when it comes in measured days, has the capacity to bring out the beauty we often keep buried deep inside us. When time is short and life more precious, we live it with passion. We show our true colors. So it was with my mother in her final years.

Diagnosed with an incurable brain tumor, she fought her way through two major surgeries and multiple chemotherapy treatments. She hit the depths of despair then picked herself up, dusted herself off, and pursued her personal "bucket list." She traveled to Europe several times, lugging big bags of medicine along with her.

She rode a donkey through the ruins of Greece. She attended concerts that moved her to tears. In her final days, her dearest friend read to her the classic books that she loved the most.

Recalling those memories, sprawled out on the blanket four months after her death, I knew that in another month the leaves would wither in brown heaps on the grass. The roots of the trees would go dormant. Winter was coming.

But in spring, the new shoots appeared on flowers and trees and signs of life were abundant. Season follows season in the perfect order of God and nature. Sometimes we need only look beyond our four walls and venture outside our window for inspiration, comfort, or in my case, all those years later, the answer to my daughter's question.

My faith allows me to believe that what it means to die is to make the transition that God intends for us with trust and grace, revealing inner beauty until the end. Perhaps more important is what it means to live.

A few years after the day my daughter and I put flowers on my mother's grave, I faced my own mortality. A late-term miscarriage caused multiple complications and serious internal bleeding. During my long recovery, the gauzy metaphors for life and death went out the window.

Like my own mother, I was under the age of forty-five and I felt cheated. Grief came in like a lion, stealing my joy of life for a time. Unlike my mother, I had survived. She had worked her way through the emotional mud. I felt it was incumbent on me to do the same.

I like to think there is a golden thread that runs through every living creature and thing on Earth. I envision a thread that links us in a mystical mosaic to one another and that which we cannot see: People we have loved and lost, people we find difficult to love—on and on—all the way to our creator. The thread looks fragile but is very strong. It is elusive in appearance but it shows up best in the dark, when times are tough.

The golden thread, I believe, is our lifeline, connecting the past, present, and future in single moments of grace. One of those "golden thread" moments came to me from a relative stranger during my posttraumatic funk. Marty Davis taught me how to raise butterflies. Butterflies taught me about the power of metamorphosis, and the joy that follows surrender.

I met Marty, a nature lover and professional photographer, who also works at Crown Hill Cemetery, during a

butterfly release at a children's grief camp. I wanted to know more about Monarchs and everyone told me Marty—aka "The Butterfly Lady"—was the woman in the know.

Marty showed me how to search for larva on milkweed, and how to protect and feed the tiny caterpillar that emerges from it. With a steady supply of milkweed, caterpillars grow three thousand times their size within two weeks. They shed their skin five times on their way to form-

ing their chrysalis and getting wings, a one-month process.

The final shedding is the most spectacular. The caterpillar hangs as if in labor, until it splits its skin, shedding everything that defines it as a caterpillar—twelve eyes, powerful jaws, sixteen legs, tentacles, and face—all of it drops off and shrivels.

"All of the things that bound them to Earth are suddenly gone," Marty noted, "and there is no turning back."

As it sheds, the caterpillar wriggles and morphs into a jade-green chrysalis encircled with gold dots that look a lot like a golden thread. Inside the chrysalis the caterpillar turns into a thick, green liquid and enters its darkest and most vulnerable state.

"What is it like to shed everything that defines them on the outside? Well, it's as if they go to sleep for a while," Marty said. But they wake up to a miracle. No longer earthbound, they are transformed—almost ready to fly.

"What we learn from the caterpillar is the phenomenon of earning wings by the very act of surrender," said Marty.

Ten days after entering the chrysalis, the Monarch pushes out upside down and backwards. Within three hours its wings are fully extended and dry, and it is ready to begin a new life, flying as high as ten thousand feet in the air.

Marty marvels at the metaphor. "On the other side of our skin is the hope for something much greater," she said. "And like the shedding of the last skin, all that

we are must dissolve in order to become all that we never were."

Monarchs released east of the Rockies after mid-August migrate two thousand to three thousand miles across North America to over-wintering colonies in the oyamel fir forests high up on the trans-volcanic mountains of Central Mexico. West of the Rockies, they over-winter in many different Eucalyptus groves along the California coast, including those in Pacific Grove and Santa Cruz. No matter where their journey begins, the timing of its conclusion is the same. The majority of Monarchs arrive in droves, in the late October sky, on or around the "Day of the Dead," All Souls Day. The Mexicans have a huge celebration, believing that the spirits of our loved ones fly on the backs of the Monarchs.

The first Monarch I raised from an egg was male—like the baby I lost. He lingered on my forefinger for several minutes—light as a feather. When he flew off into the wind, a sense of joy fluttered inside me. I let something go when I let him go. The veil of sadness—the weight of grief—lifted. It was a breakthough moment for me.

I have raised and shared butterflies ever since, believing they carry the golden thread that separates Heaven and Earth, love and loss. Their metamorphosis is a metaphor for growth, change, and the grace of surrender. I have seen them work magic with people suffering illness, job

*The memorial for Sater C. Ryder adorned with Monarch and Painted Lady butterflies.*

loss, and grief. Marty taught me how to use them as more than a hobby. They never cease to delight and amaze me.

In 2010, on the thirty-fifth anniversary of my mother's death, Marty raised enough Monarchs for a full-blown butterfly release at her grave. I took them out to Crown Hill in the early evening as the sun sank low, the same time my mother died more than three decades earlier.

When I opened the netting on the butterfly cage, the Monarchs flew away one by one and two by two until only one was left. The female crawled onto my finger and stayed. She wanted to hang out, so we just sat there.

Twenty minutes later, I was well into a one-way conversation with her when a doe joined us at the trunk of a nearby tree. The scene was enchanting, like something out a movie. I stayed another thirty min-

utes with the butterfly on my fingertip. The cemetery was about to close so I sent her on her way.

As I got up to leave, the sun setting behind a tree sent shards of light through the leaves like golden threads. Thirty-five years disappeared in an instant, and my mother felt very close. I drove out of the iron gates of Crown Hill with a smile on my face.

I believe I now know what it means to live. It means living with eyes and heart wide open to the wonders all around us. It means using our trials and pitfalls to make a golden connection with others on the journey.

And if I'm wise, I'll choose to live as though my days on Earth are measured—and live with all the vibrancy and color as the leaves in the October sky.

ANNE RYDER

# STEWARDSHIP

R. Morris Adams, Thomas W. Binford, Edward G. Dunn, William L. Elder, Susan G. Hudnut, William L. Lieber, Gayle Thornbrough, Stewart D. Tompkins, J. Reid Williamson Jr., Richard D. Wood, and Evans Wollen were the initial members of the board of directors of the Crown Hill Heritage Foundation according to the Articles of Incorporation approved and filed on March 23, 1984. Their purpose, stated in the Application for Recognition of Exemption Under Section 501 (c) (3), was to preserve Crown Hill Cemetery as a place of history and heritage for the benefit of the general public.

At the November 13, 1985, board of directors meeting, President Lieber reported, "At this point in time the foundation has received almost $5,200 and spent almost $13,700." Since that meeting, the Foundation has raised millions of dollars to plant and maintain one of the city's most beautiful and diverse tree collections; preserve the Gothic Chapel, Waiting Station, and barns and historic workshops; restore unique landmarks such as the masonry and wrought-iron fence and the Thirty-eighth Street bridge and underpass; preserve hundreds of historic monuments; restore twenty-five miles of historic roads; and share the story of the families of Crown Hill Cemetery with countless generations of Hoosiers, as well as national and international visitors to the cemetery.

*Crown Hill: History, Spirit, and Sanctuary*, an anniversary project sponsored by the Foundation, preserves 150 years of the history and heritage of Crown Hill. It will require additional millions of dollars to preserve the next 150 years of history and heritage for the generations who follow.

You can help save the memories, the beauty, and the historic treasures of Crown Hill forever with a gift through your will to the Crown Hill Heritage Foundation. Every dollar counts.

MARIANNE RANDJELOVIC

www.crownhillHF.org

In Memory of
William L. & Jane H. Fortune
originally given by their family
June 14, 2006
and
Rededicated
September 15, 2010

STRONG

HERBERT E., JR.
1925

ANN ELIZABETH
BOWMAN RUEBECK
1939

# Index

## ACKNOWLEDGMENTS

### JOHN A. HERBST
PRESIDENT AND CEO
INDIANA HISTORICAL SOCIETY

### STEVE COX
VICE PRESIDENT, IHS PRESS
INDIANA HISTORICAL SOCIETY

### RAY E. BOOMHOWER
SENIOR EDITOR, IHS PRESS
INDIANA HISTORICAL SOCIETY

### KATHLEEN M. BREEN
EDITOR, IHS PRESS
INDIANA HISTORICAL SOCIETY

### STACY SIMMER
SENIOR GRAPHIC DESIGNER
INDIANA HISTORICAL SOCIETY

### KEITH O. NORWALK
PRESIDENT
CROWN HILL HERITAGE FOUNDATION

### MARIANNE RANDJELOVIC
VICE PRESIDENT OF DEVELOPMENT
CROWN HILL HERITAGE FOUNDATION
BOOK PROJECT MANAGER

### MARTY N. DAVIS
PUBLIC RELATIONS COORDINATOR
AND PHOTOGRAPHER
CROWN HILL HERITAGE FOUNDATION

### TOM DAVIS
HISTORIAN AND TOUR DEVELOPER
CROWN HILL HERITAGE FOUNDATION

Indianapolis, Indiana
Crownhillhf.org